VIRTUOUS VICE

Edited by Michèle Aina Barale, Jonathan Goldberg,
Michael Moon, and Eve Kosofsky Sedgwick

VIRTUOUS VICE

Homoeroticism and the Public Sphere

ERIC O. CLARKE

Duke University Press   Durham and London, 2000

© 2000 Duke University Press
All rights reserved
Printed in the United States of America on acid-free paper ∞
Typeset in Quadrat by Tseng Information Systems, Inc.
Library of Congress Cataloging-in-Publication Data
appear on the last printed page of this book.

To my mother, Gerry Clarke, with love

CONTENTS

ACKNOWLEDGMENTS

I've been extremely fortunate to have benefited from the intellectual guidance and sustaining affection of so many as this project progressed. A small portion of this book originated in dissertation work completed some time ago, and I first wish to express my thanks to William Keach, Bob Scholes, Ellen Rooney, and Henry Abelove for their insightful and patient assistance in that endeavor. I am particularly grateful to Henry, whose intelligence, integrity, and affection continually guide me in matters personal and professional. He exemplifies all the best one hopes to find in a scholar, a teacher, and a friend.

Many colleagues at the University of Pittsburgh have been selfless in extending crucial advice, support, and friendship when all were needed most, and I wish to thank in particular Jonathan Arac, Paul Bové, Danae Clark, Toi Derricotte, Jane Feuer, Sabine Hake, Ronald Judy, Valerie Krips, Marcia Landy, Colin MacCabe, Dwight McBride, Marianne Novy, Carol Stabile, Richard Tobias, John Twyning, Bruce Venarde, and Sabine von Dirke. As colleagues they have provided the kind of exciting intellectual community one always hopes to have; as friends, they have made collegiality a joy. The affectionate support and confidence so generously given by the late Carol Kay were especially wonderful gifts; she made Pittsburgh a very special place to be. Jonathan Arac devoted precious time to read and comment on the entire manuscript, and his advice helped me immeasurably. More than once Ronald Judy sat me down and helped me to figure out what seemed to be intractable problems, and for this I will always be grateful. I also want to thank the editorial collective of *boundary* 2, especially editor Paul Bové, whose yearly get-togethers consistently furnish productive intellectual exchange.

I am indebted to the graduate students in my Queer Theory and Topics in Nineteenth-Century Culture seminars, and to the students who gave me the privilege to work with them and their projects. They put up with my interests and idiosyncrasies, and gave me wonderful insights into both. I especially want to thank Alison Cuddy, Joy Van Fuqua, Megan Hickey, Kara Keeling, Tony Lack, Ray Ricketts, Brian Samonek, Lisa Schwartz, Matthew Tinkcom, Elayne Tobin, and Amy Villarejo for their constant encouragement and for discussions in and out of class from which I continue to benefit. More colleagues than students, Todd Marciani and Patrick Mullen have generously listened to my ideas, read drafts, given me excellent intellectual advice, and, most of all, granted me the incalculable benefit of their friendship. They accomplished the astounding feat of making life in Pittsburgh glamorous.

Many other colleagues and friends were more than generous with their time, thoughts, advice, and support as my book developed: Nancy Armstrong, Jessica Barry, Crystal Bartolovich, Tim Brennan, Douglas Crimp, Ann Cvetkovich, Mark Douglas, Lisa Duggan, Jack Eckert, Kathy Ferraro, Diana Fuss, Larry Grossberg, David Halperin, Phil Harper, Claudia Johnson, Wayne Koestenbaum, Kevin Kopelson, Peter Lappin, Neil Lazarus, Clayborne Mitchell, Michael Moon, José Muñoz, Chantal Nadeau, Eve Kosofsky Sedgwick, Paul Smith, Cynthia Stamy, Len Tennenhouse, Keith Vincent, Michael Warner, Patricia White, and Susan Wolfson. To all, my deepest gratitude. Thanks are due Carol Stabile and Mark Unger for sharing the best of themselves with me, and the best of their food, when both were needed most. I owe a special debt to Mathew Henson's capacious intelligence—and his willingness to let me profit from it. Many of the concerns addressed here stem directly from our conversations together. Keith Green, Greg Gross, Pierre Saint-Amand, and Thom Freggens have provided both direction and diversion at the most appropriate times with a sustaining affection I will never forget. As urban compatriots, Todd Marciani, Michael Miller, Shawn O'Toole, and Janeen Potts helped me through unending revisions with their warm hearts and cold glamour. Very special thanks go to Andrea, Sarah, Paul, and Nancy Magon, and to Bríd Kerrigan for their wonderful hospitality and friendship during research trips to London, and to Norman and Yvonne Hixon, who were kind enough to escort me in search of Shelley artifacts in Bournemouth.

I owe an inestimable debt of gratitude to Keya Ganguly. She read the entire manuscript, more than once, and held my hand through the most tortured times of research, writing, and revision. She has given me advice, admonishment, sympathy, agreement, disagreement, and most importantly, her affection. Her constancy as a friend and intellectual companion are unequaled. If such things can be measured, it is only by the infinite length of love given and love anticipated.

Portions of this book were delivered as talks at a number of conferences and meetings, and I want to extend my thanks to the organizers and to the audience members of the following for generously listening and advising: the lesbian and gay studies conferences at Harvard University, Rutgers University, and the University of Iowa; Society for Cinema Studies conferences in Syracuse and New York City; the 1997 Console-ing Passions and 1998 Sex on the Edge conferences at Concordia University, Montréal; the annual Institute on Culture and Society of the Marxist Literary Group; various colloquia at the University of Pittsburgh English Department; and the Cultural Studies Common Seminar at the University of Pittsburgh. I am especially grateful to the organizers of the New York Lesbian and Gay Film Festival and the New York University Faculty Working Group in Queer Studies for inviting me to present my ideas at the 1998 Queer Publics/Queer Privates conference, whose audience also gave me the benefit of their interest and advice. The NYU faculty group also read and commented on a finished draft of chapter 1 with a level of productive engagement that one always wishes one's work to have. Many, many thanks go to Ken Wissoker and the staff at Duke University Press for their patience and support. Ann Cvetkovich and an anonymous reader went over the manuscript version of this book with extreme care and intelligence, and their suggestions were invaluable in preparing the final version.

Lastly, I want to acknowledge my mother, Gerry Clarke, to whom this book is dedicated. Her life has been and continues to be an example and an inspiration. I can only ever hope to approximate her courage, warmth, selflessness, wisdom, and incredible generosity. Thanks Mom.

An earlier version of chapter 5 appeared as "Shelley's Heart: Sexual Politics and Cultural Value," *The Yale Journal of Criticism* 8 (1995): 187–208. A condensed section from chapter 1 appeared as "Queer Publicity at the Limits of Inclusion," *GLQ: A Journal of Lesbian and Gay Studies* 5.1 (1998): 84–89. A slightly different version of chapter 3 appeared in *boundary 2* 26.2 (1999):

163–92. I thank the editors for kindly allowing permission to reprint. For financial support of this project, and much needed time off for research and writing, I thank the National Endowment for the Humanities, the University of Pittsburgh Faculty of Arts and Sciences, and the University of Pittsburgh Department of English. While working on another project, I completed the last revisions during a Rockefeller Residency Fellowship at the Center for Lesbian and Gay Studies at the City University of New York, and I thank the Board of Directors for (inadvertently) providing me with time to do so.

VIRTUOUS VICE

INTRODUCTION *Homoeroticism and the Public Sphere*

Under the social conditions that translated private vices into public virtues, a state of cosmopolitan citizenship and hence the subsumption of politics under morality was empirically conceivable. —Jürgen Habermas, THE STRUCTURAL TRANSFORMATION OF THE PUBLIC SPHERE

Publicity is the very soul of justice. —Jeremy Bentham, DRAUGHT FOR THE ORGANI-ZATION OF JUDICIAL ESTABLISHMENTS

Homoeroticism has gone public like never before. As an embodied iden-tity for public persons and media characters and as a reference point in literary and visual culture, intellectual debates, and commercial activities, homoeroticism has become a staple, if conflicted, feature of the U.S. pub-lic sphere. The national lesbian and gay press has enthusiastically em-braced this unprecedented inclusion within public forms of representation —from television situation comedies, Hollywood films, glossy magazines, and lawmaking bodies, to educational institutions and corporate market-ing practices. While enthusiastic narratives about lesbian and gay inclusion seem at first glance to be warranted, they fail to ask how this inclusion is defined, and on what terms it is granted. In its quest to secure inclusion, mainstream lesbian and gay politics in the United States has largely sought to reassure straight America that queers are "just like everyone else," and thus has restricted itself to a phantom normalcy. It is tempting to read this strategy simply as an understandable and appropriate response to a pathologizing homophobia or, alternatively, as an impoverished restriction on the part of lesbian and gay politics and media culture. Both readings have some truth to them. However, neither reading can adequately explain the problematic entanglements between homoerotic representation and the inclusive procedures of the public sphere itself. The historical and structural nature of these entanglements, and the representations they generate, form the central concerns of this book. As the "very soul of justice," the democratic ideals claimed by publicity require a critical vigilance over both their normative thrust and material distribution.[1]

From its beginnings in the worldly interests and developing self-conception of an emergent middle class, the ideal of "publicity" or "the public sphere" aimed toward democratic self-determination. This ideal sought to guarantee uninhibited communication between persons conceptualized as equal in their capacity for rational deliberation. Private individuals were to assemble freely and equally to discuss issues of public interest and exercise their powers of critical judgment. At first the ideal of publicity grew out of the informational needs and literary activities of an educated commercial class in seventeenth- and eighteenth-century Europe. It then developed into a full-fledged class ideal of social, political, and cultural organization. As this ideal gradually attained hegemony within the institutions and organizations of civil society and the state in the nineteenth century, its status as a cornerstone of a just social order seemed all but assured. Indeed, this hegemony can be glimpsed in the enabling confusion manifest in the English translations of the German term *Öffentlichkeit* (from which current discussion about the public sphere largely derives): on the one hand "publicity" or "publicness" as a normative ideal, a *quality*, and on the other "the public sphere" as a material *thing*, a spatial ensemble of places, organizations, and practices. While it is true that the ideals of publicity live in and through specific outlets, such as voluntary associations or the mass media, it is useful to view these outlets as having a *normative relation* to publicity. To identify a set of outlets and their practices as forming a public sphere is an irreducibly evaluative judgment. By insisting that the public sphere signifies a *qualitative relation* and not necessarily a distinct place or totality of venues, those disenfranchised from the venues that claim publicness can ask more insistently whether they actually embody this quality. Moreover, understanding the public sphere as a qualitative relation enables the disenfranchised to question, and to formulate alternatives to, the norms to which the quality of publicness refers. Questioning the normative definition and material distribution of publicness as a quality cannot but have an importance for counterhegemonic formulations of public interest. One of the primary historical achievements of middle-class hegemony, in fact, has been to conflate the quality of publicness with the organizations that claim to embody it, even as this embodiment may be partial, at best. This conflation was achieved at least in part by the democratic claims by which bourgeois forms of social, political, and economic organization have been justified. In this sense, "the public sphere" designates not so much a particular set of places or institutions, as the tense relation between Enlightenment ideals of democratic publicness and their material realizations.[2]

As the medium through which private people freely and equally came together to make public use of their reason, deliberating issues of concern to all in a manner open to all in principle, the bourgeois public sphere "undercut the principle on which existing [absolutist, monarchical] rule was based" and formulated new, more democratic values of social and self-governance.[3] Straddling a reconceptualized division between public and private that was rooted in the moral subject-formation of the bourgeois family and integrated within the commercial activities of the middle classes, the public sphere translated "private vices" into "public virtues": acquisitiveness, competition, and rational calculation from private commerce; companionate love, voluntary association, and self-cultivation from the intimate domestic spaces of the conjugal family. It was, in fact, the new models of subjectivity generated within the bourgeois family that provided the public sphere with a decisively moral conceptualization of the human. As Jürgen Habermas indicates, "The sphere of the public [Publikums] arose in the broader strata of the bourgeoisie as an expansion and at the same time completion [Ergänzung] of the intimate sphere of the conjugal family."[4] In the moral universe of the bourgeois family, "humanity [Humanität] had here its genuine site."[5] Together with conceiving private persons as property owners, this essentially moral conception of humanity formed a "fictitious identity" upon which social equality and the democratic nature of the public sphere were based: "The public sphere of civil society stood or fell with the principle of universal access. . . . Accordingly, the public that might be considered the subject of the bourgeois constitutional state [bürgerlichen Rechtsstaates] understood its sphere as a public one in this strict sense; in its deliberations it anticipated in principle that all human beings belong to it. The private person too, was simply a human being, that is, a moral person."[6] Despite the ideal of universal access, however, the connections between a moral conception of personhood and bourgeois political and economic relations have had proprietary implications that historically have limited social enfranchisement for many.

Precisely because many constituent features of bourgeois publicity originated in the private sphere of commerce and the intimate sphere of the family, not all private "vices" were translated into public virtues. This was especially true for those whose experiences and social position marked them as lacking the characteristics deemed necessary for full enfranchisement. Crucially, the principles of translation from private to public retained by the bourgeois public sphere have historically contradicted its own universalist, democratic ideals. While claiming to establish a "context-transcending" sphere through which to adjudicate competing interests equitably, the conversion from private to public has involved quite particular, context-specific determinations of value. For example, the bourgeois public sphere explicitly excluded women from participation, based on their supposedly inferior rational capacities and resolute identification with the domestic. Because working-class men were not seen as owning property, they too were shut out from the institutions of free rational discussion. In the United States, the explicit disenfranchisement of African slaves of both sexes was based not simply on the fact that they did not own property, but that they *were* property. Even as marriage and labor were publicly valorized, their value was at the same time inequitably distributed; women were more often than not disenfranchised by the marriage contract, and the collective interests of socialized labor were routinely suppressed if not enslaved. And today, many of the racist presumptions of public sphere participation are channeled through linguistic qualifications, to which anti-immigration and English-only movements in the United States would attest. Historically, the intimate connections between *property* and *propriety* have determined in large measure the kinds of subject positions and experiences that could be translated into the legitimate grammar of a "general" public interest.

Habermas, the primary contemporary defender of publicity as a normative ideal, has countered that while such exclusions have historically marred the realization of the public sphere's democratic principles, these principles retain a utopian capacity for "self-correction." "In the course of the nineteenth and twentieth centuries," he argues, "the universalist discourses of the bourgeois public sphere could no longer immunize themselves against a critique from within. The labor movement and feminism, for example, were able to join these discourses in order to shatter the structures that had initially constituted them as 'the other' of a bourgeois public sphere."[7] Nevertheless, it remains an open question how far the inclusive mechanisms of the public sphere can go in overcoming their historical limitations and admitting excluded groups, particularly when the very nature of such groups challenges the proprietary codes that (inappropriately) shape publicity practices. And thus it remains an even more urgent question what *effects* inclusion has in translating oppressed and/or minoritized concerns into issues of public interest. This book will seek to chart some of these effects in relation to homoeroticism and queer representation. Given the continuing purchase of public sphere ideals for conceptualizing justice, cultural vitality, and social organization (however contradictory this purchase may be), the effects of inclusion in the public sphere cannot but have an important bearing on the future of queer self-definition and its relation to the social.

Historically, the greatest impediments to queer public sphere inclusion have been twofold: first, the heterosexist tenor of the bourgeois familial morality defining proper civic personhood and universal humanity; and second, the relegation of erotic experience, which has largely shaped a queer sense of self and collective belonging, to the proprietary privacy of the intimate sphere. Acting together, these two impediments have meant that even as the public sphere both draws upon and legitimates specific forms of intimacy and erotic experience—indeed is saturated by spectacles of intimacy—those that do not conform to a heteronormative standard are demonized and repudiated. Paradoxically, the "affirming" spectacles of homoeroticism, or the embodied identities to which it is presumptively attached, that one does find in contemporary public culture largely conform to this heteronormative standard. These heroically bland affirmations pay for their admission with immiserating disavowals.

To name these affirmations as heteronormative thus marks a crucial aspect of dissent within *queer* thought and life: that sex, erotic experience, and identity formations are not necessarily coextensive. While there is (often confused) overlap between cross-sex eroticism and heteronormativity, the latter designates both something more and something less than specific acts and erotic experiences. As Lauren Berlant and Michael Warner have persuasively argued, heteronormativity names "the institutions, structures of understanding, and practical orientations that make heterosexuality seem not only coherent—that is, organized as a sexuality—but also privileged." Rather than an internally consistent set of norms, heteronormativity is more what Raymond Williams called a "structure of feeling," one that aims to produce an entitled coherence. As Berlant and Warner argue, "It consists less of norms that could be summarized as a body of doctrine than of a sense of rightness produced in contradictory manifestations— often unconscious, immanent to practice or to institutions. Contexts that have little visible relation to sex practice, such as life narrative and generational identity, can be heteronormative in this sense, while in other contexts sex between men and women might not be heteronormative."[8] By modeling homoerotic life according to a heteronormative standard, the inclusion of lesbians and gay men in the public sphere grants them a sense of entitlement by repudiating that which defies or exceeds this proprietary standard. Here we find a distorted recapitulation of the bourgeois public sphere's equation between morality and the human: instead of an egalitarian justice, a restrictive notion of moral worth now inappropriately functions as the distributive principle for social enfranchisement. Moreover, the authenticating goal of representing queers as they "really are," which is to say, "just like everyone else," dissimulates this type of moral value determination that mediates public discourse. The democratic norms of publicity intermingle with proprietary codes that, in fact, have little to do with democracy as an ideally egalitarian form of social organization and arena for self-determination. The capacity of the public sphere to "self-correct" is seriously compromised by the retention of historically particular, ideologically limiting principles for the determination of value and the distribution of equity.

To approach the salient structural and historical problems shaping the inclusion of homoeroticism, much of my investigation is focused through the category of value. The analytic and political force of this category, as one encounters it in Western Marxist thought, can suggest troubling limitations to the context-transcending claims of modern publicity. Value, I argue, provides an important analytic node for grasping the mediations by which inequalities are preserved under the cover of equality. I argue that the justice conferred by public sphere inclusion involves value relations that at the very least tend to produce a heteronormative sanitation of queer life. This sanitation cannot simply be attributed to prudery, although traditional sexual mores are certainly a factor. Rather, I argue that it can be linked historically and structurally to what I call the "subjunctive mood" of bourgeois publicity.[9]

This subjunctive mood can be located first in the claim that because the public sphere is built on universalist ideals—equal representation, participation, and access for rational discussion—it has an irreducibly counterfactual aspect. As universal ideals, they may be approximated, but never fully realized. The vagaries of history and context will continually test their validity and application. Beyond elaborating its ideals as counterfactual, however, the public sphere also demands that one act *as if* the material practices and organizations associated with the public sphere unproblematically embody the ideals of democratic publicness. In terms of homoerotic representation, publicity's subjunctive mood requires that one act as if equal representation, participation, and access are achieved through homogenized proxies—lesbians and gay men who are "just like everyone else." This subjunctive requirement compresses the complex syntax of value in determining matters of public interest and, just as importantly, representations of public interest. By opening up this compressed process of value determination, I aim to problematize publicity's utopian promise: that it is able, *through the subjunctive conceptualization of its ideals and their material embodiments,* to self-correct its historical exclusions. Even as excluded groups are brought into the fold, so to speak, the homogenization of interests and representations demanded by inclusion also indicates that it requires deferred and demonized remainders: queer persons and interests that would doubtless seem slightly out of place on a city council or in an Ikea commercial. Formulating ideals of democratic publicness as legitimately both impossible and actual, as at once "claimed and denied" in Habermas's terms, allows inadequate principles for the distribution of representational equity to operate under the cover of the very equality they deny. It is in this sense that public sphere inclusion is irreducibly bound to relations of value that are dissembled by being written in the subjunctive.

The public sphere's subjunctive mood can thus be characterized by two interrelated contradictions. The first is the contradiction between the ideal and the historical reality of the norms defining publicity. Exclusion goes against the grain of the public sphere's democratic ideals. Habermas has responded by claiming for the public sphere an ever-expanding ability to dissipate social prejudice and redress its own exclusion of traditionally disenfranchised persons and constituencies, even as the very ideals of the public sphere have historically been attached to a quite particular subject position: the white Euro-American, educated, presumptively heterosexual middle-class male who owns property. Habermas argues that "because publics cannot harden into organizations or systems, there is no exclusion rule without a proviso for its abolishment." Such a proviso stems, in turn, from the fact that "boundaries inside the universal public sphere as defined by its reference to the political system remain permeable in principle. The rights to unrestricted inclusion and equality built into liberal public spheres prevent exclusion mechanisms of the Foucauldian type and ground a *potential for self-transformation.*" [10] The public sphere can self-correct because its own ideals provide the means to critique their instantiation. To claim that the public sphere has a built-in capacity to self-correct, however, raises a more fundamental question: Will the public sphere and its norms ever *not* need to remedy their own contradictions? Or to put it another way, will the democratic ideals of the public sphere always be held hostage to their contradictory articulations and materializations, by virtue of the claim that these ideals are necessarily counterfactual anyway? In their important revision of Habermas's often overly optimistic analysis, Oskar Negt and Alexander Kluge have pointed to the fact that, at least in Immanuel Kant's classic statements concerning bourgeois publicity, the "construction of the public sphere derives its entire substance from the existence of owners of private property." [11] This constitutes one of the core prevarications of the bourgeois public sphere exemplified in Kant's political thought. In order for Kant to advance "universally valid rules of public communication," he must also "negate this material base on which the public sphere rests . . . In a word: he can constitute bourgeois publicity neither *with* the empirical bourgeois-subject nor *without* it." [12] This prevarication, they argue, indicates the extent to which the universal presumptions of bourgeois publicity were both founded on *and* set against "empirically given capitalist commodity production." [13] To illustrate the exclusions enforced by this contradiction, Negt and Kluge include an intriguing footnote where they point out that "Kant must—with considerable violence of thought—exclude *one substantial group of humanity after another* as inadequate to this 'true politics': children, women, store clerks, day laborers, 'even the hairdresser.'" [14] "The weakness characteristic of virtually all forms of the bourgeois public sphere," they conclude, "derives from this contradiction: namely, that the bourgeois public sphere excludes substantial life interests and nevertheless claims to represent society as a whole."[15] The gaps between publicity ideals and their manifestation may indeed indicate a diachronic project under construction; but historically these gaps also and perhaps more strongly pinpoint a constituent contradiction *within* this project's self-understanding. To the extent that its ideals have been articulated as irreducibly counterfactual, and therefore on their own terms *must* remain contradicted by their historical manifestation, the public sphere can only ever asymptotically approach any consistency with these ideals, even as such consistency remains an operative, indeed demanded, pretension of publicity practices. It would therefore seem that the public sphere will always have a need to "self-correct." The constitutive gap between ideal and history thus risks becoming merely a form of managed inequity. While this gap could provide the disenfranchised with the means to critique the failures of publicness, articulating publicness as "always already" counterfactual *and* requiring one to act as if it weren't, disables critique with a legitimated contradiction. In this way, the public sphere risks an infinite deferral and dissimulation of its own promise.[16]

However, the second contradiction I would point to in the public sphere's subjunctive mood concerns precisely its inclusionary promise. Were one to grant the public sphere's capacity for self-correction, this capacity represents only one element in the process of bringing groups within the public sphere's purview. More importantly, inclusion entails fundamental *transformations* in a group's self-identified interests. On the one hand, the ideal of publicness certainly contains an irreducibly transformative force that beneficially aims toward a democratization of social life and hence the elaboration of fully enfranchised civic subjects. On the other, however, the normative thrust of this ideal is often contradicted by the proprietary codes through which it is realized. The democratic promise of civic subjectivity is often contradicted by the inclusive processes that would grant it. To achieve integration within forms of public discourse, excluded groups must appear to conform to the standards of the "normal citizen" by which they were excluded to begin with.[17] This does not just entail the erasure of difference, although this does occur; publicity's conformist inertia can also render forms of difference into, for example, nonthreatening entertainment (as in the rather banal drag queens seen in a number of 1990s Hollywood films). With respect to queer life, the transformations demanded by inclusion compress and thus mystify the processes of value determination they involve. These processes can be parsed into three interpenetrating modes:

Mode One: The determination of particular interests as worthy of the public interest. The structural division between public and private has traditionally relegated sexuality, other than the publicly decorous trappings of cross-sexual monogamous marriage and other entitled aspects of a heteronormative imaginary, outside the parameters of public interest. This structural impediment, largely rooted in the class-specific nature of the private/public divide, itself signifies the specific historical content embedded within the public sphere's putatively disinterested and universally valid norms. Given this structural impediment, queer efforts to become an integral part of a (however fictional) deliberative public have more often than not necessitated self-censorship. With regard to eroticism, only those private vices that conform to a heteronormative moral code are translated into legitimate public virtues. Thus elements of queer life that do not conform to this code are expunged with little, if any, regard for the imaginative diversity of queer life. Justified at least in part by the struggle for public sphere inclusion and equal rights, the denigration of erotic nonconformity in particular by prominent lesbians and gay men over the past few years confirms the constricting requirement for a heteronormative conformity. As Amy Gluckman and Betsy Reed usefully summarize, "What good does liberation do a queen if his [sic] rights depend on no longer being a queen?" [18] Because the ideals of bourgeois publicity use unduly universalized moral codes to govern the distribution of equity, conformity to a historically particular, class-inflected, and often racially homogenized heteronormativity determines what precisely will and will not become valorized representations of queer life.

Mode Two: The mediation of queer interests by value formations unrelated to, yet mistaken for, the public sphere's ideal of participatory democracy. In the first mode, queer interests are bestowed value only insofar as they conform to the heteronormative standards retained within publicity's supposedly universal moral-political principles. In mode two, this bestowal becomes the alibi for, and thus is overlapped by, the mediation of homoeroticism through the extraction of commercial value. This mode is paradoxically the most blatant, but—perhaps for that very reason—the most unremarked. One finds it in every Absolut vodka image in lesbian and gay magazines, every corporate sponsorship of a lesbian and gay event, and in every Community Card Pack chock-full of lesbian and gay advertisements. These marketing devices, designed to expropriate economic value, are unproblematically seen to grant the political value of equitable representation. Thus they reap a "social profit" in excess of, yet originating in the drive for, the monetary profits they may realize while elaborating a lesbian and gay market. The saturation of dominant publicity forums with capitalist determinations of value—even forums defined in relation to traditional ideals of democracy—melds the political and economic value that lesbian and gay inclusion would accrue. (A similar melding could be witnessed during the events of 1989–90 in Eastern Europe, when Western media triumphantly conflated the "opening" of capitalist markets with the establishment of parliamentary democracies.) Indeed, public sphere ideals emerged coextensive with capitalism, such that publicity practices have been indissolubly woven into the fabric of specifically capitalist social formations.[19] This commercial mode of value determination thus highlights with peculiar brilliance the tense contradictions between public sphere ideals of distributional justice and equality, and capitalism's inegalitarian modes of determining and distributing value. In this regard, civic value is routed through commercial value. However, while the heteronormative standards of public legitimacy and civic equality in mode one are linked to the movements of capital, such links are complex. Modes of capitalist valuation not only overlap and supplement those of mode one, they can also contradict and outstrip them. One can see the clash between these two modes in the boycotts that "family values" groups in the United States have organized against corporations like AT&T and ABC/Disney for "affirming" lesbians and gay men in their marketing activities and corporate culture. The determination and distribution of value here does not rely fundamentally on a subject-centered morality; commercial value extraction may acknowledge moral conflicts in recognizing politically relevant economic constituencies, but also may just as easily remain blithely indifferent, even antagonistic, toward such conflicts. The larger point is that what passes as "affirmative" lesbian and gay representations are thus imbricated in economies of value that not only extend beyond the sexual, but also intriguingly complicate the very progressive, democratic ends such affirmations seek to achieve. Given the overwhelming predominance of commercialized representations in what passes for the public sphere today, this second mode crucially mediates the first and the third, yet its effects remain the most mystified of the three. We could say this mode fits the classic description of the excluded middle. Its exclusion occurs in mode three.

Mode Three: The attribution of "authenticity" to lesbian and gay publicity proxies—the "good homosexuals" of contemporary visibility politics. By claiming to present authentic representations of particular constituencies, the public sphere dissimulates the mediations through which such authenticity takes shape. Value adjudicates the question of public legitimacy, and thus determines in large measure the representational proxies that inclusion will proffer—proxies that acquire all the phantom authenticity of the native informant. Their phantom authenticity, in turn, occludes their mediation through the constricting and expropriating value-determinations of modes one and two. This occlusion allows such proxies to be coded as politically progressive in terms of achieving equivalent public representation. Authenticity under the sign of equivalence appears to displace homophobia, yet in the process displaces from critical scrutiny the mediation of queer legitimacy through inequitable value-determinations. Authenticity under the sign of equivalence, in other words, enables images that *constrict and extract* value to be read as if they unproblematically *bestow* it. Lesbian and gay visibility politics measures commercial representations, for example, only by the yardstick of "positive images." The latter, as homogenized proxies, are celebrated subjunctively—*as if* they signified equitable representation and, perhaps more important, equitable access to the means of representation. In this sense, the subjunctive mood of the public sphere becomes an alibi for practices that contradict the basic premises of democratic publicity. The dissimulation of a mediated inauthenticity appeases demands for justice, and thus justifies the subjunctive deferral of an emancipatory promise.

By focusing on the combined force of these modes, two analytic possibilities come into view. First, because value is not an ontological quality or "thing," but rather develops through the relation between systemic elements (as with the commodity whose value is established only in its exchange relation to other commodities, or with the citizen whose abstraction grounds political equivalence with others), the irreducibly social, nonidentitarian aspects of homoeroticism within each mode of value determination are more clearly brought into view.[20] Moreover, this nonidentitarian analytic possibility does not just aim to debunk the fictions of identity. It also aims to render visible the processes granting identities a public solidity, presence, and abstract authority, particularly as nonsexual identity formations impact sexual ones. Second, then, the issue of value also brings into view the entanglements between representations of homoeroticism and aspects of the public sphere whose concerns are not reducible to sexuality per se (at least as this term has acquired the fiction of a stable referent). Figuring homoeroticism within economies of value whose subject predications extend beyond the erotic—such as norms of citizenship—involves more than the removal of a prior exclusion. As the example of current marketing interest in lesbians and gay men reveals, inclusion can have far-reaching effects not exhausted by the political goal of fighting homophobia, effects that can change the shape of what "lesbian," "gay," or "queer" could come to mean.[21]

Investigating how the private "vice" of homoeroticism becomes valued as a public virtue thus necessitates conjoining value as a structure of representation with "values" as historically particular moral codes, ethical schemes, and political ideals. Bringing together these two senses of value subsumed under the idealized sign of "equivalence," as I argue in chapter 1, helps to displace the assumption, operative in the public sphere's self-conception as well as in mainstream lesbian and gay politics, that achieving equivalence in the public sphere will grant a group's interests authentic representation, and thus accurately show lesbians and gay men as they "really are." The ideal of representational equivalence has been framed and instantiated historically in a variety of ways, although generally it follows efforts within Western modernity to democratize those venues that would confer legitimate public presence and juridical protection. The promise of democratization, in fact, forms one of the most potent justifications for the norms of the public sphere. Appeals for equivalent representation, for the equitable distribution of value, have become over the past two hundred years or so a potent mode of redress for social, political, cultural, and economic devaluation, and thus an important means for legitimation. To reclaim the lesbian and gay past, to recuperate a gay cultural tradition, to offer for public consumption "positive" role models, to show that lesbians are not tortured, pathological predators, but are rather "just like everyone else": the goal of nonphobic inclusion combats devaluation and strives toward equivalence through such assimilationist measures. As the ideal of equivalent representation has developed within Western capitalist social formations, it has come to be seen as an overarching and adequate solution to exclusion and devaluation, rather than also being problematic. The issue is not whether equality and equivalence are irreparably ideological. Rather, the issue is how these ideals are articulated and instantiated within a public sphere constrained by historically particular norms, and thus structurally intricated with inequitable processes of value determination. We must ask, in other words, the extent to which the formulation of publicity ideals as constitutively, justifiably counterfactual allows inadequate principles of distributing equity to operate under the cover of democratic publicness.

By opening up these modes of value determination, we can begin to form a more complex understanding of the historical and structural dynamics underwriting both lesbian and gay publicity and forms of queer counterpublicity. The capability of the public sphere to self-correct meets its limit when its own presumptively universal norms prove incommensurate to an excluded group seeking legitimacy. Thus inclusion demands not so much a reorientation of the public sphere and its norms as it does a reorientation of that which it includes. In a certain respect this is as it should be; to be egalitarian, civic subjectivity must be grounded in yet also extend beyond the incommensurable contours of individual life histories. Civic subjectivity must be irreducibly social. However, in another respect, if the public sphere is indeed to self-correct, it must also have the capacity to alter in the face of those subjective and/or group differences informing the civic subjectivity it is to nurture. The subjunctive mood of publicity can block this kind of dynamic responsiveness. This blockage can be seen in the force with which narrow group interests, such as Evangelical fundamentalism in the United States, have been able to hinder and/or unduly affect the inclusive potential of publicity for sexual minorities in particular (often under the guise of protecting religious liberty in general). While the inclusion of previously excluded groups seems to validate publicity's capacity to self-correct, it also leaves intact—because it can legitimately dissimulate—the normalizing calculus operative within inclusive procedures. The disinterested, universal nature of publicity norms—rational deliberation, intersubjective ethics, voluntary association, fairness, equality of access and treatment—are often contradicted not only by their silent retention of moral narratives rooted in middle-class hegemony, but also by their procedural instantiation. We may thus pinpoint a fundamental flaw that can render the claim of self-correction a palliative, at best. Articulating universal democratic norms as necessarily subjunctive precludes the public sphere from embodying the democratic potential it nevertheless claims. As I will suggest throughout this book, the "incompletion" of the public sphere's egalitarian potential might not only signal an unfulfilled project of Enlightenment modernity, as Habermas has argued, but also a disabling subjunctive quality hitherto woven into the very fabric of the public sphere's self-understanding. Figuring the democratic potential of publicity as necessarily subjunctive—that it must be seen *as if* it were actual—grants inequitable and restrictively normalizing embodiments of this potential a legitimating cover.[22]

The analyses that follow thus investigate how a focus on homoeroticism can reveal the representational limits of, and dissembled transformations effected by, public sphere inclusion. These limits and transformations are framed by both contemporary lesbian and gay politics and (largely demonized) queer counterpublics, and are focused through exemplary discourses from the European Enlightenment and dynamics within nineteenth-century British cultural history. A dual focus on publicity as political ideal and historical phenomenon corresponds to the two parts of this book. The first part emphasizes the structural constraints of the public sphere, and the second focuses on particular historical examples of these constraints as they have impacted representations of homoerotic desire. However, each part is united by a primary, defining process conjoining value and representation in the public sphere: the translation of "private vices" into "public virtues." As I have indicated above, this translation is a well-known element in the historical cementing of modern capitalist social formations.[23] Apologists for capitalist commerce during the seventeenth and eighteenth centuries in Western Europe, for example, reformulated traditionally suspicious commercial interests into beneficent psychological properties harmoniously corresponding to a supply and demand economy. Yet this culture of emerging capitalism affected more than just the understanding of commercial psychology. It also established norms by which an array of elements within the middle-class individual would be judged. These in turn became universalized moral standards by which *all* persons and groups would be evaluated, and thus by which the distribution of equity and justice would be administered. Together with subjective experiences drawn from the bourgeois family, a new standard of value for humanity and the human was brought into being, naturalized, and made hegemonic.

As both a model of social organization and as a lived historical phenomenon, the public sphere has evolved from the self-conception and legitimation strategies of the middle classes, a class specificity that would challenge the universal status claimed for the public sphere's most cherished ideals. However, we must also bear in mind that to critique public sphere inclusion, one must also avoid the dangers of romanticizing alterity, for at least two reasons. First, the myriad other subject positions that queers can occupy, and thus the many other modes of value determination in which they are positioned, have meant we should not presume their exclusion to be absolute. (This is why I have emphasized homoeroticism throughout this study, rather than an ontologized and thus totalized lesbian or gay identity.) Exclusion operates differently through a number of vectors, often concomitantly with forms of privilege. Second, to charge the public sphere and its ideals with inadequacy, indeed with the mystification of this inadequacy, does not thereby justify a simplistic *rejection* of these ideals. It is as nonsensical to argue, for example, that the origin of rights discourses and ideals of publicness in bourgeois thought negates any benefits that may be derived from them, as it would be to argue that the bourgeois origins of industrialization necessitate a return to agrarian social formations. While in many regards the public sphere operates as an ideological fiction, nevertheless its norms continue to structure expectations and actions regarding justice in a quite palpable way.[24] It is in this sense that a simple refusal of public sphere norms—equal representation, for example—would be misguided. Precisely how the norms of the public sphere, like equality, may be articulated, distributed, and realized differently has been an important source of dialogue for historians, cultural critics, political philosophers, and social activists. To say the public sphere legitimates the contradiction of its own promise is also to open possibilities for transforming its self-contradictory operations altogether—and most important, possibilities for transforming them on terms *other than* their own.

Thus my emphasis on the subjunctive gaps and dislocations in the public sphere is not meant to bear the weight of a functionalist attribution or a totalizing critique: just the opposite. The subjunctive deferral intrinsic to the public sphere's claim of self-correction, in both its normative outline and material instantiations, must itself be grasped as a critical weapon, one that can be used against the stasis of deferred hopes. It can be used not in the sense of resurrecting the utopian ideal of historical consummation or a "completed world," which would simply replace one stasis with another. Nor, however, can the mere *presumption* of democratic norms, as Habermas has seemed to argue, in itself become the very sign of democracy in action. Habermas has claimed that a democratically organized publicity is at some level a pretense, a subjunctive "as if," at least in part to insure that moral-political norms remain open to debate. Only if the match between publicity norms and the institutions that claim them remains counterfactual—simultaneously claimed and denied—can debate about the realization of these norms take place and, on the basis of this debate, the public sphere "self-correct." Yet this proposes the kind of performative contradiction elsewhere criticized by Habermas: a democratic society depends upon the counterfactuality of democratic ideals.[25] To critique, as I do here, the public sphere as inconsistent with its democratic norms certainly lays claim to public sphere ideals themselves. However, such claim-making does not thereby prove that the public sphere allows for debate characterized by equality of access to discursive resources or the legitimation of diverse interests. Indeed, to claim that it does renders critique into a wholesale validation of the very thing it would change. To understand the subjunctive mood of the public sphere as the sign of the democratic organization it also denies, to legitimate the counterfactuality of democratic norms as that which insures democratic deliberation, represents a juggling act that distracts from the contradictory effects of public sphere inclusion. Critique of the public sphere's subjunctive mood cannot be held hostage by the claim that this mood is precisely what allows for critique itself; to do so would be to formalize the infinite deferral of democratic forms of life and the Enlightenment capacities for self-criticism, common understanding, and justice that the public sphere ideally embodies. The history of how publicity's egalitarian ideals take form, establish constituencies, and have been materially distributed must in turn impinge upon how we understand and transform their normative articulation. Rather than idealized as a (contradictory) space for deliberation and debate, then, the subjunctivity of the public sphere can be used against itself to turn aside weak propitiations, question alibis for inequity, and thus reimagine the dissembling and homogenizing terms by which legitimate public representation operates. The subjunctive mood of the public sphere forms not only its defining limitation. It also forms the negative, as opposed to the universally necessary, lever by which the mediation of egalitarian norms can be imagined on *other than* subjunctive terms. In this way, the potential of a publicness articulated and organized otherwise may be pried loose from dissembled democracy, expropriative practices, inegalitarian interests, and palliative "self-corrections." The question at hand is not so much how to live up to publicity ideals more fully; such a task would retain the static, ahistorical, and counterfactual understanding of these ideals. Rather, the question is the extent to which these ideals themselves can be reformulated in *response* to their less than ideal history.[26]

As my brief comments here might indicate, the question of homoerotic inclusion in the public sphere must necessarily grapple with current, rather fraught debates about the viability of the Enlightenment legacy and its relation to social justice. Certainly I cannot hope, nor do I aim, to resolve these debates. I merely wish to indicate that insofar as publicity norms continue to organize expectations for justice in a variety of arenas, the struggle to articulate and materialize them differently must displace romanticized notions of queer alterity. The central problematic that I address, therefore, does not concern exclusion so much as the procedural, inclusive norms with which lesbians and gay men have themselves become willingly entangled and with which they must come to terms. My critique of contemporary lesbian and gay conformism to the deforming effects of the public sphere does not cast this conformism simply as an external imposition, but rather as a complex dynamic. Mainstream lesbian and gay political organizations and publicity venues themselves have by no means been reticent to sanitize queer life. The representational sanitation of an assimilationist cultural and political agenda stems from efforts at *self*-representation as well. A defining element of my project, then, is to maximize the potential of antihomophobic thought and struggle to extend beyond, while retaining the critical force of, its generative circumstances.

These circumstances—from the early homosexual rights movements in late-nineteenth- and early-twentieth-century Germany, to the post-Stonewall civil rights struggles in the United States, among many other moments—have generally aimed to transform erotic life and homoerotic expression. Such transformative efforts have helped to make sex, sexuality, desire, and eroticism into newly viable experiential, analytic, and political categories. This has at the very least been a recuperative success: wresting concepts away from institutional, political, moral, and everyday contexts in which queer existences were routinely denied, denigrated, pathologized, incarcerated, or simply wiped out. More importantly, such recuperative efforts have also entailed fundamental revaluations of those concepts and practices that define and delimit erotic life. Antihomophobic revaluations require an engagement with and overturning of the irreducibly moralistic value-determinations that have made sex and its significations intelligible.[27]

Over the last quarter century in particular, antihomophobic revaluations of erotic life have centered on the oppositions closeted/out and invisibility/visibility, especially as these oppositions make sense of erotic norms and the representational exclusions they enforce. Moreover, they form an integral part of the critical armory not only in combating homophobia, but also in publicly representing the interests of queers as a constituency. The central axiological dimension these oppositions have acquired in defining queer interests has rendered them more often than not the sole arbiters of value and legitimacy—regarding the "affirmative" character of legislative agendas, media attention, marketing efforts, historical narratives, cultural texts, or many of the other arenas available for the public representation of queerness.

These oppositions have proved extraordinarily useful and productive for understanding and revising the structuring effects of homophobia. However, they do not exhaustively conceptualize the many other value relations involved in the production, circulation, and representation of homoeroticism in the public sphere. As beneficial as working toward greater lesbian and gay visibility can be, doing so more often than not fails to scrutinize the other value determinations that exceed the purview of homophobia or heterosexism. This is not to say that efforts toward antihomophobic representational inclusion can be dispensed with—far from it. However, in articulating what such inclusion might be like and on what terms it might be offered, one must come to terms with the range of representational dynamics through which this articulation may be achieved. Most important, such an articulation must examine the inclusive weight of norms neither reducible to nor utterly separable from homophobia. For example, corporate marketing aimed at (as well as offered by) lesbians and gay men is arguably nonhomophobic, but also proffers homogenized images of lesbians and gay men as a supposedly lucrative market segment. Elaborating such a market to which these images are meant to refer and appeal corresponds to an interest in extracting economic value, which certainly includes but is not limited to profit margins. It also involves a "social profit" generating the legitimation value extracted from the very real confusion such

marketing activities effect between corporate interests, subcultural formations, and what counts as progressive political change. That Disney or AT&T
can render indistinguishable an interest in market share and in progressive
social change with regard to domestic partner benefits or a generalized lesbian and gay visibility gives some indication of this legitimating confusion.
The lack of differentiation between commercial and (putatively) noncom-
mercial spheres points in fact to the problematically general character of
the public sphere itself.

The often limiting entanglements between characteristic features of the
public sphere, on the one hand, and queer struggles for public legitimacy,
on the other, coalesce in inclusion and its effects. The imperative to present
"normal" and "affirming" images of queers in corporate marketing, popular historical narratives, canons of cultural tradition, mass-distributed
films, or corporate television programming raises the important question
of what inclusion itself fails to include. When lesbian and gay identitarian
narratives acquiesce to the civic, economic, and cultural norms at work in
the calculation of valuable public representations, they also leave unreal-
ized and often simply repudiate other possibilities for imagining queer existence, not the least because this repudiation would liquidate viable counterpublics rooted in what Lisa Duggan and Nan D. Hunter have termed "sexual
dissent."[28] I will be centrally concerned, then, with the value determinations characterizing such processes of calculation and repudiation, and
their limits and possibilities for queer representation in a problematically
general public sphere. To that end, I aim to disrupt the presumption that
achieving equitable publicity for queers is merely a corrective task of reversing exclusion, erasing stereotypes, and thus achieving "realistic" representation. I will attempt to chart how understandings of homoeroticism have
been shaped by the value hierarchies embedded within the very spheres that
claim to ameliorate these hierarchies, an amelioration that more broadly
claims to provide equitable and democratic representation.

Because the materials I investigate are drawn from both contemporary dynamics of queer publicity and late-eighteenth- and nineteenth-century English and European cultural history, I will suggest points of relay between
historical analysis and contemporary critique. This requires an engagement
between historically local analyses of texts and the analytic categories that
guide these analyses—what Oskar Negt and Alexander Kluge have usefully

characterized as the "dialectic between historical and systematic methods of analysis."[29] This dialectic in turn grasps the interplay between the modern ideals of the public sphere as structures of value, and "values" in the more local historical sense of particular moral and ethical schemes. By doing so, critique can more adequately discern those historically outmoded norms, such as heteronormative moral codes, that continue to inhabit and contradict publicity's egalitarian ideals.

The first chapter will lay out the dynamics of lesbian and gay visibility politics, and will engage many of the theoretical concerns that inform the book as a whole. It begins with the conformist impulses of visibility politics, and how these impulses are related to the normalizing procedures of the public sphere. These procedures are rooted in complex and sometimes contradictory processes of determining value. Largely because of publicity's subjunctive rendering, I argue that these modes mystify the vital mediating role they themselves play in publicity's inclusive efforts. It is the issue of mediation, and its dissimulation through claims to authenticity, that best measures the adequacy of how the public sphere's justificatory premises are materialized. The dissimulation of mediation is, in fact, where one may locate the pernicious effects of bourgeois publicity's subjunctive mood—its demand that one act *as if* public sphere inclusion did not contradict its own premises.

Given this discussion about the problematic aspects of visibility politics and public sphere inclusion more generally, chapter 2 moves to a more focused theoretical engagement. It explores the problematic relation between autonomy and conformity in the public sphere in relation to the thought of Jürgen Habermas and Michel Foucault. While Habermas has admitted the public sphere's less than ideal record for living up to its own norms, he nevertheless maintains that such norms retain an emancipatory potential. Foucault, however, has argued that power relations operate within supposedly disinterested, even benevolent, discourses and practices inherited from the Enlightenment. His critique of modern sexuality as a limiting discursive formation has become especially important for antihomophobic thought. However, I argue that Foucault's discussion of homosexuality in terms of a "discourse/reverse discourse" formation cannot provide an adequate understanding of how queers might engage with norms of publicity, such as equitable public representation, while also working to overcome the limits of their normative articulation and material embodiments. By the same token, Foucault's analysis of the discourse/reverse discourse paradigm of homosexuality cautions against a too naive belief in the ability of the public sphere to mitigate the effects of social power, especially when this belief must take the form, as it often does in Habermas's thought, of a subjunctive moral imperative: to act as if social power were not a determining factor in elaborating notions of public interest. What emerges from the encounter between these two thinkers is the need to grasp dialectically the interactions among and mediating force of Enlightenment rationalities, forms of publicity, and sexual discourses.

To that end, chapter 3 stages an "exemplary" interaction of these elements in rights discourse, via the thought of Immanuel Kant. It investigates the place of homoeroticism and sexual desire more generally in Kant's humanist sexual ethics and political theory. It examines the relation between homoerotic desire and one of the fundamental forms by which modern political representation attempts to ground and distribute the equal value of subjects: the rights-based notion of the citizen. Kant's texts on these matters, I argue, can shed light on the effect political liberalism and sexual humanism have on the constitution of queers as (disenfranchised) sexual subjects. Because Kant's sexual humanism and political theory are built on the concept of the autonomous, property-owning subject—the ideal moral subject of the bourgeois public sphere—his notion of the citizen legitimates sexual subjectivity only through contractual, cross-sex, monogamous marriage. This form of marriage, Kant argues, provides the only protection against the supposedly objectifying effects of sexual "commerce." Yet it only does so subjunctively; marriage, he argues, is the only sphere in which sex can be practiced *as if* it weren't "objectifying." Because Kant's idea that sexual interaction "objectifies" another depends on conceptualizing the subject as property owner, the subjunctive nature of the moral imperative to marry secretly retains a historical class norm. Sexual humanism as enunciated by Kant importantly borrows from the bourgeois conceptualization of the citizen. As long as sexual humanism and the property-owning subject it presumes predicate the notion of citizenship, I argue, it is difficult to imagine queers becoming fully enfranchised other than through conformity to this rather traditional notion of marriage. Indeed, such conformity resonates with current efforts to denigrate queers who do not follow the marriage model of (proper) sexual expression.

With such constraints on enfranchisement in mind, each of the next two chapters details specific interactions between homoerotic desire and cultural publicity in nineteenth-century Britain. As Habermas himself has argued, the development of a literary culture in the eighteenth and nineteenth centuries was an integral part of the development of the bourgeois public sphere in general. Literature played a decisive role in shaping and translating new forms of subjectivity from the intimate sphere of the middle-class home to the spheres of public life. Arguing from a different conceptual framework, Nancy Armstrong has convincingly shown how the traditional English novel in particular sexualized the language of politics. This proved decisive in the universalization of middle-class norms.[30] The process of universalization centered on a reconceptualization of desire not only as an essential basis for the human (as it does problematically for Kant), but also as the basis for a mystified, regulatory form of social power. Developments within the nineteenth-century bourgeois cultural public sphere, focused here largely through literary history, can tell us much about the procedural mechanisms by which sexuality and public interest became entangled with middle-class hegemony and its modes of determining public value.

Chapter 4 takes up the question of homoerotic desire in relation to English nineteenth-century conceptualizations of a Western cultural tradition rooted in ancient Greece. The emphasis here is on the historical deference of homoerotic desire to middle-class sexual norms in the quest to legitimize "Greek love." I examine the imperial axiology underwriting the appropriation of Greece as a cultural sign system through which a male homophilic "identity" was mediated and legitimized in nineteenth-century England. The different articulations of "Greek love" one finds in the Regency libertine Lord Byron, and in the more staid Victorian John Addington Symonds, correspond to the different understandings of Greece itself in their two historical moments: from the Orientalized possession of the Ottoman Turks to a newly Europeanized nation rewritten as the birthplace of universalized middle-class virtues. Thus the different articulations of Greek love in Byron and Symonds reveal the class and racial dynamics affecting claims for the legitimacy of male homoeroticism as well. In their writings on homoeroticism each engaged differently with the divide between public and private; this divide in turn greatly affected how they understood the geopolitical resonance of homoerotic desire. By appealing to the middle-class norms through which a newly Westernized Greek tradition was imagined and valued, homophilic apologists like Symonds narrowed the possibilities for representing homoerotic desire to something vaguely athletic and resolutely chaste.

Chapter 5 turns from Greece to one of the "objective" forms of cultural tradition, the authoritative text of a canonical figure, the poet Percy Bysshe Shelley. Framed by attempts to articulate and legitimate a "gay literary tradition," this chapter focuses on the imbrication of sexual politics and cultural value in the Victorian canonization of Shelley. The development of Shelley criticism within the Victorian cultural public sphere reveals a mutual dependence between sexual norms and aesthetic criteria. Veneration for the poet became entangled in suspicions about his own erotic proclivities. Shelley's erotic nonconformity extended to speculations about the nature of his desire. In turn, this led to suspicions about the critics, men of letters, and enthusiastic readers who claimed undying love for the poet. I argue that public debates and anxieties about these suspicions became structurally embedded within, and thus mediated by, the "objective" form of the authoritative text. Through its pretensions to scientificity and neutrality, the apparatus of the authoritative text fetishistically displaced "Shelley-love," as it was called, onto the presumptively neutral mechanisms of cultural value. The sanitizing mediation of the authoritative text, in other words, allowed Shelley-lovers to fetishize the poet as if they were not engaging in a homoeroticized critical practice. In this sense, Shelley's authoritative texts carry the mark of this heteronormative displacement precisely to the extent that it could seem so invisible.

These analyses of value, representation, and homoeroticism in the Enlightenment and nineteenth-century England all seek to provide an inventory of the traces that have been deposited as history's legacy, an inventory that, as Antonio Gramsci reminds us, forms a determinate condition for critical self-consciousness. As I argue in the epilogue, these traces can tell us at least two things. First, they can tell us what inventories are possible of the occluded value-determinations shaping the dynamics of inclusion. Second, they can also tell us how such inventories may be used to imagine progressing beyond the limits of these dynamics. That is, insofar as the task I have set relies on exposing the limiting entanglements between antihomophobic efforts and less than progressive elements of social life—entanglements that often go by the name "complicity"—I have tried to suggest throughout how transformative possibilities might emerge. To point to the exclusionary norms structuring the institution of the citizen subject, for example, does not thereby render the question of queer participation in this institution into a simple question of acquiescence or refusal. Critique cannot simply pose the question of complicity as guilt or ideological contamination. Thus a cumulative task of this book will be to understand dialectically the predicament that the contradictions of the public sphere present to those who would be represented on their terms. This dialectical understanding indicates the untenability of a logic of representational contamination and the possibility of ideological purity this implies.

To the extent, therefore, that this book evokes the prognostic value of the analyses it performs, it must also be said that these analyses are not meant to offer definitive arguments about Enlightenment rationality, nineteenth-century British culture, or the dynamics underwriting queer representation. My intention is to pose the public sphere as a complex historical and structural problem, and to explore the critical utility of casting questions about queer representation in terms of publicity's occult structures of value. Moreover, by reflecting on some of the curious and complex relays between history and structure opened up by the issue of value, I have sought to avoid privileging either historical difference or structural continuity over time.[31] While the norming of queer life cannot be divorced from the particular historical forces at work in contemporary lesbian and gay politics, it is also useful to understand these phenomena more broadly through the value relations defining legitimate public representability in the West. An overemphasis on historical particularity cannot always or fully comprehend the structural continuities that obtain within the public sphere. By the same token, a strictly structural understanding of the public sphere can often reproduce an ahistorical and functionalist universalism. With the latter, one faces the danger of rendering historical change merely epiphenomenal to structure. This is in fact a central problem facing queer theory in its efforts to conceptualize the complex relations or "complicity" between queers and heteronormative discourses. Explaining these relations through largely ahistorical paradigms, lesbian and gay inquiry has more often than not codified these relations, especially as the contradictory norms of the public sphere are at times unproblematically reproduced on the level of theory. Such a reproduction obscures the dynamics between history and structure at work in representational economies of value. In the following pages, then, the vexing question of historical continuity versus discontinuity will remain an open one. Keeping this question open invalidates the mistaken and bewilderingly common idea that historical and structural analyses are somehow mutually exclusive.

If the relation between temporality and structure is not an account that can be settled here once and for all—if this relation must be consistently thematized when discussing the idealization, materialization, and distribution of the public sphere's norms—the same holds true for the categories used to understand the history of what has come to be known as sexuality. The contours of what counts as desire, sexuality, and eroticism will remain relatively open, determined largely by the particular texts and historical dynamics at hand. In part this openness stems from the central place given in a number of the chapters to what I call "indeterminate erotic expression." While this notion cannot receive a full accounting in the following pages, it does have a certain polemical, perhaps utopian function, originating in the imaginative rethinking of eroticism and affiliation found in queer life. It should also become evident, therefore, that my project owes an inestimable debt to work in lesbian and gay studies, the history of sexuality, queer theory, and varieties of queer activism that has questioned the commonsensical demarcations separating the nonerotic from the erotic, has recognized that categories such as sexuality and desire are relatively unstable, fluctuating over time and signifying variously within the same historical moment—in short, work that has demonstrated the incoherences and contradictions endemic to modern sexual definitions.[32] My overall aim, then, is to reflect on the value dynamics of representational inclusion that would grant these definitions a legitimately normal intelligibility. These dynamics, I argue, enforce the assimilationist imperatives for the alluring yet also limiting goal of inclusion as it currently operates. To reorient these assimilationist imperatives, to question the standards of value they circulate and enforce—such are the intellectual, ethical, and political goals this book seeks to further.

I. THE SUBJUNCTIVE PUBLIC SPHERE

ONE   *Visibility at the Limits of Inclusion*

Finally, the real me and the business me are the same.
—*Ad for* VICTORY! GAY & LESBIAN BUSINESS

Over at least the past thirty years, lesbian and gay political and intellectual struggle has focused an enormous amount of time, energy, and resources on the politics of visibility, a politics that strives for greater access to and presence within diverse cultural, economic, and political forms of representation. Visibility politics has demanded more "positive" lesbian and gay characters on television programming and in Hollywood films, promoted the election of lesbians and gay men to legislative bodies, agitated for gay-affirmative curricula within educational institutions, called for public figures who may be gay to declare themselves as such, and staged actions, such as shopping mall "kiss-ins," within the more mundane realms of the everyday. Each of these aspects of visibility politics, as well as many others, aims for both a quantitative and qualitative public representation. And each in its own way has helped to diminish the debilitating effects of homophobia, challenge intolerance where it simply went unquestioned, and gain familiarity and understanding in the face of sanctioned ignorance. A barometer as well of more directly political goals such as juridical protection and civil rights, visibility signifies lesbian and gay efforts toward social enfranchisement in the largest sense. The quest for public visibility, however, has raised important concerns about the terms on which this visibility will be offered, and the terms on which lesbians and gay men themselves attempt to achieve it. By what processes of valuation does homoeroticism gain a visible public legitimacy?

This question has acquired more urgency as national lesbian and gay organizations, publications, and prominent spokespeople demand not only that mainstream media present "positive" queer images, but also that queers themselves conform to the restrictive terms defining such images. Animating these demands is a structuring contradiction: on the one hand, visibility as a corrective realism, a circulation of less stereotypical, more "authentic" representations; on the other, visibility as fundamentally normative, a circulation of images that conform to a proprietary calculus. Prevaricating between communal authenticity and a calculated normalcy, the demands of visibility are mediated through complex processes of determining value. However much an authenticating visibility might combat devaluing stereotypes of queer life, the very claim to authenticity disavows its mediation. This disavowal tends to elevate homogenized lesbian and gay images into damagingly conformist standards of value for the very constituency they are said to mirror. Yet lesbian and gay conformity, and the current disputes surrounding it, only name the most visible end results of the evaluative processes shaping "positive" representability. If the charge of conformity leveled against a disingenuously authenticating visibility is to have any purpose beyond conjuring a mythical high ground of political rectitude, the processes of value determination that shape this conformity must bear closer scrutiny.

To that end, this chapter will explore some contemporary determinations of homoerotic value in the public sphere, in particular those by which homoeroticism and the subject positions attached to it become legitimately visible. The evaluative dimensions of visibility, and public sphere inclusion of queers more generally, can be located in the three interpenetrating modes of value determination discussed in the introduction. The first legitimates only those aspects of queer life that conform to a heteronormative propriety. It enforces a moral valuation of only particular forms of erotic expression as essentially, constitutively human. By anchoring queer legitimacy in the life narratives and social privileges that normalize narrow versions of heteroeroticism itself, the public sphere constricts queer representation to a phantom normalcy. Overlapping and supplementing this constriction, the second mode grafts a normalized homoeroticism onto economic processes of value extraction directed by the imperative to elaborate commercially valuable market segments. This grafting both enters into and reproduces a preexisting confusion between commercial publicity and democratic political representation. While predicated on the extraction of value in the form of profit margins and market share, commercial publicity has nevertheless come to function as if it were a form of political representation that democratically recognizes and equitably circulates a constituency's civic value. Presumed in and interpenetrating the previous two, the third mode of value determination grants them the appearance of justice: the valorization of publicity images as authentic. The sign of authenticity triumphantly occludes the mediation of images via processes of constriction and extraction. In turn, this reinforces a confusion between traditionally disparate representational arenas and their particular logics: for example, market representation as indistinguishable from juridical protections or access to political deliberation and decision making. This confusion is what we might call a "real fiction"; insofar as marketing efforts and commercial media now perform the labor of "political progress," we must therefore come to terms with, rather than simply decry, the politicized functions that commercial spheres of representation have taken on. In this regard, the real fictions of publicity raise important ethical and political questions for leftist critique. These questions do not ask that we choose between an expropriative mediation and an "affirming" authenticity. Rather, they demand that our modes of ethical and political judgment be attuned to the mediations by which we live now, and those by which we might live in a better future.

With this demand in mind, I will explore how publicity dynamics compress processes of value determination and their effects into narratives of legitimacy and authenticity. I will argue that this narrative compression obscures the mediating effects of value that exceed, and often contradict, the emancipatory promise of public sphere inclusion. As entry points for understanding the relation between value and the historical, ethical, and political ambivalences of both exclusion and inclusion, two questions present themselves: How is it, exactly, that representations which narrow and expropriate value—lesbian and gay "normalcy" and corporate legitimation profits from advertising, for example—are also understood to generate an unequivocally progressive political value? What can this understanding tell us about the nature of a supposedly authenticating visibility in the public sphere?

I would like to begin to address these questions by recounting a rather re-markable event that occurred on U.S. network television on April 30, 1997. This event seemed to confirm for many that giant strides had been made in a relatively short amount of time toward equitable, nonphobic representa-tion of lesbians and gay men in the public sphere. Like many others, I wit-nessed this event in a lesbian and gay nightclub. In contrast to the usually domestic quality of television viewing, this scene was organized as a public, "community" event in lesbian and gay spaces throughout North America. This particular nightclub was thus unusually crowded for a weekday night, and outfitted with two extremely large screens on which to project the tele-vision show we were there to watch. Local television news cameras vied for space with the patrons, scrambling for the best angle to record audi-ence reactions. The event was the coming-out episode of the ABC situation comedy *Ellen*, and the audience, myself included, responded with laughter, clapping, and enthusiasm. Despite reservations about the publicity preced-ing the show, I as well as others with similar reservations found it difficult not to be caught up in the very public and communal sense of affirmation—and besides, the show was funny. Together with the months-long media buildup for the episode, and the gossip that had circulated for far longer, the broadcast had the feel of a quite momentous event.

The momentous feel of this event sprang at the very least from the in-tense anticipation its publicity generated. Indeed, it would have been dif-ficult to miss the enormous amount of publicity in the United States sur-rounding comedian and actor Ellen Degeneres's decision to out her sitcom character Ellen Morgan, and the star herself, as lesbian. Before the hour-long coming-out episode of *Ellen*, rumors about Degeneres's plans, and ABC/Disney's approval, circulated for months in presumptively straight and explicitly gay U.S. weekly and monthly publications (thus occupying that curious open secret of entertainment news as really publicity in the strictly commercial sense). These rumors had been featured on ABC's *Enter-tainment Tonight* and the E! channel's *The Gossip Show*. Double entendres about Ellen Morgan's sexuality had been written into the show's scripts during the entire 1996–97 season. The month of April saw a media blitz over the coming-out episode: Degeneres was featured on the cover of the April 14 issue of *Time* magazine and the cover of the May issue of *Out*; she was interviewed by television journalist Diane Sawyer on the April 25 episode of the ABC news magazine 20/20, followed by an interview with Degeneres and her parents after the revelatory episode of Ellen; and there had been many articles about the show and its star in the New York Times, Entertainment Weekly, People, and the Advocate, to name just a few national publications that regularly feature U.S. entertainment news and publicity.

According to the news-oriented publicity and the celebratory reporting of the lesbian and gay press, these events were important because Ellen Morgan became the first lead character in a U.S. sitcom to be openly gay or lesbian, and Ellen Degeneres became the first star of a U.S. sitcom to declare that she is herself lesbian. Finally, U.S. network television had a lead lesbian character in a prime-time show, and more importantly, one who was not tortured, pathological, predatory, homicidal, suicidal, serial-killing, drug-addicted, prostituted, pathetic, scheming, devious, or simply bad to the core. For these reasons, the coming out of the two Ellens acquired a tremendous political value in the struggle for legitimate, affirming, nonphobic inclusion of lesbians and gay men in the public sphere.

Yet the progressive sheen of this event represents only the finished patina glossing over complex, and often contentious, processes of value coding, both before and after the anticipated revelation. For example, the week following the April 30 episode featured Ellen coming out to her parents. During a strained discussion at a Los Angeles restaurant, Ellen's father expressed anger and resentment at his daughter's revelation, saying that "Your brother Steve had the same childhood and he turned out perfectly normal." Ellen turned to her father and, with exasperation, declared, "I'm normal." Despite her declaration, her father abruptly left the restaurant. Following a later, awkward discussion between the two in the basement of her parents' home—as her father fiddled with a model train set circling "Morganville"—Mr. Morgan unexpectedly arrived at a support group for lesbian and gay parents and their children, attended by Ellen and her mother; he had had a change of heart. The episode ended with Mr. Morgan, defending his daughter against a homophobic parent in the group, proudly exclaiming a slogan from the activist group Queer Nation: "She's here, she's queer, get used to it!"

Apparently, Mr. Morgan's use of the Queer Nation slogan was meant to indicate that he no longer feared for his daughter's normalcy. In this sense it underscores the confluence of Ellen's self-designation as "normal" and similar emphases in national lesbian and gay politics. There are, of course, generic televisual factors in this confluence. The constraints of the situation comedy dictate that even a dramatic conflict be presented not only with humor, but also in a way that allows for its humorous resolution within half an hour. Moreover, one of the basic premises of *Ellen* was that the title character was anything but normal. If she were, the show would hardly be a comedy. Week after week, Ellen Morgan consistently entangled herself in extraordinary circumstances played for comedic effect. For example, the February 18, 1998, episode featured Ellen's attempts to convince her South Asian neighbors that she is not strange. Needless to say, her attempts failed: they watched her play a game of Twister on the roof of her house with her best friend; as a friendly gesture, she delivered to her neighbors a gift basket with cheese, bread, a banana, cereal, paper towels, and toilet paper— all the while unaware that she inexplicably had a bindi-like red dot on her forehead; and finally, locked out of her house and stuck on her roof wearing a chicken suit for a friend's birthday party, she used a tree to climb into the second story of her neighbors' house while they were holding a wake, tried to make small talk, and was promptly and indignantly asked to leave. Given the extraordinary strangeness that defined Ellen Morgan as a sitcom character, her lesbianism was in fact her most ordinary characteristic. The logic of the show rendered Ellen's lesbianism the only normal thing about her.

Yet the generic constraints of the situation comedy cannot completely account for the show's emphasis on a normalized, albeit socially challenged, lesbianism. Understandably, lesbian and gay responses to a pathologizing homophobia have historically been much the same as Ellen's response to her father's fears. They have sought to render homosexuality less noxious, debilitating, and dangerous than clichéd representations have made it out to be. Degeneres herself had enunciated the rationale for emphasizing lesbian and gay normalcy in her *Time* interview preceding the coming-out episode:

> If other people come out [because of her decision to do so], that's fine. I mean, it would be great if for no other reason than just to show the diversity, so it's not just the extremes. Because unfortunately those are the people who get the most attention on the news. You know, when you see the parades and you see dykes on bikes or these men dressed as

women. I don't want to judge them. I don't want to come off like I'm attacking them—the whole point of what I'm doing [by coming out] is acceptance of everybody's differences. It's just that I don't want them representing the entire gay community, and I'm sure they don't want me representing them. We're individuals. It's like seeing scary hetero-sexuals on talk shows—it's like saying Joey Buttafuoco represents the heterosexual population.[1]

While claiming not to judge the "extremes" like dykes on bikes or drag queens, Degeneres compares them to a "scary heterosexual" like Joey Butta-fuoco (who, it should be noted, is a convicted felon). Thus bull dykes and drag queens are implicitly "scary" for two reasons. They are scary because, according to Degeneres, they have historically comprised the queer images offered in bad faith by mainstream media. However, given her comparison with Buttafuoco, they are also scary in and of themselves. On the one hand, Degeneres voiced a concern for a more accurate diversity of representation. On the other, she voiced an *evaluative* judgment, indicating rather forcefully that scary homosexuals not only need to be displaced from public attention, but also need to be implicitly repudiated.

In this regard, the *Ellen* event captured a central contradiction in visi-bility's pronounced emphasis on lesbian and gay normalcy: figuring public sphere representation as at once accurate and evaluative, diverse and par-tial, transparent and yet restricted to idealized metaphors. Reacting to a history of stereotypically mincing pansies and predatory dykes, visibility politics demands not just *more* images of queers, but qualitatively "normal" ones whose partiality is understood as a corrective accuracy. A 1996 article in the national lesbian and gay magazine the *Advocate* makes the interest in "quality" explicit: "As images of lesbians and gay men appear on tele-vision with increasing frequency, the struggle for visibility on the tube turns from one of quantity to quality."[2] This turn suggests that mainstream les-bian and gay publications understand visibility politics to have won some measure of progress in the "numbers game"—how many lesbian or gay sit-com characters, for example, are offered up during a particular television season. While "quality" programming could mean anything from the Gay Games on ESPN, Gucci on QVC, or sanctified gay nuptials on *Touched by an Angel*, it is relatively clear what quality would ideally *not* include: the scary homosexuals singled out by Degeneres. As Degeneres points to the "extremes" as exemplars of the queer Cain to her Abel, she also disavows pronouncing judgment on them. The problem, according to Degeneres, is that they just get too much media attention, and thus inappropriately stand in for all queers. Even if we take her disavowal of judgment in good faith, we are left with the issue of public representation compelling her jokey animosity, which is to say we are left with the issue of what constitutes a group's public representativeness. To respect queer diversity, Degeneres claims, queer publicity must be closely guarded lest a small minority represent the entire "community." Yet the very repudiation of "extremes" supposedly safeguards a more diverse, accurate, and representative publicity. Importantly, the sanitizing effects of visibility's irreducibly evaluative dimensions cannot be fully measured by the claim of correcting stereotypes. The singular importance of the two Ellens coming out to a national public, I would argue, lies not so much in the fact that they declared themselves lesbian, but more in the way these declarations both enforce and dissimulate the conformist calculations built into them.

The conformist calculations of the Ellen event, and of lesbian and gay visibility politics in general, indicate more than a particular individual's or group's narrow conception of politics or failure of political will (although the October 1998 decision by the national U.S. lesbian and gay organization Human Rights Campaign to endorse conservative Republican Senator Alfonse D'Amato indicates that both are too often the case). These calculations are importantly made possible by a defining historical feature of bourgeois publicity: camouflaging an essentially *moral* view of public representation as an *equitably democratic* one, and thus rendering moral value judgments the very precondition for equitable and legitimate public presence. Under cover of a truly representative publicity, the conformity of visibility politics recapitulates the historical problem of premising the public sphere's ideally democratic and equitable representation on a moral conception of the human.

At stake in modern definitions of the human is enfranchisement in the largest sense: the point at which all forms of official and unofficial social membership and participation converge. Alongside the political institutions of the state, the public sphere has become an important arena for regulating enfranchisement. Acting as a kind of social foreman, publicity distributes the value of enfranchisement, imaginary or otherwise, through what Janet E. Halley has termed "practices of categorization."[3] Such categorizations pinpoint the role of value in determining the contours of the abstract political identities, such as the citizen, by which we live. More importantly, they contribute to the supplementary social character of something like citizenship, which is to say beyond simply the right to vote or hold office. Through practices of categorization, modes of determining value establish what and who will be judged worthy of social enfranchisement. By constraining such enfranchisement by a moral determination of value, the public sphere betrays its democratic and universalist promise.

Universalist strains in contemporary political philosophy persuasively maintain that abstract political identities and the universalist guarantees attached to them are in some form necessary in pluralist democratic societies. Without them, regressive minority interests would have an even greater foothold by which to hijack national politics. In addition, the ability to adjudicate equitably between competing interests and cultural traditions would be severely restricted. However, the ability of particular value determinations, such as proprietary codes of public and private, to regulate abstract political identities does call into question the defining opposition of post-Kantian universalism: the distinction between a context-transcending morality (the realm of justice) and a context-specific ethical life (the realm of community). *Modes of value determination mediate between and thus cut across these two realms.* This mediation is particularly apparent in the polysemic movement of the term "morality" itself. It can prevaricate between universal principles and narrow standards of behavior. While the moral premises of the early bourgeois public sphere were often articulated differently and underwent various permutations, such premises have been historically lasting in two respects: in constitutional states where individual liberties are protected through notions of a universal, inalienable human worth; and in societies where middle-class codes of propriety have acquired a certain naturalized hegemony.[4]

The intersection of these two notions of the moral can be seen in the way value determination regulates social enfranchisement. The abstract universality of the citizen—in political institutions but also in the public sphere more generally—depends on a prior valorization of particular "moral" characteristics as essentially, universally human. Moreover, the ideally rational procedures and argumentative burdens of democratic deliberation are themselves often encoded with proprietary norms constituting "the moral." That the characteristics of context-transcending political identities or deliberative procedures are drawn from context-specific arenas, such as property ownership, ethnic heritage, or cross-sexual eroticism, and then valorized as universally human, reveals the extent to which value determination regulates the abstraction to civic equivalence. Thus the manner in which the abstractions of civic equivalence are both *determined and regulated* needs to be continually scrutinized. While (problematically) retaining a universalist morality as a defining element of "post-traditional" societies, Jürgen Habermas has also correctly noted that anyone "who in the name of universalism excludes another who has the right to *remain alien* or other betrays his own guiding idea."[5] A moral categorization of human value supposedly elaborates a universally applicable and thus equitable mode of judgment. However, this mode can also unduly restrict enfranchisement by attributions of moral worth. Under the cover of the universal, it can be used to designate morally worthy persons, rather than equitable social participants.

This is to say that moralizing enfranchisement has important repercussions for the distribution of equality—not only in an ideally autonomous public sphere, but also in legal and political institutions. Practices of categorization, and their impact on an enfranchisement grounded in notions of equality, interpenetrate diverse public discourses and institutions, from commercial media and social movements, to legislative deliberation and judicial action. In a society at least conceived as democratic, enfranchisement must be based on some principle of value by which persons can be viewed as equal. The principle attributing a specific value to the human also becomes the principle by which human equality is distributed. A moral determination of human value can restrict the distribution of equality through judgments about who, and what attributes, are more *worthy* of such equality. One is thus forced to view moral worth *as if* it were an adequate ground for distributing representational equity and maximizing participation in a radically plural social polity. If moral valuation is treated *as if* it were adequate to democratic notions of citizenship, social belonging, and a critically debating public, the promise of equity can be thwarted. This subjunctive "as if" allows asymmetrical enfranchisement to be justified, at the very least because such enfranchisement would depend on attributions of moral worth.

Regulating enfranchisement through moral worth contributes to the severe ideological retrenchments seen in the U.S. public sphere, as in the bludgeon of "family values" that has bullied political debate and constrained the national media for some time now. In debates over welfare, immigration, crime, education, or many other matters of public interest, such retrenchments reinforce the vast reach and retarding effect that moral worth can have in complex societies. In this sense, Degeneres's implicit recognition that publicity operates via proxies conforming to moral judgments renders her argument about representational diversity disingenuous, at best. Able to restrict itself to the evaluative designation of individuals, a moralized enfranchisement can severely inhibit the ability to construct an expansive definition of group belonging, establish viable political constituencies, and elaborate equitable modes of social participation for competing interests. Utilizing morality as if it were an appropriate distributional principle for equal representation can provide a pretense for violating the very promise of such representation. Enfranchisement, in the largest sense, atrophies under the weight of regulatory moral judgments.

Recapitulating the origins of publicity ideals in the subject formation of the bourgeois family, a moral determination of human value is both a historically generative *and* residual aspect of publicity. While a moral determination of human value represented a radical challenge to the arbitrariness of monarchical rule and feudal class arrangements, more often than not it now lags behind and hinders the very democratic ideals that it originally helped to foster. The ideal of the bourgeois public sphere aimed toward democratically organized discussion, self-determination, and a critical self-reflexivity regarding the grounds for generating social norms. At its best, this ideal has provided responsive arenas of self-determination for citizenship as an irreducibly social subjectivity. Conceived as an equitable mode of social participation and developmental arena for citizenship, publicity simultaneously arose with and promised more than the moral worth of a privatized individualism.[6] In this sense the ideal of the public sphere exceeds and outstrips its historical moorings in the intimate sphere of the bourgeois family—with regard to the public sphere's ideal role in securing both public *and* private self-determination. Distributing equity according to residual notions of moral worth, however, ambushes what was originally a historically progressive capacity of publicity: the socialization of private persons into participatory citizens. Publicity risks becoming stunted when the distribution of equity is determined according to moral judgments of individual worth. This stunted development finds an echo in what Lauren

Berlant has persuasively documented as the privatization and infantiliza-
tion of citizenship in the United States, such that images of the ideal citizen
have contracted *ad absurdum* to the fetus and the child. Because they are
moral innocents, which is to say "unencumbered" by any particular life narrative, the public sphere is discharged of having to adjudicate their worth.
In this way, a fatuous infantilism becomes the norm for the proper citizen.[7]

To critique a moralized enfranchisement, however, is not to argue against
universal moral-political principles *per se*. Rights discourse, for example,
still has a critical utility in securing enfranchisement. However, the polysemic characteristics of the moral enable the public sphere to utilize narrow standards of behavior as the universalist cornerstones of a democratic
society. If the public sphere is to be responsive to cultural heterogeneity,
it cannot mistake inappropriately generalized moral schemes for representative deliberation, or an ontologized self-enclosure for social participation. If enfranchisement is to be conceived and practiced as a dynamic
form of social participation, in which a fluid responsiveness exists between
concrete cultural life, abstract political identities, and universalist political
guarantees, it cannot be constrained by an ontological designation of moral
worth. An ontologized moral value cannot provide adequate grounds for
an equitable, dynamic, and mutual conversion between private and public,
person and citizen. In this sense, treating contingent moral frameworks as
if they were universally valid and binding can obstruct a democratic publicity.

With regard to queer politics, a strictly moral determination of human
value, and thus legitimate representability, impedes critical public reflection on eroticism in particular, which in any case has been a matter of public
relevance for some time now. This constitutes a signal failure to realize
the transformative capabilities not only of a democratically conceived public sphere, but also of antihomophobic thought and struggle. The latter
points away from the limiting historical entanglement of publicity ideals in
the moral subject formation of the bourgeois family. Significantly, a moral
determination of representational value also disables any productively dia-
logic relation between concrete subcultural formations and the generalized
social competencies, like ethical deliberation, ideally inhering in participatory citizenship. That is, a restrictively moral value-determination impedes
any role queer counterpublics might have in shaping the contours of public interest, and moving political culture beyond what Berlant terms "dead

citizenship": notions of social belonging that have no connection to actual, vital sociocultural resources.[8] By subjunctively offering a moral grounding of publicity *as if* it were an equitably democratic one, visibility politics and the public sphere with which it engages betray their own best possibilities.

This betrayal is most pronounced with regard to queer eroticism. The integration of erotic experiences into moral narratives of proper citizenship delimits much of what is at stake in queer publicity. One of the most imaginative aspects of queer life, the fluidity of eroticism and the range of options made available for thematizing and practicing it, has been rendered damagingly discordant with public sphere inclusion. Detaching eroticism from ontologized categories and the social privileges that come with them— that is, articulating eroticism as relatively indeterminate—is itself seen as a major threat to achieving such inclusion. One important reason for this, I would suggest, is that erotic expression indeterminately related to ontological categories and their social privileges is incompatible in a quite important and fundamental sense with a strictly moral determination of human value. This is to say that aspects of queer eroticism and their importance in the formation of queer constituencies can reveal the extent to which a moralized enfranchisement is now incompatible with its original historical promise.[9]

Caught within the terms of this incompatibility, a vocal group of lesbian and gay writers and spokespeople have publicly argued that queer erotic diversity should be restricted to already valorized, heteronormative forms of erotic attachment and expression. They present this restriction as the sine qua non of inclusion within the public sphere as well as achieving equal rights: moral conformity as the very precondition for enfranchisement. For example, the prominent gay columnist and author Bruce Bawer has often derided in national lesbian and gay magazines and in his own books the "sex-centered" aspects of queer culture. With the parsimony of a moral valet, Bawer views the spectacle of Pride Day parades in New York City as "silly, sleazy, and sex-centered, a reflection of the narrow, contorted definition of homosexuality that marks some sectors of the gay subculture."[10] He presents himself as the spokesperson for a silent majority of lesbians and gay men. The homosexual majority for whom Bawer presumes to speak, he believes, would constitute a much more diverse constituency than that presented by Pride parades. This constituency falls in love, serves its country, attends church, goes to work, buys houses, mows lawns, showers, shaves, recycles—in short, engages in the vast heterogeneous multitude of activities that presumably define the universality of "normal life." And why shouldn't they do these things? While one may detect the whiff of banality in such activities, the quarrel is not with them per se—even the extraordinary may be ritualized into banality.[11] Rather, the more important point of contention is the ease with which Bawer restricts relevant issues for a democratic public to historically constipated moral standards that he nevertheless presents as universally "normal." What really disturbs Bawer, and the mythical majority for whom he presumes to speak, is not so much that gay men (he only mentions men) choose to be sleazy—although he really does prefer that they not be—but more that they choose to be sleazy in public: "Unfortunately, however, this wasn't a private party; it was a public spectacle."[12] The placards carried during this particular Pride parade "suggested that the march was intended, at least in part, to be a political statement directed at the heterosexual population. But if this was the case, what could explain the grotesque appearance and vulgar behavior of so many marchers, who were, quite frankly, a public-relations nightmare?"[13] According to Bawer, heterosexuals do not bear the burden of equitable and self-reflexive debate aimed toward common understanding. Queers must bear this burden entirely by themselves. His argument reproduces, indeed affirms, the entitlement of "normal" heterosexuals as those-who-must-be-persuaded, on their terms. In this sense publicity may claim to embody reasonable argument and equitable democratic representation; yet positioning moral equivalence as if it were adequate grounds for representational equity mandates an undue burden for queers to legitimate themselves according to a dominant heteronormative propriety.

Certainly this propriety includes what are understood to be traditional sexual mores, especially proscriptions against acts and preferences not reducible to the gender of object choice. Yet the propriety delimiting visibility politics is much more than a heterosexist prudery. Its narrow vision of queer experiences and persons correlates with the constriction of hetero-eroticism itself within moralized aspects of social legitimacy, aspects which in and of themselves exceed the sexual (even as they may be sexualized): property relations, financial arrangements, inheritance laws, legally sanctioned contractual agreements, caregiving, commercially viable market attention, and codified divisions between public and private, to name just a few. This constriction renders only certain heteroerotic arrangements into defining norms of erotic life. Lesbian and gay visibility politics has measured homoerotic expressions according to these narrow norms. It is therefore not simply "heterosexuality" that provides the standard for lesbian and gay normalcy, as if this category could both exhaust the possibilities of cross-sex desire and expression, and bear the full weight of guilt (a limiting term itself) for such conformity. Heteroeroticism is just as constrained by the incompatibility between erotic indeterminacy and a moral grounding of representational equity. Nor is it so much that visibility expunges any and all notions of lesbian and gay difference *from* heterosexuality. Public representations coded as "positive" often maintain an at least minimal distinctiveness to lesbian and gay "being," as a peculiar sensibility or simply as a form of humor, even as these are linked to activities marked as traditionally heterosexual (like parenting, as in the 1996 Disney film *The Birdcage*). Particularly with regard to public representation, the great feat of heteronormative narratives lies not so much in the proscription of particular erotic acts, objects, and forms of attachment (although they certainly do this), as in the quite singular way particular erotic acts, objects, and forms of attachment are *presumed on moral grounds* to be synonymous with property rights, patriotism, consumption patterns, political alliances, reproductive choices—in short, with the array of elements attached to a moral view of enfranchisement. As Bawer makes clear, until queers displace the immoral centrality of sex, desire, and eroticism from their consolidation as a constituency, "to many of them [heterosexuals] we'll continue to look like a somewhat lower order of being whose personal lives can't possibly be morally equivalent to their own. And thereupon hang our rights."[14]

Public offenses against erotic propriety, it would seem, violate (a moralized) human value and thus the very basis for achieving equal rights. Bawer, and many others like him, voice a defining feature of this first mode of value determination: a moral understanding of the human as the very ground for legitimate social belonging. In this regard, the moralizing of enfranchisement significantly reveals the degree to which public discourse cuts across often disparate spheres and institutions, such as judicial protection, legislative action, and media representation. In relation to the political sphere, a moralized enfranchisement explains in part why right-wing groups in the United States have understood lesbian and gay rights as "special rights." It reveals the extent to which ideally universal moral principles undergirding abstract political identities can carry with them exclusionary notions of the general and the particular, the "normal" and the "special." A moralized enfranchisement also helps to explain the types of rights lesbian and gay politics have focused on: the right to marry, serve openly in the armed forces, parent, dispense with private property as one pleases, or any other activity already valued as morally worthy in which a particular individual, as group representative, might engage. Coupled with the denial (on largely moral grounds) of the aforementioned rights to queers, these goals make a certain sense. However one might disagree with or wish to abjure enjoying the right to serve openly in the military, for example, to take issue with a focus on military service or marriage does *not* mean that queers shouldn't have access to such a right. Rather, the point is that visibility politics may begin with naming a visceral anxiety, fear, and hatred—what we have come to call homophobia—but by no means do its legitimation strategies end there. Such strategies have increasingly focused on integrating homoeroticism *only* within the institutions, narratives, and practices of sociosexual belonging hinged by a morally legitimate personhood, rather than working on behalf of more politically expansive and culturally responsive forms of enfranchisement. Notions of social and political equality do not exist in a vacuum even as they may claim a universal, suprahistorical neutrality. By moralizing equality, one submits to the merely given yet universalized standards of what one is being made equal *to*. Equal rights lose the elasticity they should ideally have in relation to a dynamic social and cultural terrain. In this way, rights themselves become petrified.

The petrifaction of rights can be glimpsed in the much publicized call by Andrew Sullivan, former editor of the *New Republic* and poster boy for gay conservatism, to focus antihomophobic struggle on the right to marry. Sullivan argues that "quick and easy sex" is, at bottom, "a desperate and failed search for some kind of intimacy, a pale intimation of a deeper longing that most of us inwardly aspire to and deserve."[15] For this reason, queers must recognize that the forms of indeterminate erotic expression they have elaborated for themselves stem *only* from the denial of marriage rights. In other words, exclusion has bred pathological erotic attachments, and only after we have been granted the right to marry will we be able to achieve "real love," "real commitment," a "sexuality that embraces the whole person in a relationship of love and fidelity": "Marriage is not, whatever its enemies say, a means to tame or repress or coerce gay men and women. On the contrary. It is, in fact, the only political and cultural and spiritual institution that can truly liberate us from the shackles of marginalization and pathology. . . . It is the institution more than any other that links the equality of politics with the intimacy of the heart." [16] For lesbians and gay men, marriage represents nothing less than "integration into the human race." [17] More than any other civic right, Sullivan argues, marriage would place queers on an equal social footing with all other citizens. Yet his restrictively moral understanding of both sex *and* political culture goes against the expansive effects he presumably thinks marriage rights would have. Sullivan proposes a trickle-down ethics, the belief that "law can affect culture indirectly by its insistence on the equality of all citizens." [18] This is indeed an accurate assessment, but only to the extent that an exclusive focus on rights that institutionalize heteronormativity would damagingly constrict the possibilistic dimensions of equal rights themselves.

This constriction is particularly striking in gay journalist Gabriel Rotello's recent call to establish a system of social rewards that would encourage gay men in particular to turn away from indeterminate erotic expression. Arguing on stunningly specious epidemiological and "ecological" grounds, Rotello claims that the only way that gay men can ward off the disaster of HIV and AIDS is through sexual "moderation" and "balance"—by which he means the erotic practices one presumably finds among marrying heterosexuals (and, Rotello condescends to add, among lesbians as well). One of the chief ways that sexual "restraint" and "responsibility" can be encouraged is through granting lesbians and gay men marriage rights: "In a culture where unrestrained multipartnerism has produced ecological catastrophe, precisely what is needed is a self-sustaining culture in which people feel socially supported *within their identities as gay men* to settle down with individual partners for significant periods of time." [19] One wonders here which is the carrot and which is the stick. According to Rotello, in order to enjoy a right one must first prove oneself worthy of it. Marriage and full parental rights "are not cure-alls but *prerequisites* in any serious attempt to create a sustainable culture among gay men." [20] Because indeterminate erotic expression—what Rotello refers to as promiscuity—is supposedly a necessary *and* sufficient cause for epidemics like HIV infection and AIDS, the social rewards of marriage and parenting rights become moral prophylaxes against natural catastrophe. Along with other forms of social enfranchisement, rights in this view are constricted to preexisting and unreflexive notions of moral worth, even as Rotello presents these notions under the cover of historical and scientific authority. This constriction prevents aspects of civic life from constructively responding to and interacting with the innovative erotic and affiliative practices of queer culture. (Indeed, such practices themselves have arguably had a positive impact on cross-sexual erotic life as well, and *include* but crucially *are not limited to* monogamous arrangements.) Both Sullivan and Rotello would render aspects of civic life functionally normative in the narrowest sense.

In this regard, focusing queer politics and public discourse on marriage rights tends to enforce heteronormativity as the moral measure by which eroticism in general can become publicly relevant. Again, the question is not whether queers should have access to marriage; of course they should. Nor is it a question of rendering monogamous arrangements and indeterminate erotic expression mutually exclusive for everyone at all times. This view, advocated by so many publicly prominent lesbians and gay men in recent years, is not only destructively divisive but also breathtakingly foolish. Rather, when enfranchisement is moralized—in this instance according to a dominant heteronormative standard—marriage becomes one of the only rights deemed worth having, and conversely *only those who desire to marry are deemed worthy of rights.* Rotello happily embraces this punitive vision of rights. He explicitly argues that to provide "status to those who married and thus implicitly penalize those who [do] not" is absolutely necessary to a "responsible" gay culture.[21] In this way heteronormativity atrophies the ability of rights, publicity, and sexual dissent to realize dialogically the transformative potential of each. As queers are abstracted as both citizens and media images, their abstraction is constrained by the moral justification of heteronormative standards as those of civic equality *tout court.* In the process, queer practices and persons unrelated or antagonistic to their normative counterparts are not only disenfranchised, but also become the repudiated, debased remainders hindering social equality itself: drag queens, promiscuous clones, bull dykes, "shrill" activists, and the like. Grounding publicity and its promise of social enfranchisement on moral worth not only reproduces a normalizing distillation of "positive" images out of the diversity of queer life. It also morally divides the spectrum of queer erotic and affiliative life, and renders stillborn queer efforts to revitalize what constitutes public interest.

The *Ellen* event brought to the fore the restrictively moral practices of categorization underlying visibility politics within the public sphere. Yet it also revealed a condition of representability both supplementing and exceeding such practices. To state the obvious, *Ellen* was a corporate television program underwritten by advertising dollars. Publicity for the show as media event, as well as the show itself, had an irreducibly commercial element. The moral determination of value underwriting lesbian representability in this instance was overlapped by a commercial determination of value. Besides their general organization as capitalist enterprises, contemporary media determine commercial value through the relatively recent practice of market segmentation. This practice has transformed identifiable social groups, including but not limited to minorities, into markets targeted by businesses and represented within a commercial cultural public sphere. The determination of such groups as commercially valuable market segments grounds their representability. Thus, by elaborating queers as a profitable market segment, commercial value in this mode determines the distribution of their representational equity. The commercial value of queer representation, in fact, has become not only one of the most celebrated and successful aspects of visibility politics, but also one of the most contentious. By way of illustration, I want to point to an event preceding Ellen's coming out that acutely registered the ambivalence and hostility many queers feel about a visibility so promiscuously caught within commercial culture.

In late June 1994, hundreds of thousands of lesbians, gay men, drag queens, bisexuals, queers of all kinds, and their friends, families, and supporters converged on New York City to commemorate and celebrate the twenty-fifth anniversary of the Stonewall riots. This commemorative celebration was underwritten by a number of organizations and corporations. One of these, *Out* magazine, sold T-shirts with the following upbeat message: "Stonewall 25: New and Improved for the 90s." What might be new or improved about a '90s Stonewall, however, became a matter of contention over that weekend. As a challenge to the rainbow-drenched official Stonewall parade past the United Nations, the New York chapter of the AIDS Coalition to Unleash Power (ACT UP) organized a counter-march (conservatively estimated by New York City police at 10,000) to protest not only the ongoing and deadly inattention to AIDS, but also, and more pointedly, the commercialization of this historical marker as a rather cynical improvement on the original. Lesbian Contradiction of San Francisco, for example, handed out stickers at the ACT UP protest that read "Queer Liberation . . . a Movement, not a Market!" Another graphic listed the many mainstream and lesbian or gay businesses underwriting the Gay Games alongside a glaringly blank list of businesses supporting lesbian and gay civil rights.

The controversy during that weekend over what a '90s Stonewall might or had come to mean indicates, on one level, the profound importance historical narratives have acquired for queers. Such urgent and intense investments in history—its meaning, remembrance, value, and circulation—point toward the legitimating function that modes of representation, like historical narratives, have acquired in relation to subordinated groups, not the least for the political and economic value they can generate.[22] This fact was not lost on ACT UP/NY and the other groups who derided the official Stonewall events as politically diluted by their complicity with capital. ACT UP/NY, of course, had been concerned not just with official versions of lesbian and gay political history. Its own history of active engagement with dominant forms of representation and, especially, their efforts at self-representation have demonstrated the value of questioning the conditions under which public representability is conferred on disenfranchised groups.[23] ACT UP/NY and affiliated art and video collectives have understood that publicness in the United States involves fundamental dynamics of valuation and devaluation. Through their critical attempts to generate (often ad hoc) forms of counterpublicity to an officially heteronormative social and cultural terrain, these groups have shown that such dynamics often reorient what a "valuable" queer representation will look like. They have understood that these dynamics necessitate a vigilance over publicity's normative contours. Responding to images of people with AIDS (PWAS) in corporate television programming and museum institutions, for example, Douglas Crimp has insisted that "images of people with AIDS created by the media and art photographers alike are demeaning, and . . . are overdetermined by a number of prejudices that precede them about the majority of the people who have AIDS—gay men, IV drug users, people of color, poor people."[24] In addition to recognizing that mainstream representations of PWAs are demeaning, we must also, Crimp argues, "recognize that every image of a PWA is a *representation*, and formulate our activist demands not in relation to the 'truth' of the image, but in relation to the conditions of its construction and to its social effects." [25] Crimp indicates here the importance of questioning not the authenticity of images of PWAs, or of queers in general, but rather the value relations governing how such images are produced, as well as the effects they may have for particular constituencies and audiences.

The kind of critical consciousness toward representation that Crimp invokes, however, has not seemed to be an important concern for mainstream lesbian and gay political organizations and publications. Responding to a history of stereotypes proffered by Hollywood films and television programming, organizations such as the Gay and Lesbian Alliance Against Defamation (GLAAD) and national magazines like *Out* and the *Advocate* have fallen over themselves to congratulate the culture industry for instances of increased "sensitivity" and especially of "realistic" and "positive" representations of lesbians and gay men. One important factor in the increased shift toward a normatively constrained queer visibility is the shift in the groups that tend to dominate media attention. Over the past several years radical, media-savvy organizations such as ACT UP, Queer Nation, and Lesbian Avengers have had a decreasing amount of public presence and share of participation within visibility politics. This is not just because such groups tend to be relatively short-lived. It is also because there has been an inversely proportional rise in public presence of more mainstream, assimilation-driven, and fund-raising-oriented advocacy groups such as GLAAD and the Human Rights Campaign, as well as slick national lesbian and gay publications underwritten by corporate advertising dollars.[26] In this regard, grounding publicity in commercial value can determine *who* generates queer "representativeness." Supplementing the moral restrictions of the first mode, the commercial valuation of visibility also determines *material access* to enfranchisement.

While lesbian and gay political organizations struggle for entrée into corridors of mainstream political power and corporate visual culture, national lesbian and gay publications have replaced the "in your face" tactics characteristic of queer activism in the early 1970s, the late 1980s, and early 1990s with elaborating and vying for a readership-cum–market segment. Within the cultural public sphere in particular, commercial value determines who generates queer representation because such representation understands itself, in turn, to represent a commercially valuable demographic. This demographic, the mythically well-to-do lesbian and gay market segment, is organized as a liberal-centrist voter bloc, and known best by its supposedly superior taste, interest in fashion and music, frequent vacations, brand-name loyalty—in short, its cultivation of a consumer culture "lifestyle."[27] Some indices of the construction of an explicit lesbian and gay market segment include the following: advertising campaigns produced exclusively for lesbians and gay men by large corporations such as AT&T, but also by smaller companies, especially those producing liquor and clothing; the emergence of lesbian and gay credit cards, such as Point-One Link, Uncommon Clout, and Rainbow Visa Cards; financial services targeting lesbians and gay men by companies such as Scudder Investor Services and the Working Assets Corporation, among others; the appearance of public relations, advertising, and marketing firms, such as WinMark, Strubco, and Landmark Enterprises, that target lesbian and gay consumers; the establishment of large lesbian and gay business expositions; and the appearance of lesbian- and gay-oriented product catalogs, such as those produced by Shocking Gray, Don't Panic, Tzabaco, 10% Productions, Greenwood/Cooper, Phoenix Rising, M2M, and the Community Card Pack.[28] Each of these aspects of market segmentation—and there are many more— indicates the extent to which commercial representation coordinates the value of lesbians and gay men as a simultaneously political, cultural, and economic constituency.

Two consequences of this coordination stand out as relevant to understanding and rethinking visibility politics and queer publicity more generally. First, this coordination reinforces an indistinction between economic and political spheres of value determination. The lesbian and gay market segment, and the forms of public visibility it generates, is offered unproblematically as a political constituency. The attachment of erotic norms to (a moralized) civic equivalence in the first mode provides commercial representations of lesbians and gay men with the political cover of democratic equity and access. Second, however, this coordination also represents the historically radical nature of capital: the capacity to socialize persons and groups beyond the confines of "tradition." Commercial value determination may follow the moralized contours of visibility from the first mode, but it is under no compulsion to do so. Capital generates different orders of value than those organizing kinship, community, or a self-enclosed consciousness. Yet visibility politics mistakes commercial publicity as a democratically authentic representation of persons and groups.

The first consequence arising from the convergence of economic and moral determinations of value is a variation of their historical convergence in bourgeois ideals of publicity. Habermas has pointed out that the bourgeois public sphere established an intimate connection between the moral individual, the property owner, and the enfranchised citizen: "The fiction of a justice immanent in free commerce was what rendered plausible the conflation of *bourgeois* and *homme*, of self-interested, property-owning private people and autonomous individuals per se. The specific relationship between private and public sphere, from which arose the duplication of the selfish *bourgeois* in the guise of the unselfish *homme*, of the empirical subject in that of the intelligible one, was what made it possible to consider the *citoyen*, the citizen eligible to vote, under the twofold aspect of legality and morality." [29] The identification of commerce and property ownership with moral individualism and political self-determination allowed capitalist economic relations to appear all the more natural and just. In this respect the melding of the political and economic functions of lesbian and gay commercial publicity echoes, in altered form, earlier apologetics for the market as an expression of human nature. Bourgeois ideologies, Habermas argues, have historically been able to "assume a universalistic structure and appeal to generalizable interests because the property order has shed its political form and been converted into a relation of production that, it seems, can legitimate itself. The institution of the market can be founded on the justice inherent in the exchange of equivalents; and, for this reason, the bourgeois constitutional state finds its justification in the legitimate relations of production." [30] The correlation of market value and political equivalence, the correlation of consumption and citizenship, allows commercial representations to function *as if* they were democratic arenas for self-determination. This correlation has advanced such that "in liberal capitalism, there occurs a peculiar transfer of socially integrative tasks to the separate, unpolitical steering system of the market in such a way that the elements of tradition that are effective (at first for the middle class) for legitimation (rational-natural law, utilitarianism) become dependent on an ideology that is itself built into the economic basis—namely, the exchange of equivalents." [31] Thus the decoupling of political legitimation and capitalist economic forces dissimulates their intimate connections. As Negt and

Kluge argue, this dissimulation enforces the misrecognition of the "public sphere of production" as merely following system imperatives. The bourgeois public sphere was founded on such public spheres of production, yet it effectively disavows this foundation as "nonpublic," part of the private sector of individual interests and market forces. At the same time, the so-called system imperatives of capital borrow from the legitimated ideals of the bourgeois public sphere, such that *"power relations in the production process that are not in themselves capable of being legitimated are injected with the generalized interests that have become legitimate and are thereby presented within a context of legitimation."* [32] This injection of supposedly general, public interests affects not only the production context of capital, but also the system of capital as a whole, including distribution and consumption. In this way, market representation for traditionally underrepresented groups appears legitimate in the context of achieving a "public" visibility. The commercial determination of value enables civil and political equivalence to metamorphose easily into a socialized exchange value for persons and groups as markets, and vice versa.

The presumed fungibility between political and economic equivalence thus further calls into question visibility's narrative about correcting queer stereotypes. This narrative is unable to grasp the collusion between the political value and the economic value of lesbian and gay visibility. Indeed, forms of economic representation have arguably become the most "affirmatively" attentive to lesbians and gay men. The elaboration of lesbians and gay men as economically useful market actors should make us aware that the usual way value is thought about in relation to queers—homophobia or affirmation—is by no means the only way that value is an operative category for understanding their public representation. Commercial value determination forms an essential, if unremarked, moment in lesbian and gay public sphere inclusion. Coupled with the moral restrictions enacted in the name of normalcy (or indeed survival), the correction of stereotypes is imaginarily disinvested of its relation to capital.

In this way, the narrative of correcting stereotypes remains relatively indifferent to the *types* of arenas through which queer images are offered. This indifference was exemplified in the reaction of Judy Dlugacz, president of the lesbian-owned and -oriented company Olivia Cruises and Resorts, to ABC's denial of advertising time to her company during the coming-out episode of *Ellen.* ABC had issued a statement saying that "discussion about same-sex lifestyles is more appropriate in programming." Befuddled by ABC's justification, Dlugacz was quoted as saying that "I'm tongue-tied as to how they could make the differentiation between programming and advertising."[33] Dlugacz's response shares with the narrative about combating stereotypes an indifference toward specific economies of value other than that which organizes the opposition homophobia/affirmation. The differences, ethically or otherwise, between queer images in corporate advertising and queer images in alternative video, for example, cannot be thematized by this binary. Moreover, the inability to thematize such differences reproduces the dubiously generalized character of the public sphere itself, such that programming and advertising seem indeed to have become functionally the same. Organized by this inability, visibility politics remains unable to account for the diversified dynamics of representational inclusion. Perhaps the most telling index of this inability is the problematic attribution of a politically progressive quality to economic relations that are expropriative in character.

To become equally a valuable market is on one level to become an economically useful demographic by which commercial cultural representations measure their appeal. On another level, the success of this appeal doubles back so as to contribute to the corporate legitimation profits to be had from sponsorship of the Gay Games or contributing money to AIDS charities. The indistinction between representation as a consumer-based market niche and as a traditional political constituency both aids *and* obscures the extraction of these legitimation profits. This in turn aids in the misattribution of a democratic justice to capitalized representational forms. The expropriation of value, in the form of profit margins and market share, becomes the alibi for having any public representational value at all.

One can find a glowing affirmation of this alibi in Grant Lukenbill's enthusiastic 1995 handbook to lesbian and gay marketing phenomena, *Untold Millions: Positioning Your Business for the Gay and Lesbian Consumer Revolution*. Here Lukenbill cheerfully lays out the confluence of commercial value and political value effected by such phenomena. The gay and lesbian "consumer revolution," he argues, will "ultimately result in a seismic shift in popular culture."[34] This shift requires marketing professionals "to allow a wider, more realistic range of America's spiritual and emotional character to be explored in relationship to sexual orientation, personal identity, and how importantly they relate to product marketing" (7). Should marketing pro-

53

fessionals choose to take advantage of the ethical and political dimensions of marketing to lesbians and gay men, the results would be historic indeed: "A dynamic infusion of economic opportunity for American business is now invading the entire commercial spectrum—one that is more historic than the appearance of gay male walk-on parts in soap operas and more substantive than the subjugation of lesbians in straight male erotica: the power of the gay and lesbian consumer dollar and all that it represents" (2). This power can translate not only into "increased revenue for the business you own or work for," but also into "credibility to a corporate image in need of one or make a company more attractive for prospective employees, partners and associates, or lucrative government contracts—even mergers" (2). This credibility identifies the melding of political agendas with commercial interests, such that corporations can earn a social profit in excess of monetary profit. Thus Lukenbill advises corporations to factor in the "alienation" and "cynicism" many lesbians and gay men feel toward mainstream culture, including business culture: "Marketing and employee communication strategies that take into consideration the influence of these factors can sidestep the pitfalls and leverage the benefits of their management approaches and product or service offerings, and thus increase the success of their business, management, and consumer marketing planning" (111). According to Lukenbill, the lesbian and gay "consumer revolution" presents a win-win situation precisely because the economic is irreducibly bound to the political. The fight for human rights, Lukenbill claims, "is now becoming an economic process as much as it has been a political process" (182). Because these processes are so intertwined, the "business leaders who are taking a stand and establishing or reaffirming their commitment to gay and lesbian emancipation are taking a stand for their own economic prosperity as well" (182). Yet for all that, Lukenbill seems to have inverted his own appeal. The value of lesbian and gay "emancipation" for corporations in no intelligible way *precedes* or *informs* an interest in their own economic prosperity. The political interest that accrues from corporate attention forms only the final appearance that the commercial determination of value, as a process, takes on.

To return to Stonewall 25, the events during that weekend revealed too well that commercial recognition via commemorative historical events—presumed to provide correctives in the name of accuracy—bestows political value through extracting economic value. The importance of corporate sponsors for such events underscores this point. As lesbians and gay men are explicitly organized as a potentially lucrative market segment, their economic value is expropriated with the same hand that underwrites the heroism of their history. And as ACT UP/NY and others pointed out, such conditions of possibility for representation and recognition have far-reaching effects on lesbian and gay political agendas. In other words, ACT UP and groups like it have questioned the subjunctive quality of public sphere inclusion: the dissimulated inadequacy by which the public sphere ideal of representational equivalence is distributed. While mainstream lesbian and gay organizations and publications are critical of distorting images and stereotypes, they also seem to retain a belief that their vigilance is simply a matter of cleansing homophobia. The net effect, it is presumed, will be more accurate and unbiased images.

The question of accuracy, however, not only obscures the functional confusion between political and economic forms of representation. It also fails to understand adequately what could very well be the contemporary historical importance of this confusion. This brings me to the second consequence of the mutual coordination of queer economic and political value: the trend, pointed out by Habermas, for capitalist dynamics to take over the functions of "social integration." Because commercial value determination relies on socialized affiliations and identities, particularly with regard to the elaboration of market groups, it contains the potential to outstrip the regulative moral value constraining publicity in mode one. In other words, commercial value determination routes practices of categorization through its own order of value. As groups are organized as markets, they acquire what we might term a social exchange value. Unlike attributions of moral worth, the conversion of constituencies into market segments achieves a level of abstraction adequate to (a capitalized) social equivalence. The fungibility between political and economic equivalence has enabled not only a confusion between the two; it also has enabled economic representation to take over the functions (and, to a certain extent, the promise) of enfranchisement, which has otherwise found itself inappropriately constrained by moral value. Unlike the moribund moral categorization of persons and behaviors, commercial value determination is simultaneously abstract, as an order of equivalence, and concrete, to the extent that market-based representation can present itself as responsive to subcultural formations, individual needs, and "cultural trends." [35]

That capitalist valuation entails such social effects is not to say anything particularly new. Negt and Kluge have effectively revealed the intimate connections between capitalist economic relations and the democratic ideals of bourgeois publicity. In its critique of absolutist feudal social arrangements, they argue, the "revolutionary bourgeoisie attempted, via the emphatic concept of public opinion, to fuse the whole of society into unity. This remained as a goal. In reality, although this was not expressed in political terms, it was the value abstraction founded on commodity production that forced society together. The extent to which the public sphere holds society together was therefore never gauged." [36] In this regard, Negt and Kluge follow Marx in noting the radical capacity of capital to generate networks of connection that can undermine traditional hierarchies.

Marx noted such effects in his working-through of an analysis of capitalism in his *Grundrisse*. He argues that capitalism *socializes* exchange value in such a way that it can both reorient existing forms of social connection and replace them with new ones: "The reciprocal and all-sided dependence of individuals who are indifferent to one another forms their social connection. This social bond is expressed in *exchange value*, by means of which alone each individual's own activity or his product becomes an activity and a product for him; he must produce a general product—*exchange value*, or, the latter isolated for itself and individualized, *money*. On the other side, the power each individual exercises over the activity of others or over social wealth exists in him as the owner of *exchange values*, of *money*. The individual carries his social power, as well as his bond with society, in his pocket." [37] The ability of exchange value to generate social bonds represents one of the historically radical effects of capital. Because "exchange value is a generality [*Allgemeines*], in which all individuality and peculiarity are negated and extinguished," capitalism creates conditions "very different from that in which the individual or the individual member of a family or clan (later, community), a naturally or historically enlarged individual, directly and naturally reproduces himself, or in which his productive activity and his share in production are bound to a specific form of labour and of product, which determines his relation to others in just that specific way" (G 157). In a developed system of exchange, "the ties of personal dependence, of distinctions of blood, education, etc. are in fact exploded, ripped up. . . ." (G 163). Even as commercial value determination may be (arguably) concrete, as it appears to be in market segmentation, it bears no obligation to tradition on its terms. Marx observed that new forms of interconnection enabled by capital are in fact preferable to "the lack of any connection, or to a merely local connection resting on blood ties, or on primeval, natural or master-servant relations" (G 161). Indeed, capitalism has generated not only the conditions of possibility by which marriage, for example, lost many of its traditional functions, but also those conducive to modern homoerotic association. John D'Emilio, for one, has persuasively shown how the institution of wage labor greatly facilitated the historical opportunities for the formation of lesbian and gay communities via enhanced social mobility, the dissolution of the family as an economically necessary social unit, and the creation of large metropolitan centers, among other factors.[38] The material conditions that displace tradition extend from the conversion of concrete social elements into abstract equivalents that characterizes capitalist modernity. Commercial value determination does not necessarily follow a traditional moral determination of human value as the basis for the conversion from private to public, nor as the grounds for generating and distributing equivalence. A socialized exchange value is an "all-sided mediation" (G 156) indifferent to questions of moral worth. In this way, it can generate the type of simultaneously generalized and socially responsive equivalence that ideally premises political enfranchisement. Marx's diagnosis seems particularly apt as capitalist value determination has also overtaken traditional notions of community via market segmentation. Not only can it displace these notions, it can also colonize and thus fundamentally reorganize them.

However, while capitalism can foster associational freedoms not tied to tradition as well as forms of social equivalence relinquished by the political sphere, it does so only partially and without the democratic procedures promised by political equality. By taking over the tasks of "social integration," commercial value determination can also inhibit the very promise of participatory self-determination it holds out, in at least two ways. First, the extraction of value is neither an equitable nor democratic principle of enfranchisement. By basing the conversion into social equivalence on the extraction of commercial value, this second mode also requires debased remainders. Those whose social- or self-definition resists their determination as commercially valuable do not achieve recognition within capitalized representational forms, such as marketing. Commercial equivalence distorts equality insofar as it is based on a "comparison [*Vergleichung*]" of potential commercial worth, rather than "real communality and generality [*Gemeinschaftlichkeit und Allgemeinheit*]" (G 161). In this sense, the associational freedoms made possible under capitalism carry with them material inequities precisely because these freedoms are presented *as if* they are held out to all: "In the money relation, in the developed system of exchange . . . individuals *seem* independent . . . , free to collide with one another and to engage in exchange within this freedom; but they appear thus only for someone who abstracts from the *conditions,* the *conditions of existence* within which these individuals enter into contact. . . ." (G 163–64; original emphasis). Second and perhaps most obviously, commercial value determination does not provide access to representation in a way recognizable as democratic. While the conflation of consumption and self-determination may provide, directly and indirectly, freedoms not delivered by political systems—what is in fact called "lifestyle"—this conflation also mystifies the fact that many aspects of capitalism are not commensurate with democratic participation.[39] Rather, access to capitalized economic representation is determined by the extent to which social- and self-definition accord with the taxonomies organized by commercial value. Inclusion within commercial cultural publicity requires conformity to these taxonomies. Filmic images of drag queens, for example, became a relatively profitable and arguably forward-looking aspect of commercial entertainment in the early to mid-1990s (even with dubious outfits and a drag affect just this side of *echt*). However, the success of these images was also dependent on converting drag into what Ronald Judy has termed, in a different context, a "commodified affect."

The interrelated possibilities and limits of a commercial determination of value can perhaps best be glimpsed in the production and circulation of commodified affect. This affect articulates identification and social belonging as adjacent to and yet incommensurate with traditional notions of community (and thus also begs the question of what relation there may be between what Marx termed "real communality and generality"). Commodified affect is, Judy argues, something by which one "can belong with millions of others in an asynchronic moment of consumption of the same affect, the same passion."[40] Its production and circulation signals "the end of morality as the basis for identity beyond commodification."[41] For Marx, this possibility was for the most part only negatively thematized as alienation. As an irreversible historical phenomenon, however, the elaboration of "lesbian" and "gay" as commodified affect signals both more and less than either "alienation" or "community." This affect grounds social groupings via the sign formations generated by commercial value—lesbian and gay product catalogs, "theme" films, sitcom characters, celebrity "role models," mass-mediated gay events, and the ubiquitous red ribbon and rainbow flag. Via these sign formations, commodified affect becomes communicable on a global scale, and in this way seems to generate representational enfranchisement. Condensed in the euphemistic use of "lifestyle," it embodies both the promise and the challenge of contemporary commercial publicity.

The commercial determination of value operative in the public sphere requires that we come to terms simultaneously with both the limitations *and* the historical importance of capitalized representation. At the same time that it determines value only according to commercial worth, it can radically dissolve constipating moral perspectives and enable, albeit in distortion, the associational freedoms and representational equivalence largely abnegated by social and political institutions. The type of "objective social bond" generated by capital, Marx argued, still has an "alien and independent character," which "proves only that [individuals] are still engaged in the creation of the conditions of their social life, and that they have not yet begun, on the basis of these conditions, to live it" (G 162). On the basis of its historically radical character, this second mode of value determination presents commercial worth as if it adequately grounds an equitably enfranchised social life. It thus dissembles the partiality of its own promise. By viewing commercial value as if it were an appropriate principle for distributing equity, visibility politics aids in the culture industry's partial and distorted delivery of social enfranchisement. Moreover, by remaining indifferent to the specificity and reach of capitalist economic representation, visibility politics is unable to apprehend that such representation operates according to a historically pregnant order of value, one different than traditional notions of community.[42]

These brief and by no means exhaustive comments on the economic dimensions of visibility have two purposes. First, they are meant to displace the totalizing centrality of closeted/out, invisibility/visibility, homophobia/affirmation as the defining political and intellectual arbiters of queer value. While the social force of these binaries has not dissipated, thinking and acting solely on their terms restricts the kind of imaginative reach antihomophobic efforts should have. And second, my comments are meant to indicate that supposedly discrete realms of value production are intimately, indiscretely related to each other, as the political coding of market activities suggests.[43] The confusion between a traditionally conceived political public sphere and other arenas of public representation in capitalist social formations indicates a historical development of great ethical and political significance. This is not to absolve commercial value determination from its distorting effects. However, it is to say that critiques of commercial value need to be formulated according to appropriately attuned modes of judgment. Such critiques should not fall prey to what Hegel termed the "terrorism of pure conviction." The radical historical aspects of capital necessitate that the left be as creative in its ethical thinking as in its political thinking. It is as inaccurate to think that with capitalism "history has come to a standstill" as it is "ridiculous to yearn for a return" to a time unencumbered by, say, the circulation of commodified affects: "The bourgeois viewpoint has never advanced beyond this antithesis between itself and this romantic viewpoint, and therefore the latter will accompany it as legitimate antithesis up to its blessed end" (G 162). Living in the history of capital requires reflexivity about the modes of judgment by which we understand this history. Indeed, insofar as commercial value determination has the capacity to render moot a moralized representativeness, a capacity that has had profound, irreversible effects both benefiting and hindering queer life, it should focus our attention even more. My brief comments on commercial value determination, then, are offered in the spirit of reopening the historically and ethically complex question of capital as it impacts queer public visibility. We might say that the socially integrative functions of capital as it operates now indicate an important phase in the sign-formation of value. The condensation of meaning is even greater, the subjunctive slippages even more pliable, between political, economic, and subcultural practices.

Secretion

The previous two modes of value determination highlight the mediations that contour publicity. And both indicate that visibility's narrative of correcting queer stereotypes fails to comprehend adequately the complex dynamics of public sphere inclusion. But perhaps this narrative has not received its due. That is, perhaps it is too easily dismissed as an illusory prevarication, an imposed fiction behind which lurk less than ideal motives: neoconservative moralizing, capitalist profiteering. I do not intend the preceding analysis to rest with such a simplifying diagnosis; this would fail to consider adequately three things. First, it would fail to consider the very real felt need for the abstract identities by which we live, such as the participatory citizen, to be commensurate with their promise and thus responsive to the forms of cultural life they are called upon to protect and encourage. Second, it would also fail to consider the very real objective force that the correction of stereotypes has as an organizing narrative of a queer culture charged by the ambivalences of exclusion. This narrative cannot simply be designated as a damaging illusion. And third, this designation would thereby fail to step outside the opposition between inequitable mediation—moralized enfranchisement, commodified affect—and a romantically authentic visibility. That is, by casting the correction of stereotypes as mere illusion, and thus implicitly conjuring a more true form of immediacy, this diagnosis would run the risk of disabling antihomophobic thought from displacing the authenticating effects of the very value determinants it would critique. As Theodor Adorno reminds us, casting the real objective force of exchange value, as both commercial and sociopolitical equivalence, simply in terms of "a deception, accedes to the ideology of universal humanity [*Allmenschlichkeit*], and clings to forms of an immediate togetherness, which are historically irretrievable if in fact they ever existed otherwise."[44]

Because of the risk of these analytic failures, it is incumbent to analyze both the authenticating effects of contemporary publicity, and the historically imposed ambivalences of exclusion that have given the question of authenticity a particular urgency for queers. This brings me to the third mode of value determination, one that interpenetrates the previous two: valuing public sphere representation as authentic. In many ways the historical formation of publicity ideals and practices has nourished this view. For example, by conflating the moral individual, the property owner, and the citizen, bourgeois publicity could mistake itself as the transparent conveyor of prior interests, rather than the mediated conversion of these interests into publicly legitimate forms. In this way the translation of private vice into public virtue could be understood as a mirroring correlation, rather than a transformative mediation. This historical problem is recapitulated in the principles of value, and the categorizations they entail, by which enfranchisement is regulated. As the arena for ideally safeguarding the mutual determinations between concrete social life (like queer counterpublics) and abstract identities (like the citizen), the public sphere and its orders of value regulate enfranchisement.

Authenticity as an *effect* of this regulation can be located in two aspects of publicity. First, as Habermas has indicated, capitalism and liberal democracy entail systemic processes of conversion that establish equivalence: the former through the social exchange value of market segments, the latter through the formal equality of participatory citizens. Equivalence importantly *socializes* markets and citizens, which are nevertheless posited as bearers of a presocial value: a market segment as an association of ontological affects and needs, the citizen as atomized moral individual. The attribution of an a priori worth confuses the extent to which transformative determinants of value regulate equivalence. This confusion allows public sphere representation to be coded as if it were a transparent circulation of authentic interests, particularly as commercial and political equivalence tend to merge in publicity practices. Second, then, this coding itself stems in part from the intermingling of moral and commercial value-determination. While the latter, as I have argued, is not necessarily tied to the former—indeed is importantly discordant with it in many respects— the confusion between political and economic representation allows them to conjoin. The politicized characteristics of commercial publicity allow moral and commercial value to become at least *functionally* commensurate. While their orders of value are historically and logically distinct, they have also become practically true analogs. The objective force of their analogical relation is further cemented by the presumption that their principles of value, both moral and commercial, seem to offer immediately an anterior worth. Together with publicity's historical misrecognition of itself as transparent, the principles of value that undergird publicity tend to reinforce public representation *as if* it presents an untrammeled authenticity.

To illustrate how principles of value have authenticating effects, I would briefly point to Marx's historic insights about the commodity as a particular value-form within a circuit of equivalence. First, Marx points out that the ability of commodities to circulate equivalence is an effect of their relational form:

> The natural form of the commodity becomes its value-form [*Wert-form*]. But, note well, this substitution only occurs in the case of a com-

modity B (coat, or maize, or iron, etc.) when some other commodity A (linen etc.) enters into a value-relation with it [nur innerhalb des Wertverhältnisses], and then only within the limits of this relation [Beziehung]. Since a commodity cannot be related to itself as equivalent, and therefore cannot make its own physical shape [ihre eigne Naturalhaut] into the expression [Ausdruck] of its own value, it must be related to another commodity as equivalent, and therefore must make the physical shape [Naturalhaut] of another commodity into its own value-form.[45]

A commodity becomes a value-form only when it has entered into a relation of equivalence with something else, and this something else thereby becomes a value-form as well. Equivalence is established not through comparable qualities *already* in value-forms, but rather through their relation to each other, as well as in their mutual relation to a universal equivalent, a principle of value that grounds the comparability of difference. Value, Marx importantly argues, is neither ontological nor presocial. The "physical shape" (Natur + Haut—"skin") by which a value-form seems to exude a prior quality is only the solidified appearance of a relation. To read off the "skin" a naturalized value is to succumb to the subjunctive rendering of value *as if* it were a natural or authentic property. It is to misrecognize an a posteriori relational effect for an a priori ontological attribute. This misrecognition extends to the excessive social signification that equivalents acquire: within the value-relation between two commodities, each "signifies more than it does outside [this relation], just as some men count for more when inside a gold-braided uniform than they do otherwise."[46] However, the enfolding of this excessive signification within a prior ontologized worth is not a mere illusion, but takes on an objective force of its own—what Jeremy Bentham, in a rather different context, termed a "second order fiction."[47]

Marx's analysis of value in both *Capital* and the *Grundrisse* brings out a general contradiction within nineteenth-century capitalist societies: the contradiction between the reigning ideology of bourgeois individualism and the dynamics of capitalist social formations. These dynamics generated socialized forms of equivalence that gave the lie to the autonomous and moralized bourgeois subject. An equality of competitive, atomistic individuals, Marx argued, was an equality contradicted by its retention of a bourgeois standard of the citizen. Bourgeois civil society could only ever effect what might be best termed a managed inequity. It thus stalled, and thereby dissembled, its self-proclaimed project of "human emancipation."[48] Despite the many discontinuities between Marx's political writings, particularly his early essays, and his later work in the *Grundrisse* and *Capital*, one can discern a minimal continuity: his persistent concern with the systemic, contradictory presence of historical, class-based norms in modernity's promise of universal economic, political, and social equivalence.

This contradictory presence is captured in Marx's reference to commodities as "social hieroglyphics," enigmatic significations whose representational occlusions it is the task of critique to displace. In this regard, the category of value can provide a powerful analytic lever by which to pry open the subjunctive dissemblance of equity. As Marx demonstrates so exhaustively throughout *Capital*, the capitalist value-form is a problem to the extent that inequivalences are reproduced subjunctively as if they were equivalences. To accede to the subjunctive mood defining representational equivalence in capitalist social formations is to accede to their historical and structural limits. In the public sphere, these limits reside most clearly in the value hierarchies secreted—both suppressed and surreptitiously reproduced—within its regulation of enfranchisement.

Today the secretion of these hierarchies inappropriately conflates the demand for "realistic" queer images and the demand that they be "normal." Charged by a history of demeaning stereotypes and the desire to rectify them, lesbian and gay visibility politics demands an authenticity the public sphere is all too willing to propitiate. The public sphere's own "jargon of authenticity," to use Adorno's term, propitiates claims for a better life by "fastidiously prolong[ing] the innumerable events which are to make attractive to men a life by which they otherwise would be disgusted—and which they would soon come to consider unbearable."[49] To prolong its form of managed inequity, the public sphere regulates enfranchisement subjunctively, as if it delivered the authenticity it promises: "If . . . one forgets the apparatus of mediation [*vermittelnde Apparatur*], then the jargon of authenticity, which takes pleasure in this situation, is committing itself to the philosophy of As if [*bekennt sich . . . zum Als ob*]. . . ."[50] By disavowing mediation, authenticity evaporates its artifice through a pretense of immediacy.

By displacing the public sphere's claims to authenticity, we can better question its subjunctive formulation—the legitimated contradiction between what it promises and what it delivers. This also means, however, that inclusion should not simply be cast as an either/or proposition. The question as to the viability or desirability of publicity can't be settled "in theory"—an idealist impulse to assume that it could be—but rather in the engagement between theoretical reflection and the histories to which publicity practices belong. The *potential* validity of public sphere inclusion should not be held hostage by a subjunctive dissemblance. In this regard grappling with the authenticating value of publicity entails coming to terms with the ethical complexities of leftist critique raised by inclusion.

This latter point is worth amplifying. To simply *charge* visibility politics with a restrictive sexual conformity or complicity with commercialism has its own limits. First, it cannot explain how it is or what it means, for example, that commercial representations have acquired political functions. And second, it cannot progress very far beyond a simplistic calculus of ideological purity and contamination: the mistaken idea, for example, that one can simply choose to be outside capital. Reducing analysis in this way to a game of paintball—once you're stained, the game is over—can only bemoan, rather than fully understand, the conditions it evokes. Eve Kosofsky Sedgwick has shown the conceptually weak and implicitly consumerist evaluations built into such a calculus—"straining eyes to ascertain whether particular performances (e.g. of drag) are really *parodic and subversive* (e.g. of gender essentialism) or just *uphold the status quo.* The bottom line is generally the same: kinda subversive, kinda hegemonic."[51] Sedgwick's point, as I understand it, is not that one should necessarily refuse judgment of something like commercialism altogether—as if one could. Rather, the question of lesbian and gay conformism to heteronormative standards or complicity with capital cannot be reduced to failures of political will or, alternatively, to instances of false consciousness or bad faith. Rather, it is incumbent to recognize the ethical and political ambivalences that accompany a tradition of exclusion: the ambivalence of wanting what one has been denied—marriage rights, military service, Hollywood films, corporate advertising—at the same time that what has been denied often proves to be less than what one may want. The very real gains and pleasures won by successfully abating the effects of an abject demonization such as homophobia should not be underestimated. They nourish the very real desire for something like "authentic" representations. Nor, however, should we underestimate the extent to which these gains and pleasures are often paid for with expro-

65

priative practices and second-order exclusions, which are often justified by claims to political expediency—usually figured as the need to combat homophobia by representing lesbians and gay men as "normal," "just like everyone else." Such politically strategic claims exemplify the need for progressive politics to grasp the structural and historical dynamics of public sphere inclusion. That one often finds simultaneously progressive and conformist aspects in struggles for social justice should form the initial problematic, rather than the conclusion, in analyses of disenfranchisement and its redress.[52]

This simultaneity, as well as the ambivalences for which it is a historical symptom, indicate that a critical analysis of visibility politics must abjure simplistic or totalizing ethical gestures. One may critique dominant elements of social and political discourse, such as equal rights for marriage and military service, for being less than progressive in and of themselves. However, because these elements are also part and parcel of homophobic discrimination and the struggle for full enfranchisement, they are, to borrow from Gayatri Chakravorty Spivak, those things one "cannot not want." Such ambivalence points to the stubbornly difficult histories of oppression, as well as the attempts to progress beyond them. To the extent that the modes of value determination outlined above interpenetrate each other, simply invoking conformism or complicity cannot adequately convey the historical and structural complexities of "social integration," not the least because neither invocation adequately makes clear its own set of ethical presumptions. This inadequacy is perhaps most glaring with regard to queers and a commercial determination of value. As Michael Warner usefully observes, "Gay culture in this most visible mode [consumer culture] is anything but external to advanced capitalism and to precisely those features of advanced capitalism that many on the left are most eager to disavow. Post-Stonewall urban gay men reek of the commodity. We give off the smell of capitalism in rut, and therefore demand of theory a more dialectical view of capitalism than many people have imagination for."[53] Critique lives, however obliquely, within the space of its object, and thus is necessarily entangled within the value relations that give its object an ethical and political urgency. Any critique of lesbian and gay conformism, then, inhabits not only the contemporary structuring of visibility politics, but also the diversified modes of value determination that make it possible, intelligible, and powerful: visual pleasure, struggles against phobic stereotypes, corporate marketing and media images, and the affirming authenticity presumed to inhere in these images—lesbians and gay men "as they really are." The persistent critique of "what one must inhabit," as Spivak reminds us, requires an "incessant recoding" of these "diversified fields of value." [54]

How we might recode the relations between homoeroticism and the public sphere requires engaging with the modes that mediate and thus constitute the tenor of enfranchisement. As I have argued here, the subjunctive mood of the public sphere allows inclusion to be administered according to conformist and inequitable standards of value—that is, administered *as if* these standards equitably distribute enfranchisement. Habermas has claimed, in fact, that the procedures securing enfranchisement in the public sphere *necessarily* have this kind of counterfactual element. He has argued for a contingent universality within the discursive procedures of deliberative democracy, such that "impossible" ideals of justice become at least hypothetically applicable to all. Much like Kant's categorical imperative, we are required to test principles of justice according to whether they *could* be universally justified. Because this universality remains only counterfactual, both "claimed and denied," he argues that publicity practices can remain open to democratic revision. Theoretically, the necessary gap between ideal and reality gives democratic debate room for "ideal-typical" principles to measure how justice is applied and practiced.

Yet Habermas has also maintained that conformity to the procedural norms of liberal democratic pluralism is a necessary precondition for a just social order. Even if the application of publicity ideals contradicts their basic premises, we are required to act as if they did not, if only because these ideals must be retained as our best hope for democracy. He would seem, then, to be open to the criticism that he in effect justifies the "society of normalization" and its disciplinary techniques of power so forcefully exposed by Michel Foucault. Why precisely would Habermas argue that deliberative democracy and the autonomous public spheres that nourish it necessarily involve a subjunctive dissimulation by which a disenfranchising conformity would appear just? Why would the very definition of a just democratic social order contain the possibility of its own contradiction? Do Foucault's reflections on power and "normalization" offer a useful counterpoint to the subjunctive tenor of enfranchisement? What are some of the consequences of Habermas's and Foucault's thoughts on conformity for understanding queer publicity? These are questions the next chapter will seek to address.

TWO   *Autonomy and Conformity*

It is, in the most precise sense of the word, the Idea of his Human Nature [Menschheit], hence something infinite, to which in the course of time [man] can approximate ever more closely, but without ever being able to reach it. —Friedrich Schiller, ON THE AESTHETIC EDUCATION OF MAN

Schiller's evocation of human nature as an impossible ideal exhibits two general aspects of Enlightenment thinking about self-determination. First, it exhibits the impulse to ground moral and political self-governance in abstract, universal principles. This impulse was arguably forward-looking insofar as it set an ideal standard of the human according to which Man could continually transcend himself as he was, both individually and socially. Thus it could elaborate, against the arbitrariness of feudal social arrangements, universal moral-political principles of the human that could ground the equality of all. Along with its promise of unfettered individual development and political equality, however, Schiller's evocation also confirms the irreducibly regulative aspect of Enlightenment ideals of the human. Because such ideals are impossible, they can become evaluative standards against which behaviors and institutions will be continually judged. Even as they can protect self-determination and social equality, moral-political principles can also function as norms by which persons themselves are judged as worthy or unworthy of the very enfranchisement these principles would guarantee. Subject to a regulative ideal, self-determination becomes irreducibly bound to judgments of value.

These two aspects of self-determination as an Enlightenment thematic have animated debates over the tension between individual freedom and social equality in modern plural societies held together more by political administration than by communal traditions. This tension has also structured contemporary debates in political philosophy over whether ideally context-transcending moral principles or a communally rooted ethical life should have priority in defining the nature of enfranchisement. This issue touches on the viability of dissent in marking out the contours of abstract political identities, such as the citizen, and thus in developing an enfranchisement appropriate to plural societies. The character of enfranchisement addressed by these debates can be cast as a problem of judgment: What principles of value undergird the process by which persons are converted into equal and free social participants? Where is the meeting point between individual freedom and social equality in judgments about the public interest? By what criteria of judgment can one adjudicate between these two aspects of enfranchisement?

Because the public sphere helps to regulate enfranchisement, it also operates as a mode by which such questions, and the judgments they both ask about and require, are shaped in public discourse. Haunting the public sphere's engagement with these questions, however, are the limits imposed by two interrelated legacies of publicity: first, the subsumption of politics under morality; and second, the often tendentious relation between the private and the public. By understanding politics to be ideally guided by universal moral principles, such as innate human dignity and worth, the quality of publicness requires judgments as to what constitutes a valid principle applicable to all. While promising to adjudicate between competing interests, such judgments also provide space for more narrow and "commonsensical" conceptions of the moral to be formulated *as if* they were universalizable. This space constitutes the subjunctive quality of universal moral-political principles and allows, indeed requires, judgment to intercede within the process of forming and applying such principles. This need for judgment intersects with the translation of private vices into public virtues underlying publicity as a historical phenomenon. This translation requires criteria that will guide judgments about which elements of the private sphere are publicly relevant and thus how they may be generalizable. Such criteria are often drawn from rather particular experiences and understandings of the private; they can involve narrow standards of moral value, which in turn determine the conversion from private to public, the constitution of norms, and judgments about the public interest. We could say, then, that moral judgment is a "practice of value" that regulates enfranchisement.[1] Moral judgment as the contested space between ideal and reality, indeed as a space within idealization itself, enables universal principles to hold out the promise of self-determination with one hand while paradoxically demanding conformity with the other.

With regard to sexuality, these two legacies of the public sphere are especially problematic. Sexuality and sexual dissent in particular make salient the dissimulation of narrow evaluative standards of behavior ("sexual morality") as both socially desirable and universally applicable. This dissimulation renders morality into the sphere not of autonomy but of heteronomy, a coercive imposition of behavioral codes. A heteronormative sexual morality is able to present itself inappropriately as if it were a universal prerequisite for enfranchisement. In this way, the narrow moral standards regulating enfranchisement not only demonize varieties of sexual nonconformity integral to individual or group self-definition. They also legitimate conformity as the very prerequisite for a supposedly equitable and democratic inclusion within the public sphere.

These aspects of the public sphere indicate that the inclusion of queers cannot be reduced to the lifting of a prior exclusion. Inclusion has involved a conformist inertia toward inegalitarian standards of value, standards that nevertheless are presented as universally binding because they are figured as constitutively human. To investigate further this conformist inertia, this chapter will engage the thought of two figures, Jürgen Habermas and Michel Foucault, who have presented powerful yet often diametrically opposed rereadings of the Enlightenment legacy as it relates to contemporary political discourse. While arguing that both thinkers provide politically vital analyses of such discourse, this chapter will explore specific limitations in their thought for understanding fully publicity's regulation of enfranchisement.[2]

Both Habermas and Foucault present powerfully enabling paradigms for thinking through inclusion, or "social integration," as a problematic. Habermas presents one of the most cogent analytic reworkings of universal moral-political principles, like human rights, such that they are anchored in both social participation and personal autonomy. At the same time, Foucault's later work on ethics usefully challenges political discourse to reconceive "power" via what he terms "practices of freedom." Alongside the strengths of each, however, I hope to sketch here a clearer picture of their limitations for understanding the homogenizing effects of public sphere inclusion, both specifically for queers and more generally, as well as the theoretical resources needed to articulate inclusion differently. Where Habermas tends to uphold a dubious symmetry between ideal and reality to recuperate the rational potential of publicness, Foucault tends to create a functionalist symmetry that would call such potential into question. The limitations and possibilities each thinker provides for thinking about inclusion as a problematic have important repercussions for queer politics and self-understanding. These limits and possibilities highlight the need to understand the larger social, political, and economic processes within which queers are imbricated alongside of but also beyond evocations of subcultural identity, minority status, or "community." How might the experiences, resources, and problems posed by queer politics reorient self-determination as a relevant Enlightenment thematic?

The Ideal-Typical

As odd and nerdy as it may sound, I often think of Habermas when teaching alternative AIDS videos to my undergraduate students in an Introduction to Popular Culture course. Despite the inequities of power between teacher and students, the classroom at times can be an ideal arena for the exchange of ideas. It can embody, at some time and in some form, Habermas's notion of "communicative action" and "intersubjective rationality," those critical capacities central not only to the public sphere but also to the discourse ethics that for Habermas emerges from publicity ideals. I mention teaching alternative AIDS videos in particular because they point to difficulties these ideals encounter in practice, difficulties that reflect not just on the vagaries of context but more importantly on the very normative articulation of these ideals.[3]

Two videos seem especially instructive in terms of the classroom exchange that invariably takes place after they are screened: *Doctors, Liars, Women: AIDS Activists Say No to Cosmo* (dir. Jean Carlomusto and Maria Maggenti, 1988), and *Like a Prayer* (dir. DIVA-TV, 1989). The first documents the efforts of a women's group within the New York chapter of ACT UP to protest an article published in an issue of *Cosmopolitan* magazine that claimed heterosexual women are at such low risk of HIV infection from unprotected vaginal intercourse that they should not be concerned about safer-sex practices. Naturally enough, this outrageously dangerous claim spurred the women's group within ACT UP/NY to take action: they met with the author, a psychiatrist with no training in or experience with HIV or AIDS, and confronted him with extraordinarily persuasive countervailing evidence and arguments; they attempted (rather unsuccessfully) to air their disagreements on a local talk show; and they staged an informational protest outside the New York headquarters of *Cosmopolitan*. *Doctors, Liars, Women* thus powerfully documents a disenfranchised group's efforts to engage equitably in a life-or-death debate within the public sphere, and is itself an important document of self-representation in the face of the failures of public discourse. The students who speak about this video—and many do—uniformly praise the strategies of the activists, and strongly disapprove of the protested article, the activists' lack of access to debate over it, and thus the tactics by which the media attempted to silence them. Indeed this video inspired at least a few students to become involved in HIV/AIDS activism.

Like a Prayer has had a rather different reception among my students. It documents the protest staged by ACT UP/NY against New York's Cardinal John O'Connor and the Catholic Church, in particular their moral opposition to homosexuality and the use of condoms. The students are treated to powerful images of queer street theater and protest: queer clowns wandering the streets to humorously ridicule the church's antihomosexual campaign; a gay Jesus extolling the virtues of safer sex; and outraged activists occupying St. Patrick's Cathedral in New York City and, at one decisive moment, "desecrating" a host wafer. This moment in particular grabbed the attention of the news media at the time (all but ignoring everything else about the protest, including the reasons it was staged). The video also documents these media reactions, as well as some of the disagreements within ACT UP itself over the "desecration." Despite similar concerns over restrictions to self-representation and dangerous public discourse regarding HIV and AIDS as *Doctors, Liars, Women, Like a Prayer* is met with a great amount of hostility by my students. There is near unanimity among them that this video depicts the worst kind of political protest. Not only does it offend religious sensibilities, they argue, but also it presents the most repulsive tactics they could imagine. The students who speak about this video object that they were, to say the least, unpersuaded. If the activists wanted others—Catholics? heterosexuals?—to be persuaded, my students argue, they went about it in entirely the wrong way.[4]

When I first planned to screen these two videos, it did not occur to me that they were so diametrically opposed as so many of my students continually think them to be. I still do not think they are: both forcefully document moments in the struggle against homophobia and sanctioned ignorance about HIV and AIDS. But their differing receptions by the students who speak in class about them is instructive. One video, it would seem, presents activists engaging in acceptable forms of rational argumentation, while the other presents activists engaging in unfamiliar, theatrical, and "offensive" protest. It would seem that one meets a particular normative burden of persuasion, while the other most resolutely does not.

Thus I think of Habermas when I teach these videos not just because the classroom can ideally embody, in some fashion, the rational debate that publicity and discourse ethics aim to foster and protect. I also think of him because the vastly different reception of these two videos indicates problems of value in the normative content and practical orientation of publicity ideals and discourse ethics. Two objections to Habermas's otherwise compelling and extraordinarily thorough defense of a normatively procedural model of deliberative democracy are exhibited in my pedagogical anecdote. First, the normative definition of publicity ideals can carry with it a potentially conformist demand that the disenfranchised be like those from and by whom they are disenfranchised. This demand appears in the inequitable distribution of the burden to persuade—who bears it, and on what terms. While rational argument itself is not necessarily in dispute, inequitably distributing the burden of persuasion indicates that conformist value-determinations can operate under the alibi of "reasonableness." The operation of value appears in the conflation of "conduct" and procedure in argumentative burdens and interpretive norms. Conflating conduct and procedure can legitimate restrictive notions of moral worth and greatly constrict the possibilities open to and the effects of political struggle, even in a strongly deliberative democracy. Second, the normative content of publicity is thus not as open to self-critique as Habermas claims. Because the ideally universal procedural norms of democratic deliberation in his model are justified as *legitimately* counterfactual, one is forced to conform to these norms even if they are what is in dispute. Both of these objections revolve in some measure around the role of value in forming idealizations, as well as in mediating between ideal and reality, norm and context.

To explore these objections in more detail, I want to focus particularly on the ideal-typical status Habermas gives the public sphere, and the extension of this status to aspects of his discourse ethics. Habermas has provided one of the most systematic and compelling defenses of a discursively based, procedurally normative democracy. Displacing the instrumental rationality of the Enlightenment (exemplified in the harnessing and exploitation of labor power under capitalism), Habermas views communication as a more democratic, nonappropriative practice of rationality whose kernel can be found in Enlightenment ideals of bourgeois publicity. This kernel Habermas variously terms "interaction," "communicative action," "communicative liberty," and "intersubjective rationality." While granting many of the criticisms against his earlier overidealized vision of the bourgeois public sphere, particularly those by historians and feminist critics, Habermas nevertheless has retained bourgeois publicity's ideal of a democratic, discursive agreement among equals. He has thus sought to elaborate the procedural—as opposed to substantive—norms that would make central the determining role of communicative action in democratically deciding matters of public interest. "If there is any small remnant of utopia that I've preserved," Habermas has stated, "then it is surely the idea that democracy—and the public struggle for its best form—is capable of hacking through the Gordian knots of otherwise insoluble problems." [5]

Habermas has traced the public struggle for the best form of democracy in the West back to the earliest articulations of the bourgeois public sphere. Since its publication in German in 1962, however, *The Structural Transformation of the Public Sphere* has been criticized for presenting a rather idealized vision of its object. Such criticism has usually focused on the contradiction between the norms of bourgeois publicity and their historical materialization—the contradiction, that is, between its democratic principles of free and equal access and expression, and the constitutive exclusions of the public sphere in its historical unfolding. This contradiction forms what we might call the historical counterfactuality of the public sphere as an ideal, a part of what I have termed its subjunctive mood. However, the subjunctivity of the public sphere is indicated not only by the contradiction between norm and reality but also by this contradiction's constitutive place in the normative definition of publicity ideals. The contradiction between norm and reality can be legitimately dissimulated because the ideals of publicity are articulated as only ever counterfactual to begin with, and thus they carry an at least implicit subjunctive compulsion to view them as if they were actual.

This dissimulation can be seen most clearly in critiques of the public sphere that have focused on the enfolding of bourgeois economic interests within the supposedly general, universal interests of publicity.[6] As early as two years after the publication of Habermas's book, Theodor Adorno pointed out that the bourgeois public sphere was not a "fixed" but rather a polemically normative and politically ambitious phenomenon. Echoing Gramsci's characterization of the bourgeoisie's universalizing impulses — "everyone will be bourgeois"—Adorno similarly (and characteristically) renders into a slogan the public sphere's voracious subsumption of all within its normative calculus: "what was not part of the public sphere, should become so."[7] This ambitiously hegemonic aspect of the ideal of publicity originated as a critique of absolutist political regimes, and in this sense necessitated that "the public sphere and democracy [be] joined together. Only under the guarantee of democratic rule through free expression can the public sphere develop; only if it is public, something over which the citizen has the capacity to vote, is democracy conceivable."[8] However, Adorno is quick to indicate the distance between the bourgeois public sphere as an ideal and as a historical phenomenon: "The public sphere itself, however, is in its actual development caught up within the economic forms of bourgeois society; its 'profit' is gained through the commercial industry that provides popularized information. Through this the theoretically universal concept of the public sphere is mixed in practice with a moment of limits and particularities. It largely obeys the material interests of the institutions through which it lives."[9] Adorno's critique echoes Habermas's own argument that the bourgeois public sphere disintegrated through the commercialization of properly political, morally normative public institutions. However, Adorno's critique also points toward a more fundamental problem: that the bourgeois public sphere was *structurally and constitutively* tied to particular class interests and processes of value extraction from the very beginning.[10] The counterfactual distance between ideal and reality would then not be a sign of the public sphere's incompletion, the historical blockage of its normative potential. Rather, it would signal that the public sphere served at least in part as an idealized mask for the universalizing presumption of a hegemonic, minority class interest.

The public sphere's idealized conceptualization cannot be divorced from its history—would be in fact the very *sign* of its historicity. Even as the bourgeois public sphere formulated principles that ideally could transcend their ideological instantiation, as Habermas has claimed, Adorno's argument implies that this "context-transcending" claim had the potential to mask, and indeed did mask, inequitable publicity practices.[11]

A more sustained consideration of these problems can be found in Wolfgang Jäger's 1973 study, *Öffentlichkeit und Parliamentarismus: Eine Kritik an Jürgen Habermas* (The Public Sphere and Parliamentarianism: A Critique of Jürgen Habermas). Jäger argues that by understanding the bourgeois public sphere as an "ideal-typical" category, Habermas is forced to reproduce substantively and methodologically the class interests disguised in publicity's universalizing presumptions. Because of the ideal-typical nature of his investigation, Jäger claims, Habermas must assume that "historical reality can be grasped with relative impartiality," thus reproducing methodologically the bourgeois presumption that the "private interests of individuals extended into objective interests."[12] Jäger specifically takes Habermas to task for claiming that in nineteenth-century Great Britain, and in the British Parliament in particular, one finds a "model case" of the public sphere's ideal development (one that, Habermas maintains, would only later be compromised by the bureaucratization and encroachment of commercial interests on Parliament as a deliberative body). By examining the history of agitation for parliamentary reform and the writers who defended the English constitution—Edmund Burke and Walter Bagehot in particular—Jäger underscores the extent to which economic and class interests had always formed a decisive factor in parliamentary decisions. "The political distribution of power," he argues, "reflected the economic distribution of power."[13] By reproducing the terms by which the public sphere was idealized in the nineteenth-century British liberal tradition, Jäger argues that Habermas thus *follows* this tradition in erecting a "phantom" (*Trugbild*), a public sphere whose democratic pronouncements dissimulate the more naked exercise of power and the hegemony of bourgeois interests.[14] Publicity's democratic ideals were, in fact, essential to the success of bourgeois hegemony.

The historical difficulties brought up by Jäger can be traced through what Charles Tilly has termed the "parliamentarization" of popular protest from the mid-eighteenth to the mid-nineteenth century in Great Britain. Tilly investigates discursive processes of "claim-making," arguing that these processes underwent fundamental transformations as they increasingly looked to Parliament—as the presumptive organ of democratic representation and deliberation—to redress sociopolitical injustices. The process of parliamentarization certainly involved some accommodation on the side of legal and judicial authorities, particularly through the gradual extension of the franchise in 1832, 1867, and 1884. Yet it also involved the abandonment of previously successful forms of popular claim-making, such as seizures of grain and attacks on poorhouses. Indeed, the 1867 Reform Law, which extended the vote to some working-class men, was passed in large measure because established interests in Parliament believed threats to property or of revolution no longer existed. Through the Reform League, the working class had become, in the eyes of many aristocratic and middle-class lawgivers, conciliatory and "responsible." The inclusion of working-class interests, of increasing working-class access to the means of political representation, necessarily involved a *transformation* of those interests. Thus Tilly concludes that "[n]o one should confuse parliamentarization with the advent of justice and democracy." [15]

Tilly's study therefore suggests some validity to Jäger's point concerning Habermas's methodology. The contradiction between publicity as norm and reality is also complicated by the assimilationist strictures governing the processes of inclusion that would seek to redress this very contradiction. The public sphere's idealized norms of rational deliberation and democratic representation would seem themselves to be extensions of the exercise of bourgeois interests, at least in terms of the nineteenth-century British Parliament. To accede to these normatively universal procedures for the public articulation of general interests was also, therefore, to conform to the historically particular—which is to say class-specific—uses to which they were put. This example drawn from nineteenth-century British political history suggests that the processes of conversion by which social elements become publicly relevant and legitimate have historically been entangled within conformist value-determinations that may operate under the guise of universal moral-political principles and "reasonable" deliberative procedures. The point is not that attacks on poorhouses or seizures of grain should necessarily have continued as preferred modes of social criticism and demands for legitimacy. Rather, the point is that the procedural norms of rational deliberation have historically encoded substantive, often exclusionary norms regarding conduct and propriety.

The force of Adorno's and Jäger's critiques brings up a further methodological point about Habermas's ideal-typical understanding of bourgeois publicity. Jäger argues that Habermas misuses Max Weber's concept of the ideal-typical; he inappropriately uses the ideal-typical, Jäger argues, as an objective descriptor of empirical reality, rather than an interpretive methodological tool. This forces Habermas to reproduce the idealization of publicity and its norms found in bourgeois thought itself. On this point, however, Jäger's critique is somewhat less convincing. Weber developed the "ideal-typical" as a heuristic category, one that could reveal the "interpenetration of value-spheres": "Its function is the comparison with empirical reality in order to establish its divergences or similarities, to describe them with the *most unambiguously intelligible concepts*, and to understand and explain them causally." [16] Importantly, Weber underscored that ideal-typical categories were in no way concepts that one could use to support the objectivity of one's research, and that such categories always had an irreducibly *evaluative* dimension to them. Ideal-typical constructs are merely useful ways of comparing disparate historical phenomena. They can be used to form a "representation of value [*Darstellung von Wert*]," but should not themselves reproduce this value *as if* it were objective.[17]

In *Structural Transformation*, Habermas uses the public sphere not only as a category by which to *describe* sociohistorical dynamics but also as a category for political critique. It has for Habermas an explicitly *normative* function. Thus the last half of the book focuses on the disintegration of the norms of publicity under the influence of state bureaucratization and, more importantly, the reifications of cultural forms and everyday life under advanced capitalism. This latter point, as Pete Uwe Hohendahl has argued, "logically presumes a condition of standardized norms whose retrieval is desirable. Therefore, Habermas' model of the public sphere has a double function. It provides a paradigm for analyzing historical change, while also serving as a normative category for political critique." [18] This returns us to Jäger's methodological critique: To the extent that Habermas defends a reformulated notion of the public sphere as an evaluative ideal, rather than simply as an "objective" empirical fact, Jäger's critique seems unfounded. Habermas himself admits that with regard to the exclusion of women and the working class in particular, "bourgeois democracy . . . from its very inception contradicted essential premises of its own self-understanding."[19] However, for Habermas this admission does not diminish the public sphere's capabilities to adapt: "From the very beginning the universalistic discourses of the bourgeois public sphere were based on self-referential premises; they did not remain unaffected by a criticism from within because they differ from Foucaultian discourses by virtue of their potential for self-transformation."[20] This potential for self-transformation reveals the normative, fundamentally axiological dimension Habermas attributes to the public sphere as an "ideal-type." Simply put, the public sphere contains a utopian possibility, he argues, that should neither be discarded nor discounted: "The ideals of bourgeois humanism that have left their characteristic mark on the self-interpretation of the intimate sphere and the public, and that are articulated in the key concepts of subjectivity and self-actualization, rational formation of opinion and will, and personal and political self-determination, have infused the institutions of the constitutional state to such an extent that, functioning as a utopian potential, they point beyond a constitutional reality that negates them."[21] These ideals can point beyond their ideological rendering, Habermas argues, because they are grounded in the communicative capacity for self-critique:

> To be sure, this *utopia of reason, formed in the Enlightenment,* was persistently contradicted by the realities of bourgeois life and shown to be a *bourgeois ideology.* But it was never a mere illusion; it was an objective illusion that arose from the structures of differentiated lifeworlds [*Lebenswelten*] which, while certainly limited in class-specific ways, were nonetheless rationalized. To the extent that culture, society, and personality separated off from one another as Mead and Durkheim said they did, and the validity basis of communicative action replaced the sacred foundations of social integration, there was at least *an appearance of posttraditional everyday communication* suggested by the structures of the lifeworld. It was, so to speak, a transcendental apparition — determining bourgeois ideology, while yet surpassing it. In it, communication was represented as standing on its own feet, setting limits to the inner dynamics of autonomous subsystems, bursting encapsulated expert cultures, and thus as escaping the threat of reification and desolation.[22]

The ideal of an intersubjective communicative action ideally found in publicity, Habermas argues, can transcend its ideological realization because it can establish an evaluative standard against which these inadequate realizations themselves can be judged. In this respect Habermas is quite clear that publicity, and the communicative rationality ideally inhering in it, is both "objective" *and* ideal.

The Transcendental Apparition

For Habermas the kind of communicative action sustaining publicity forms the meeting point between the normative and the factual. Habermas maintains that an intersubjective communicative action can be found in any everyday speech context oriented toward understanding; it is an actual, cognitively structured practice. Because it is intersubjective, this practice also necessarily involves ego-transcending *idealizations* that make understanding possible. Adequately testing the validity of our assertions involves an irreducibly social ideal of reaching understanding. Communicative action is thus a two-sided coin whose factual and normative sides cannot be utterly separated from each other. The actual practice of an intersubjective communication oriented toward understanding, Habermas maintains, contains a context-transcending ideal that both allows mutual understanding to occur, and forms an evaluative standard against which the validity of democratic deliberative procedures and the moral-political principles that guide them may be judged. The idealizations presupposed in intersubjective communication are not so much "objective" criteria themselves as empirically sustained norms by which to measure the democratic vitality of social and political institutions.[23]

The "apparition" of communicative action characterizing democratic publicness, however, brings up a problem related to Jäger's methodological criticism. This problem concerns the role of value in both forming and instantiating ideal moral-political principles, whose context-transcending claims Habermas grounds in intersubjective communicative rationality. In his work on discourse ethics, Habermas has transformed what had become a strongly criticized aspect of *Structural Transformation*—the gap between the public sphere as ideal and reality in the unfolding of its historical existence—into a constitutive yet more limited aspect of democratic deliberative procedures. Discourse ethics emerged from his sense that the intersubjective and communicative ideals of the public sphere had not been properly thought through. He has argued that the exclusive focus on instrumental reason distorted, or rather concealed, other modes of Enlightenment rationality that were not expropriative. He extended this argument in the late 1960s in his reconsideration of Hegel's Jena *Philosophy of Mind*, and importantly his work here signals a distinct turn from the Critical Theory of Theodor Adorno and Max Horkheimer. He wanted to avoid what he saw as their totalizing critique of Enlightenment rationality by pinpointing a nonobjectifying form of reason latent in Enlightenment thought: one that is intersubjective and not subject-centered, as in philosophies of consciousness. In this sense discourse ethics strives to be a reconstructive, "postmetaphysical" theory.[24]

For Habermas, the pragmatically universal norms of discourse ethics embody the *procedural* means by which the historical exclusions of the public sphere can be overcome. Morality thus becomes a procedural sphere of rational deliberation, rather than a trancendent realm of duties.[25] To allow equitable inclusion within the public sphere despite the distorting effects of preexisting prejudices and inequities of social power, this procedural sphere and its norms must be able to transform competing private interests into a discursively agreed-upon public interest. Precisely because these norms entail a "weak" universality, "the shadow of a transcendental illusion," they must be "approached in a sufficiently skeptical manner": "Communicative reason is of course a rocking hull—but it does not go under in the sea of contingencies, even if shuddering in high seas is the only mode in which it 'copes' with these contingencies."[26] His theory of communicative action provides "an empirical approach in which the tension of the abstract opposition between norm and reality is dissolved."[27] By pointing to these communicatively based procedural norms that have built-in mechanisms for self-critique, Habermas claims for the public sphere an ability to "self-correct" the historical distortions of its democratic premises.

However, even as communicative action "dissolves" the tension between norm and reality, Habermas has conceded that any full adequation between universal moral-political principles and their historical realization is impossible. The universal claims to validity embodied in rational procedures of deliberation are fundamentally counterfactual: "[I]f we want to enter into argumentation, we must make these presuppositions of argumentation *as a matter of fact*, despite the fact that they have an ideal content to which we can only approximate in reality."[28] Habermas makes an even stronger case for the necessarily counterfactual premises of the public sphere in the procedural processes by which it would move toward full democratic inclusion: "In fact, we can by no means always, or even only often, fulfill those improbably pragmatic presuppositions from which we nevertheless set forth in day-to-day communicative practice—and, in the sense of transcendental necessity, from which we *must* set forth. For this reason, sociocultural forms of life stand under [*überstehen*] the structural restrictions of a communicative reason *at once claimed and denied*."[29] In this formulation, "sociocultural forms of life" must "stand under" the procedural norms of intersubjective communication. This would mean, for example, that no one set of interests would automatically have priority within public discourse. All must submit to the equalizing force of an intersubjective communicative rationality and its universalizing presumptions. Thus the ability to mediate between "the universal and the individual is provided by the *higher level intersubjectivity of an uncoerced formation of will [Willensbildung] within a communication community existing under constraints toward cooperation [unter Kooperationszwängen stehen].* . . ."[30] These constraints toward cooperation ideally insure that no one set of interests receives a presumptive authority within deliberative procedures. Such constraints, in the guise of context-transcending communicative norms, regulate the adjudication of competing interests.

Yet Habermas also wants to insure that the universal moral-political principles that are presupposed by and emerge out of discourse ethics are responsive to particular contexts and demands. This responsiveness would include the demand for autonomy *on the terms of those who lay claim to it*. In his more recent writings on political theory, he makes clear that "the intended equalization of actual life circumstances and positions of power should not lead to *normalizing* interventions that perceptibly restrict the capacities of the presumed beneficiaries to shape their lives autonomously."[31] The liberal version of rights, for example, "misconstrue[s] the universalism of basic rights as an abstract leveling of distinctions, a leveling of both cultural and social differences. These differences must be interpreted in increasingly context-sensitive ways if the system of rights is to be actualized democratically."[32] The question of interpretation here is crucial. For Habermas, the universal principles arrived at through intersubjective communication only intermingle with context-specific norms when considering how to *apply* such principles. The deliberative moment of arriving at universally valid principles, he argues, lifts one out of one's own context. In this way, Habermas insists that the "moral" questions involved in such deliberation are distinct from the "evaluative questions" tied to a "concrete historical form of life." [33] Because communication oriented toward understanding requires splitting off the realm of the moral from the realm of value, Habermas maintains that "the dialogue roles of every speech situation enforce a symmetry in participant perspectives." [34] This symmetry is achieved only when participants are able to abstract from their own particular life narrative and context. Within this moment of abstraction, Habermas argues, participants are able to arrive at (at least provisional) agreement on norms that may be applicable to all: "For, although they may be interpreted in various ways and applied according to different criteria, concepts like truth, rationality, or justification play the *same* grammatical role in *every* linguistic community." [35] It is only *after* a context-transcending deliberation that the norms it generates are reinserted into practical life: "This much is true: any universalistic morality is dependent upon a form of life that *meets it halfway*. There has to be a modicum of congruence between morality and the practices of socialization and education." [36]

But can moral questions be distinguished from evaluative questions? Do the value determinations found in specific life contexts only factor in *after* context-transcending deliberation regarding moral principles has taken place? Other aspects of Habermas's thought would seem to contradict this distinction. For example, he has argued that interpretation and judgment are internal to processes of reaching understanding. "Mutual understanding about the contestable existence of states of affairs," he has argued, "can be reached by participants only *on the basis of an evaluation* of the truth of sentences." [37] While he concludes, with Wittgenstein, that this internal relation between "meaning and validity" within communication is not necessarily tied to any particular empirical context, it does involve conformity to specific rules of argumentation: "[T]he identity of a rule in the multiplicity of its realizations does not rest upon *observable* invariances, but upon the validity of a criterion according to which rule-conforming conduct can be judged." [38] In this sense, "constraints toward cooperation" necessarily involve evaluative judgments. Such judgments pinpoint the eruption of value within ideally universal communicative procedures and the norms they produce. "The rational potential of speech," Habermas has argued, "is interwoven with the *resources* of any particular given lifeworld." [39] The context-transcending promise of intersubjective rationality rooted in communication is irreducibly intermixed *from the start* with the preexisting "resources" of a society at any particular moment in time.

While the role of judgment constrains Habermas's ideal of a symmetrical and intersubjective communicative rationality, it also affects the universal moral-political principles this rationality would generate. Because such principles can only have an illusion of universality, they can be potentially "claimed and denied" by the force of existing power differentials, the "resources" of a given "lifeworld": "This amalgam of background assumptions, solidarities, and skills bred through socialization constitutes a conservative counterweight against the risk of dissent inherent in processes of reaching understanding that work through validity claims [*Geltungsansprüche laufenden Verständigungsprozesse*]."[40] Prejudicial value-orientations, like heteronormativity, can constrain the very procedures that one would expect to ameliorate such orientations. Context-specific norms no longer affect moral-political principles only *after* agreement on them has been reached and the search for their application has begun. Such norms can constrain an ideally context-transcending deliberation as well. While guarding against the possibility that minority interests might inappropriately overwhelm the democratic formation of consensus, "conservative counterweights against dissent" can also inequitably distribute deliberative resources and burdens.[41]

These difficulties in Habermas's model raise vital questions about such resources and burdens: Who bears the burden to persuade? Who enjoys the entitlement of the one who must be persuaded? What terms structure this distribution of burdens and entitlements? By *whom* are universal moral-political principles claimed, and by *what* are they denied? These questions are particularly relevant to social groups whose relation to signification itself fails hegemonic standards of moral conduct. The "good homosexuals" found in mainstream lesbian and gay civil rights lobbies, for example, certainly measure their successes by the normalized face they can present to Congress. Yet their normalization allows them to engage in rational deliberation only insofar as such deliberation is *already* constrained by a heteronormative construction of what is reasonable communication. The success of such groups has more to do with conforming queerness to heteronormative standards for fund-raising purposes than they do with either representing a diverse constituency or actually transforming the heteronormative terms defining public discourse about sexuality. As the example of student reactions to *Like a Prayer* indicates, the significations of political struggle can fail to meet the burdens of "reasonable" discursive engagement because such burdens can encode prejudicial norms.

Habermas has made clear that political struggle is central to the processes of validity-testing ideally guaranteed by universal norms of communicative action. Political struggle, then, is central to combating disenfranchisement: "Liberating ourselves from the merely presumptive generality [*Allgemeinheit*] of selectively employed universalistic principles applied in a context-insensitive manner has always required, and today still requires, social movements and political struggles; we have to learn from the painful experiences and irreparable suffering of those who have been humiliated, insulted, injured, and brutalized so that nobody may be excluded in the name of moral universalism. . . ." [42] However, when the universalist contours of communicative rationality are claimed and yet denied by specific value-orientations, like heteronormativity, political struggle against such orientations may very well come off as nonsensical, unpersuasive, or indeed offensive. If the universality of procedural norms must be approached subjunctively, *as if* they were actually universal, then the inequitable burdens legitimated under their cover cannot also be a subject of effective debate *except on the terms of those who have already predetermined the contours of "the universal" and the "moral."* Habermas's model legitimates a mode of participation that may effectively constrain an autonomy of, and thus an expansive rationality for, political signification. Conformity to inappropriately universalized norms can thereby regulate self-determination—indeed, can appear as if it were itself the exercise of autonomy.

To be sure, Habermas often stresses that the ideally universal presuppositions at work in communicative rationality "must still be conceptualized in such a way that their tensions remain irreducible"; one must stress both their "idealizations and their failures." [43] Such failures must be kept in mind in order to evaluate adequately whether they live up to their promise. Only in this way, he has argued, can the "other" *remain* other on his or her own terms. However, these failures do not only take place *after* moral-political principles have been formed; this formation itself may fail its own paradigm. Judgment as a practice of value in *both forming and applying* idealizations represents a blind spot in Habermas's thought. Even within the ideal deliberative arena of communicative action, "Once the other appears as a *real* individual with his own unsubstitutable will, new problems arise."[44] It is beyond the scope of discourse ethics, Habermas admits, to deal adequately with these problems, other than his own weak invocations of "compromise." Indeed, we could say that the invocation of compromise signals what may well be a quasi-theological aspect of Habermas's thought. "The structure of linguistic intersubjectivity," he has argued, "makes harmony between the integration of autonomy and devotion to others possible for us—in other words, a reconciliation that does not efface differences."[45] Such "harmony" begs the question of who must be conciliatory and on what terms. If the specific differences at hand require a fundamental change of certain value-orientations in the public sphere, as queer struggle at its best has, then the ideal of reconciliation may prove inadequate to realize such change. In the end, reconciliation may recapitulate a core problem in Habermas's paradigm: the subjunctive dissimulation of democracy within the public sphere. Against its own democratic ideals, his paradigm unwittingly justifies confusing context-specific norms and universal principles, conduct and procedure, autonomy and conformity.[46]

Discourse/Reverse Discourse

In light of both its power and its limits, Habermas's work is valuable to queer thought for at least two interrelated reasons. First, it provides a strong rationale for engaging with, rather than simply dismissing, the Enlightenment norms that continue to inform public discourse and political practice, despite all their manifest contradictions. Second, it also strongly symptomatizes the potential for context-specific norms and prejudices to be dissimulatively retained within ideally universal moral-political principles. The subjunctive quality of the public sphere's inclusive procedures, as well as the privilege thus reserved for the force of historically particular social norms, together open a space for the operations of power. It is the issue of power that, in fact, Habermas has said differentiates his thought from Foucault's. In *The Philosophical Discourse of Modernity* Habermas criticizes Foucault for presenting a "totalizing" critique of the Enlightenment. This critique is totalizing, he argues, because Foucault postulates a primordial, functionalist conceptualization of power pervading all relations among social actors, even the self-relation of subjects. This conceptualization leaves no room for the "utopian possibilities" promised by modernity and the Enlightenment legacy. For example, the discourse of rights forms an important part of this legacy, and Habermas persuasively contends that, despite its many inconsistencies, the promise of rights cannot be dispensed with: "[W]e should not be too skeptical as far as the practical validity of universalistic moral principles is concerned. There is hardly a constitution nowadays which does not have a section, written or unwritten, setting out fundamental rights. And it is obvious that—when something crucial is at stake—these basic rights are precious and dear to us, whatever the individual may otherwise claim." [47] Despite the usefulness of Habermas's position here and elsewhere, it is also compromised by the unconvincing (and often unsubstantiated) attacks on poststructuralist critique one finds throughout *The Philosophical Discourse of Modernity*.[48]

Foucault's own comments on Habermas are instructive in this regard. While admitting his admiration for Habermas's work, he has termed Habermas's critique a form of "blackmail" that casts rationality as a zero-sum game and thus disables one from asking productive questions: "I think that the central issue of philosophy and critical thought since the eighteenth century has been, still is, and will, I hope, remain the question, *What* is this Reason that we use? What are its historical effects? What are its limits, and what are its dangers? How can we exist as rational beings, fortunately committed to practicing a rationality that is unfortunately crisscrossed by intrinsic dangers?" [49] Following Foucault, we could turn Habermas's critique of poststructuralism against him. Habermas sees a "performative contradiction" in poststructuralists using rational discourse to critique Enlightenment rationality. Yet the communicative norms of the public sphere themselves contain an irreducible performative contradiction insofar as they are fundamentally counterfactual, both claimed and denied. The subjunctive mood of the public sphere, as both practiced and reformulated by Habermas in his discourse ethics, actually embodies the performative contradiction that he so consistently damns in critiques of Enlightenment rationality.[50]

The questions raised by Foucault return us to the issue of conformity characterizing queer inclusion within the public sphere. If Habermas's theory provides a glimpse of this conformity, how have the analyses generated by lesbian and gay studies, the history of sexuality, and queer theory addressed the conformist effects of assimilation within the public sphere?

In large measure these analyses have provided powerful explanatory para-digms about the dynamics of representational inclusion and exclusion. Many of the most influential of these analyses have generally followed the paradigm regarding sexuality, identity-formation, and the power of dis-cursive norms found in Foucault's *The History of Sexuality, Volume 1*. This paradigm posits a complicity between regulatory and liberatory discourses of homosexuality emerging from late-eighteenth- and nineteenth-century Europe. In the interest of denying any "pure" position from which one might critique something like homophobia, queer theory has produced theoretical tools by which we might make visible the assimilationist im-pulses behind queer visibility itself. However, the explanatory power of much of queer theory has also turned into something of a liability. More often than not it only figures "complicity" synchronically and symmetri-cally as a kind of Manichean law; one important effect of this figuring is the hypostatization of the dynamics it would explain. It is in this sense that Foucault's influential figuring of complicity, I would argue, remains incomplete. His understanding of power as not simply a coercive and limit-ing force but more a relation that generates possibilities *beyond* this rela-tion, is compromised in his discussion of the reverse-discourse paradigm of homosexuality.

Foucault's compelling narrative of homosexuality's discursive "inven-tion" in late-nineteenth-century Europe formulates this invention as a part of the tactics and objects characteristic of sexuality as a relatively recent discursive formation. Within the multiplication of new objects of sexual knowledge, homosexuality was but one, yet its defining importance in the twentieth century would accord it greater emphasis in Foucault's investi-gation. Proceeding from the hypothesis that power (*pouvoir*) characterizes and subtends sexual discourse as a type of relation, Foucault posits a basic antinomy to the operations of homosexual discourse: on the one hand, a regulative ideal whereby homosexuality entered an ontological arena so that those persons designated as such could become objects, not only of knowledge but also by extension of those institutions whose power de-pended on knowledge of this sort; and on the other, a liberatory ideal, or " 'reverse' discourse" (*discours "en retour"*) whereby the subjects thus con-structed as objects of knowledge grasp their discursively imposed subjec-tification and transform it into an affirmation of the designation that this ideal had imposed: "There is no question that the appearance in nineteenth-century psychiatry, jurisprudence, and literature of a whole series of discourses on the species and subspecies of homosexuality, inversion, pederasty, and 'psychic hermaphrodism' made possible a strong advance of social controls into this area of 'perversity'; but it also made possible the formation of a 'reverse' discourse [*discours "en retour"*]: homosexuality began to speak on its own behalf, to demand that its legitimacy or 'naturality' be acknowledged, often in the same vocabulary, using the same categories by which it was medically disqualified." [51] The regulatory discourses of homosexuality provided the conditions of possibility for the formation of a reverse discourse of homosexual legitimacy. More importantly, Foucault hinges both discursive formations not simply by their shared object of knowledge but also by their collusion within the operations of power: "There is not, on the one side, a discourse of power [*pouvoir*], and opposite it, another discourse that runs counter to it. Discourses are tactical elements or blocks operating in the field of force relations; there can exist *different and even contradictory discourses within the same strategy; they can, on the contrary, circulate without changing their form* from one strategy to another, opposing strategy." [52] Power (*pouvoir*) is the principle that guarantees the potential exchangeability of even the most contradictory discourses of sexuality, allowing them to circulate from one strategy to another "without changing their form."

There are two interrelated points to make about the status of power as a principle of exchange in this passage. First, within the context of Foucault's discussion of homosexuality specifically and his overturning of the "repressive hypothesis" generally, the exchangeability of differently freighted discourses is a principle particular to the discourse/reverse-discourse dynamic of homosexuality. This distributive principle of exchange called power, then, establishes the overarching rule to only one aspect of sexuality as a discursive formation: the relation between opposing elements *within* a formation. Second, however, the rhetorical framing of this principle would belie this specificity. Rather than a local observation about the functioning of one element within a larger discursive formation, the relation between discourse and reverse discourse becomes paradigmatic of the interrelated dynamic between power and discourse in general. Whether we understand Foucault's formulation to be primarily local or general, however, the theoretical consequences of this formulation are similar. If the exchangeability and formal equivalence of ethically and/or politically quite distinct discourses remains local to homosexuality, this equivalence would require reevaluating the utopian possibilities mainstream lesbian and gay organizations seem to think inclusion would bring. If the exchangeability of discourses is general, the consequences may be more far-reaching but would not be substantively altered.

In the wake of Foucault's paradigm, queer theory has often stressed the irreducible complicities between homophobia and gay-affirmation, heteronormativity and antihomophobia, complicities located in the (il)logic of identity-formation. The category of complicity has in fact become a defining, and vexing, problematic through which homophobia and opposition to it may be conceived. How does this category organize our understanding of the formal and substantive relations between differing discourses? To what extent does it describe and to what extent might it hypostatize the phenomena with which it is concerned? How can this category accommodate shifts within discursive formations, between different or competing ones, or historical transformations on each of these levels?

To address these questions, I will offer four objections to the discourse/reverse-discourse paradigm. First, I argue that this paradigm involves an indifference of form to content. Second, it thereby cannot adequately conceptualize historical discontinuity and change. Third, Foucault's paradigm thus renders homosexuality somewhat impermeable to the effect of other types of discourses. And fourth, together these objections indicate the extent to which Foucault's paradigm tends to reproduce the problem of formal equivalence.

The first consequence of Foucault's formulation, one that relates as well to the problematic of complicity within queer theory, has to do with *form*: how discursive structures, the structural relation between discursive elements, and between discourses themselves, are conceptualized. Recall that in Foucault's formulation, the nexus of power/knowledge (*pouvoir/savoir*) characterizing discourses in general allows for the structural equivalence of discourses that may be substantively, strategically opposed. Contradictory discourses can exist "within the same strategy" and they can "circulate without changing their form from one strategy to another, opposing strategy." The possible structural equivalence postulated here within the economy of discourses, strategies, and power implicitly disregards the asymmetries *between* discourses, between elements within or strategies across discourses, and between larger discursive formations. To the extent that discourses can circulate and be exchanged across a divergent field of ethical and political valuations, Foucault's paradigm posits an irreducible *indifference* toward the asymmetrical effects these valuations may exact on discourses themselves.

Second, to the extent that the structural equivalence of discourses and their deployments enforces an indifference to their substantive specificity, Foucault's paradigm remains relatively unable to conceptualize historical discontinuity.[53] The antinomy of a regulatory discourse of homosexuality and a liberatory one becomes in Foucault's analysis a double bind. The formal equivalence of discourses insures a certain repetition of the operations of power, regardless of the particular content of the discourses at hand. Thus, there is a formal contiguity and exchangeability between heteronormative and gay-affirmative discourses insofar as both inhabit, indeed constitute, the field of force relations. In this sense, inclusion necessarily entails at least a structural complicity with those devaluing discourses on which exclusion is based. The double bind of this structural complicity would seem to explain, at least in part, the conformist thrust of contemporary lesbian and gay visibility politics. Reverse discourses do not necessarily transform regulatory ones. Indeed, the former only displace the latter through a structural repetition of the dynamics of power/knowledge central to identity-formation. Because such a repetition would be understood in Foucault's paradigm as part of the dynamics inhering in discourses and their strategies, oppression and resistance, indeed history itself, each thereby becomes merely epiphenomenal to power and the operation of discursive formations. Historical change, in other words, would remain insignificant relative to the machinery of discursive power. This is not to say that Foucault, in other texts, does not take account of historical change; quite the contrary. *The Archaeology of Knowledge* plots the "evential engagements" of discourses: archaeology "does not believe, therefore, that a system of positivity is a synchronic figure that one can perceive only by suspending the whole of the diachronic process. Far from being indifferent to succession, archaeology maps the *temporal vectors of derivation.*"[54] In *The History of Sexuality, Volume 1*, however, power is elevated to a formal, distributive principle of equivalence and exchange such that the discourse/reverse-discourse formulation suspends diachronic processes, and thus becomes precisely the kind of synchronic figure against which Foucault had earlier cautioned. The formal equivalence of discourses effects an indifference to their particular value-codings, rendering discourses structurally exchangeable. This paradigm of discursive equivalence thus hypostatizes the relation between regulatory and liberatory deployments of homosexuality, and thereby locks both within the disciplinary contours of sexual identity-formation.[55]

My third objection concerns the extent to which the synchronic figuring of discourse/reverse discourse is analytically unable to account for the effects of other discourses and their dynamics on sexual identity-formation. To return to the example of corporate marketing toward lesbians and gay men broached in chapter 1, the rules governing this activity do not necessarily, or even probabilistically, conform to the practices of, say, progressive queer resignification, although marketing attention is certainly hailed by many as political progress. This may very well be true—but only if understood *exclusively* in terms of sexual discourses. When understood in relation to capitalist marketing practices, dynamics other than queer affirmation come into play. Predicating such "affirmative" marketing attention, capitalist value-determination cannot be exhaustively explained by the antinomies of power circulating between regulatory and liberatory discourses of homosexuality. By locking the discourse of homosexuality within a synchronic figuring, Foucault's paradigm cannot account for "affirmative" resignifications whose logics exceed and can reorient the opposition homophobia/affirmation. Indeed, the contemporary relevance of corporate attention to lesbians and gay men indicates the need to displace the synchronic, self-enclosed figuring of sexual discourses.[56]

My fourth point comes from the cumulative effect of the previous three. This effect can be seen initially in the odd echo between the methodological difficulties of Foucault's paradigm and the particular political goal animating contemporary visibility politics: equivalence. The strategy of equivalence central to the reverse discourse of contemporary lesbian and gay visibility demands an equality and exchangeability between, and thus a structural indifference to, varieties of sexual expression and identification. In their struggle for this equivalence, lesbian and gay civil rights groups remain themselves indifferent to the particular representational modes through which inclusion is achieved, be it the U.S. Army, AT&T advertisements, or the Republican Party. If the goal of an antihomophobic reverse discourse is a formal equivalence of subjects under systems of value like the law or economic representation, then the *substance* of reverse discourses would seem strangely to coincide with their *formal* equivalence to regulatory discourses. It would seem that antihomophobic or gay-affirmative strategies, in their search for inclusion on the terms of equivalence, reproduce in their very substance the formal equivalence and exchangeability of opposing discourses.

On the face of it, this coincidence would also seem to provide a useful explanation for the conformist character of contemporary visibility politics. The lesbian and gay repetition of dominant norms would be an effect not so much of a regulatory imposition but more an effect of the isomorphism between even the most opposed discursive strategies. Superadded to this isomorphism would be the *substantive* repetition of the equivalence of discourses in the very goal of rendering homosexuality equivalent to heterosexuality—in terms of all the privileges and rights either explicitly marked as heterosexual by definition, as in companionate marriage and its perks, or de facto marked as such by virtue of the exclusion of lesbians and gay men from enjoying them.

But what if Foucault's paradigm in *The History of Sexuality, Volume 1* were seen not so much as an explanation for visibility's conformism but rather more as a paradigm that tends to codify the dynamics underwriting this conformism? What if, in other words, the assimilationist understanding of equivalence in contemporary visibility politics, as well as the theoretical paradigm that would render this goal epiphenomenal to the formally equivalent operations of power, were both to varying degrees *affiliated to* the logic of equivalence—a logic that insistently posits history and difference as merely epiphenomenal to structures of equivalent exchange? Might it be possible, in other words, that Foucault presents a theoretical repetition of the simultaneously historical and structural problem of formal equivalence itself? If so, it could be said that when the elucidation of complicity between differing discourses is brought alongside the assimilationist emphases of visibility politics, then the explanatory framework of discourse/reverse discourse formalizes, renders necessary, and thus implicitly legitimates these emphases as well. This framework would implicitly legitimate these assimilationist emphases insofar as the relatively recent historical dominance of equivalence as a political, civic ideal of the public sphere is *theoretically* reproduced as a kind of law governing the terms according to which discourses operate.

At this point I would like to emphasize that my discussion of the problem of equivalence in Foucault is not meant to supplant a relative prioritizing of structure over history with a privileging of history over structure. Rather, I have attempted to point out the following. In *The History of Sexuality, Volume 1*, Foucault provides a paradigm of homosexual articulation that renders history and historical change epiphenomenal to the antinomial operations of structure. In this paradigm we do not have a way to account for the disappearance of certain norms over time, nor for the appearance of new ones. To the extent that this is true, this paradigm presents a relatively flawed conceptualization of structure as well, since the complex and differently determining relations *between* history and structure remain unthought. Moreover, the synchronic figuring of homosexual discourse/reverse discourse prevents this paradigm from accounting for the effect of other discourses on the formation of homosexuality.

I have wanted to argue that such problems indicate an affinity between this paradigm and the logic of formal equivalence. Foucault's account postulates an economy of discourse and forms of signification; the force of the *excesses* produced from within this economy, however, remains synchronically bound within it. It is not as if one would need to repeat Hegel's formulation in his *Logik*—the identity of identity and nonidentity, or in this instance, the identity between the normative discursive production of the subject and the resignification or undoing of this production. Indeed, the important point about equivalence is that it need not, nor usually does it, posit a *substantive* identity between different elements within a system of equivalent exchange. However, such a system *does* insure their mutual value, their exchangeability; within this system, difference is tolerated, but as "tolerate" implies, rarely makes any difference *to* this system itself. In this sense, equivalence posits an overarching *formal* identity between groups and persons by which their universality and equality as legitimate subjects are made effective. They are identical in their *value*, not in their "substance." This raises the important question of what it is that provides the evaluative standard for this formal identity. Because equivalence purports to guarantee the equality and thus the potential exchangeability of all subjects, however, such standards are obscured. It is on this formal level of universal exchangeability that "assimilation" enforces similitude to mystified norms.

I would suggest, then, that Foucault's paradigm, rather than helping to indicate a beyond to the damagingly normative discourses it makes intelligible, in fact tends to codify the very system it might explain. This codification is where we might see a lurking affinity between his paradigm and the logic of equivalence as the dominating premise of liberal pluralism. It is this premise, and its valuing of toleration, inconsequential difference, and inclusion without systemic change, that to my mind animate much of the conformist character of contemporary lesbian and gay visibility politics.

Resignification

Faced with these difficulties, many queer theorists have engaged with the discourse/reverse-discourse paradigm to find a way out of the double bind presented by a formal discursive equivalence and exchangeability. More specifically, many have attempted to elaborate nonidentitarian modes of thinking that are critical of, and critically different from, the antinomial binding of discourse/reverse discourse. In this way, queer theorists have evinced a critical attention not only to the possibilities for self-determination that may be gleaned from Foucault's paradigm, but also for the various articulations of sexuality and eroticism across time.[57] By attempting to account for a critical agency from *within* the discourse/reverse-discourse paradigm of homosexuality, however, much of queer theory has similarly remained unable to account for the effect *other* discourses and historical forces might have on the relation between heteronormativity and queer politics.

If Foucault's paradigm tends to inscribe the limits of a liberal vision of inclusion, how might we describe these limits? Judith Butler has provided an apt formulation: "In this sense, radical and inclusive representability is not precisely the goal: to include, to speak as, to bring in every marginal and excluded position within a given discourse is to claim that a singular discourse meets its limits nowhere, that it can and will domesticate all signs of difference."[58] If the successful domestication of difference is only a pretended success, nevertheless such a pretension is where the logic of formal equivalence as equitable exchange can cover over the continuation of inequity. As I have argued with regard to Habermas, particular historical norms are retained within economies of value thought to guarantee equality. Because this retention is hidden underneath the cover of equivalence, discourses and institutions claiming to guarantee equality attempt to domesticate difference according to the standard set by the norms they retain. In this sense, equivalence in itself cannot figure a beyond to static, inconsequential difference. Rather, it attempts to assimilate any difference in "excess" of the standards guiding the measure of equality. In fine, equivalence has become the ruse for managed inequity.[59]

If, as Butler argues, underrepresented groups erroneously assume in their search for equivalent inclusion that "a singular discourse meets its limits nowhere" and assume that any single discourse can "domesticate all signs of difference," how might we conceptualize the extent to which any discourse may or may not have the capacity to do so? What precisely are the limits to the procedures of inclusion? If managed inequity, as I have called it, is a structural characteristic and effect of modern equivalent representation, how might it be figured as both a synchronic *and* a diachronic problematic? In other words, how might the asymmetries of structure and the displacements of history covered over by equivalence be foregrounded? What correlates of lesbian and gay visibility—cultural, political, historical, economic—are rendered unmarked and left unacknowledged by the very representational forms through which this visibility is achieved?

To address these questions requires a twofold focus. First, to grasp the excesses of a conformist sense of identity—the "scary homosexuals" repudiated by Ellen Degeneres, for example—that are negated and devalued by the normalizing mechanisms of equivalence requires attending to processes of value determination. These processes often define what will count as valuable within a lesbian and gay politics so insistently focused on a normalizing assimilation. Second, these processes of value determination generate the determinate contradictions in which these excesses struggle to make their claims licit. To that extent, one can afford neither the leisure of simply conforming to the procedural norms of the public sphere, such as those embodied in liberal pluralism, nor simply refusing them altogether.

Because much of Foucault's other work on sexuality and power is not confined to the discourse/reverse-discourse paradigm, it provides an important resource for moving beyond the either/or of a static complicity. His later essays, lectures, and interviews engage the question of judgment as an "ethical" practice of value, such that judgment becomes in fact a tool for elaborating modes of self-determination, rather than for legitimating conformity. The important question for queer politics, Foucault has argued, is "not whether a culture without restraints is possible or even desirable, but whether the system of constraints in which a society functions leaves individuals the liberty to transform the system. . . ."[60] Movements for "sexual liberation," he points out, may start off as "movements of affirmation," but "these movements are displaced in relation to sexuality, disengaging themselves from it and going beyond it." [61] The goals of such movements should focus not on a functional equivalence and legitimacy, but rather on "fabricating other forms of pleasure, of relationships, coexistences, attachments, loves, intensities," such that sex is no longer understood as the "universal secret." [62] Indeed, this is what varieties of gay liberation and queer activism have encouraged and made possible. By focusing on a normalizing equivalence, however, mainstream lesbian and gay politics and media culture refuse to "transform the system" of constraints in which queers find themselves. That is, they have largely failed to grasp the task of judgment as a practice of value deployed on behalf of an ethical intervention. Their enthusiasm for disciplining a socialized homoeroticism refuses to grasp, indeed repudiates, the excesses of identity-formation as possible alternative models for sociality itself. As Foucault has noted, "It is the prospect that gays will create as yet unforeseen kinds of relationships that many people cannot tolerate." [63]

The excesses of identity-formation within systems of equivalence point not only to the distance between what such systems promise and what they deliver. More importantly, these repudiated excesses might also be used to formulate alternative principles for equality and social connection. In other words, the abjected practices and modes of life repudiated by assimilation hold out the potential of reformulating the contradictory systems that disenfranchise them. However, left with either Habermas's coercively counterfactual democracy or Foucault's synchronically symmetrical figuring of complicity in *History of Sexuality, Volume 1*, such reformulations will remain stalled.

Ironically (and much to Habermas's consternation), Foucault engaged late in his career with the "popular" political writings of Immanuel Kant, a figure that for both Habermas and Foucault became central in their differing efforts to break through the stalemate between autonomy and conformity in the Enlightenment legacy.[64] Consequently, the next chapter will focus on Kant to inaugurate the historical investigations of homoeroticism and value that will follow. Habermas's and Foucault's engagement with Kant raise fundamental questions regarding the extent to which practices of value inhere within the universalist contours of the moral, and the extent to which these contours may be progressively reshaped. Such questions can be formulated according to the particular concerns of each thinker: Following Habermas, How might we reshape the negative freedoms of liberalism such that autonomy is indissolubly bound to social participation? Or following Foucault, How might we reshape the formal equivalence of liberal rights as a "practice of freedom" integral to queer life?

II. PRACTICES OF VALUE

[T]he scales of the heart seem to be especially natural when they condemn unnatural love among men (though curiously enough not among women). The woodpile with the witch upon it fit in quite well with a sense of justice popular at the time but not at all with that of those few who wanted to extinguish the flames. —Ernst Bloch, NATURAL LAW AND HUMAN DIGNITY

Over the past few years, gay male promiscuity has become a subject of intense debate in U.S. lesbian and gay media. Particularly after the formation of the group SexPanic! in New York in the summer of 1997, the issue of gay sexual practices spilled onto the pages of not just national lesbian and gay magazines such as *Out* and the *Advocate*, but also more mainstream national publications such as the *New York Times* and the academic magazine *Lingua Franca*. Most reports drew lines between, on the one hand, sex radicals and queer theorists who seek to protect the public viability of alternative erotic practices, and on the other, gay journalists and writers who see promiscuity and public sex as nothing short of irresponsible, infantile, and life-threatening. Even more than in the early years of the AIDS epidemic, gay men in particular are being urged to restrict their erotic behavior to the confines of monogamous committed relationships. This is done not only on (quite specious) epidemiological grounds, but also on behalf of what many see as the growing tolerance and acceptance of lesbians and gay men by straight America. Gay male promiscuity and other "nontraditional" forms of erotic behavior, it is claimed, threaten the fragile gains won in efforts to present lesbians and gay men as "just like everyone else" and thus to gain civil rights. But what exactly are the connections between erotic propriety and the proper citizen? Why, in other words, would enfranchisement in the fullest sense exclude certain modes of sexual practice?

In this chapter I will suggest that the answer to this question lies partially in the continuing legacy of a sexual humanism firmly tied to Enlightenment norms of civic life. In the modern humanist idealization of erotic love, sex should be a medium of love's expression. The material cause of love itself is ideally matrimony; its final cause must at the very least tend toward the potential for sexual reproduction. Love without sexual fulfillment can be poetic but is nevertheless tragic. Sexual love outside the confines of ecclesiastical and/or legal recognition is sinful, a sign of weakness, a defiance of authority and tradition for the sake of impulsive passion. Sex without love, however, cannot be pardoned by even the most secular of viewpoints. It is never adequate to its promise or its capacities. Sex for its own sake is (so it goes) base, coarse, brutish, venal, fleeting, animalistic, grotesque— a defilement of body and soul. It "objectifies" persons, it *degrades*. In every way it is inhuman.

Sexual practices not tied to monogamous, contractual marriage or its semblance, practices that I have referred to descriptively and polemically as indeterminate erotic expression, have therefore traditionally been antithetical to a humanist view of erotic propriety. Two objections leveled against indeterminate erotic expression by a humanist sexual morality maintain this antithesis: It lowers humans to the level of animals, and it renders them as objects, or property. Both violate an ideal species propriety integral to sexual humanism, if not humanism in general. To charge indeterminate erotic expression with impropriety appears universally valid by conceptualizing erotic behavior in terms of human distinctiveness. It is at this level of abstraction or idealization, however, that these improprieties and the injunctions they imply—that humans not be like animals, that humans distinctively *own*, and so cannot themselves *be like*, property—also make clear the indebtedness of this morality to the intellectual and political history of middle-class formation. An integral part of such formation lies in Enlightenment ideals of political organization and civic life. What is most striking, in fact, about humanist understandings of erotic propriety is the language of Enlightenment *political* humanism underpinning the notion of a sexual subject: one who requires respect and equality, duty to oneself and others, the unambiguous exercise of consent, and, perhaps most importantly, the enclosure of these qualities within legally sanctioned contracts. Mutual regard, unfettered free will, and legal constraints determine the boundaries not only of the modern citizen subject but also the modern sexual subject. Sexual humanism vividly displays the congruence of sexual and political subjectivity, not only in their ideal, proper forms but also in their practical historical unfolding. Civic values and sexual values seem to share the same object and aim: the complete unfolding of the truly human.[1]

The ideal and historical congruence of sexual and civic norms can illuminate the value determinations underlying the Enlightenment norm of the citizen subject. The social conditions that enabled this norm, as Habermas has argued, are those of the classically conceived bourgeois public sphere, specifically as outlined by Immanuel Kant. This sphere was composed of "freely competing commodity owners" whose private autonomy, property ownership, and male sex predicated the basic outline of bourgeois civil society.[2] The division between public and private that organizes bourgeois civil society entails value determinations designating certain behaviors and psychological inclinations as either vicious or virtuous; it presupposes fundamental moral distinctions. Describing Kant's formulation, Habermas argues that the "translation" or "placing over" (Übersetzung) of elements from private to public involves recoding elements of subjectivity from the intimate sphere so that they become the basis for the public good. This "placing over" that revalues private elements in turn allows for a "state of cosmopolitan citizenship" (weltbürgerlicher Zustand). Thus, according to Habermas, from this concept of the citizen follows the subsumption (Subsumtion) of politics under morality.[3] The realm of social power is brought under the subject-centered realm of moral laws, such that politics and notions of the public good revolve around moral categories deemed proper to the autonomous individual.

This subsumption also involves a process of revaluation, whereby politics will now be judged, as in morality, according to the freedom, rationality, and autonomy of the subject. These qualities endow the subject with the capacity to own (manifest in property ownership), which in turn becomes a principal if often occluded sign of the enlightened citizen.[4] Following from Kant's formulation, Habermas describes both the cosmopolitan citizen and a morality-based politics as enabled by the translation of private vices into public virtues. However, we might go further in this formulation to suggest an intimate congruence between the conceptualization of the humanist sexual subject and the Enlightenment citizen subject. This congruence can be located within these revaluing processes of translation and subsumption—but how do these processes take place? On what logical moves and assumptions are they predicated?

I want to suggest that how we answer this question carries important implications for a conceptualization of "sexual citizenship." By sexual citizenship I mean to evoke a subjectivity through which sexuality as a "private vice" would become a legitimately recognized "public virtue" within the modern state and civil society. A conceptualization of sexual citizenship is an important one for queers insofar as the protections and rights they seek would at least implicitly confer public legitimacy to traditionally devalued forms of erotic expression, and would thereby grant public recognition that such expressions are worthy and equivalent (even if they remain within the domain of a protected autonomy). Such recognition would include but could also exceed even the most expansive notion of state-sanctioned belonging and enfranchisement such as citizenship. But can the Enlightenment notion of the citizen subject accommodate the revaluation of homoeroticism? If it can, on what terms and with what effects? By delineating Kant's reflections on freedom, rights, citizenship, and the public good through his reflections on proper and improper sexual expressions, this chapter will raise the following question: What would hinder, and what would enable, indeterminate erotic expression to fit within the contours of citizenship?[5]

By understanding my purpose here to be the formulation of a question and, in turn, the suggestion of some possible answers, I mean to signal the heuristic value that Kant's texts can have for the issues I will raise. Kant's understanding of rights, particularly his idea that rights are grounded not in nature but rather in reason alone, by no means exhausts the differing conceptualizations of rights circulating in Europe and the newly formed United States during the latter part of the eighteenth century, nor for that matter those circulating today. While his thoughts on civil society are in many ways paradigmatic of Enlightenment thinking, there are some important differences—for example, his disagreement with Christian Wolff on the role of pleasure as a "private vice" that could be translated into a "public virtue." Additionally, there are important divergences between Kant's sexual morality and those of his contemporaries and students, most notably Johann Gottlieb Fichte.[6] Thus, I do not mean to construct a *genetic* argument about Kant's formulation of the citizen and the contemporary issues that inform my analysis here. Kant did not necessarily produce the contemporary citizen subject, but there are important implications for thinking about citizenship in the way that he did. There are significant resonances among Kant's thinking on sexuality, its relation to rights and civil society, contemporary discussions about equitably integrating queers into the public sphere, and the effects this integration would have on the future of sexual freedom and queer self-definition. These resonances, I argue, suggest a number of difficulties relating to this integration and the terms by which it might be achieved. How are the universality and rationality of rights constrained by a heteronormative sexual morality? Where might a dominant discourse of rights meet its limits with respect to sex?

Commercium Sexuale

The heuristic value of Kant's texts aligns with the pedagogical context where my investigation begins: a series of lectures on ethics that Kant delivered between 1756 and 1794 to his male students at Albertina University in Königsberg. Kant never published these lectures himself. They have come to us through his students' lecture notes, which were subsequently published in the twentieth century. In 1924, the Kant scholar Paul Menzer took three of these manuscripts of students' lecture notes—those by Federico Brauer, Theophilus Kutzner, and Christoph Mrongovius—and, basing his text on Brauer's manuscript (because Menzer believed it to have greater comprehensiveness, internal coherence, and consistency with other texts by Kant), with supplements from the other two, published a hybrid text titled *Eine Vorlesung Kants über Ethik*. These lecture notes were taken, according to the dating of the manuscripts, between 1780 and 1782.[7]

According to Menzer's hybrid text, two lectures appear under the section "Ethica," one titled "Duties toward the Body in Respect of Sexual Inclination" (*"Von den Pflichten gegen den Körper in Ansehung der Geschlectsneigung"*), and the other *"Crimina Carnis"* (*"Von den Criminibus carnis"*). In these lectures, Kant instructed his young male students on their ethical duty to refrain from masturbation, sodomy (here defined as cross-species sex involving humans), prostitution, concubinage, fornication, adultery, and same-sex sex. While Kant's injunctions formed the negative or prohibitory aspect of the men's duty to their bodies, marriage formed the positive aspect. Only matrimony, Kant is said to have argued, can provide a context in which *any* form of sexual activity could be practiced without debasing humans to the level of the nonhuman.

That Kant thought sexual activity should be an important philosophical subject is not particularly surprising. In general, he was continuing a well-established line of thought in Western ethics, secular and Christian. It is somewhat more surprising that so-called crimes against nature should occupy lectures within this pedagogical context (he indicates his reluctance to discuss such "shameful" topics). Moreover, Kant repeats many of the formulations attributed to him here in a more truncated fashion in his 1797 *The Metaphysics of Morals (Die Metaphysik der Sitten)*. Even more intriguing are the connections, both implicit and explicit, that the lectures and *The Metaphysics of Morals* create between sexual ethics and the political rights ideally enjoyed by citizens, rights that help to define the intersection of politics and morality in the state and the bourgeois public sphere. As his argument sets out to show in *The Metaphysics of Morals*, politics and morality are intimately joined. One cannot have a sound political philosophy, Kant argued, without having foundational principles in the realm of morals. Because any just political order must be grounded in freedom of the will, political theory and the modern state itself must be established according to moral principles.[8]

Before moving to the connection between Kant's sexual ethics and his overall moral and political theory, however, we need to understand more fully the bases for his injunction against any form of sexual activity other than that which occurs within contractual, cross-sexual, monogamous matrimony. This injunction stems first from Kant's conceptualization of the innate dignity of "humanity" (*Menschlichkeit*), a dignity that proceeds from the ability to reason and, concomitantly, the freedom of the will. Second, it stems from his understanding of sexual desire as an animalistic, and not a properly human—that is to say rational—activity and impulse. Sexual desire in itself, Kant reasons, "exposes mankind to the danger of equality with the beasts."[9] I will return to the specific contours of Kant's argument about humanity's innate dignity, and its connections to reason and freedom. For the moment I want to concentrate on his conceptualization of "sexual inclination" (*Geschlechtsneigung*) in *Lectures on Ethics*.

Because Kant claims that sexual inclination in itself lowers humans to "equality with the beasts," he must justify this claim with a theory of sexual desire and activity that places them within an animalistic or natural economy of value. In other words, he must understand this inclination as a shared attribute among animal beings that grants each equal value with respect to their sexual activity. However, because Kant also claimed that without sex "a human being would be incomplete; he would rightly believe that he lacked the necessary organs [Werkzeuge], and this would make him imperfect as a human being" (Lectures 164/206), he must also therefore formulate the conditions under which a distinctively human sexual expression could be possible. He must formulate, in other words, a human economy of value in which humans would be uniquely equal with each other vis-à-vis erotic expression and not lowered to the value of animals guided only by lust. Kant justifies his animalistic understanding of desire with the notion that in sexual relations a person becomes an "Object" (Objekt). From this, he concludes that contractual monogamous marriage between men and women represents the only sphere in which sexual desire's objectifying effects may be mitigated, and thus in which sexual desire could be transformed into a properly human attribute.[10]

In his lecture "Duties toward the Body in Respect of Sexual Inclination," Kant begins by defining sexual inclination as the one directed "immediately" (unmittelbar) toward other humans. Other humans are direct "Objects of its pleasure" (Lectures 162/204). One may enjoy the service of others in contracted labor; however, "we do not find at all that a human being can be made into an Object of pleasure except through sexual inclination" (Lectures 163/204–5). In this respect, sexual inclination is to be firmly distinguished from "true human love," which requires "good-will [Wohlwollens], affection [Gewogenheit], promoting the happiness of others and finding joy in their happiness" (Lectures 163/205). Because sexual inclination is only an "appetite" for another human, the virtuous fellow-feelings of true human love do not follow here. Sexual appetite makes a person an Object who then may be cast aside "as one casts away a lemon which has been sucked dry" (Lectures 163/205). This objectifying appetite, however, may be combined with true human love, and only in this combination does sexual desire "carry with it [führt . . . mit sich]" the virtues of love. By itself, however, sexual inclination values a person only as a means and not as an end (Zweck) in him- or herself, and as such can only bring about a "degradation [Erniedrigung] of humanity." When a person is rendered into an Object by another, their relation is immoral; as an Object, a person "can be used by any and all" (Lectures 163/205). The sexual inclination a man feels for a woman, for example, does not regard her as a human (*Mensch*), but rather purely as a "sex." In this way, "humanity is sacrificed for sex" (*Lectures* 164/206). Sex, in fact, is utterly unique in this regard. In no other way, Kant argues, have humans been determined (*bestimmt*) by nature to be Objects of pleasure for each other.

The problem of what Kant terms *commercium sexuale*, or sexual "commerce," can thus uniquely illuminate the problem of freedom that runs throughout Kant's major critiques and "popular" writings.[11] On the one hand, humans cannot be Objects, yet on the other, they are also desiring beings with inclinations. Moreover, as rational beings humans have the capacity to choose freely (*Willkür*), and from this capacity, Kant argues, it follows that humans are in the unique position to *own*, not just in terms of property, but also in terms of human consciousness. How might the inalienable freedom of the subject be conceptualized so that objectifying inclinations—private vices—can be "subsumed" into a human economy of value in which an equality of free subjects can be guaranteed, and thus erotic expression be humanized? What is the distributive principle by which the freedom of the atomistic, acquisitive individual can be reconciled with an equality *among* such individuals?

This is the problem Kant posed in his essay "Toward Perpetual Peace" regarding the organization of the state: "Given a multitude of rational beings requiring universal laws for their preservation, but each of whom is secretly inclined to exempt himself from them, [the task is] to establish a constitution [*Verfassung*] in such a way that, although their private inclinations conflict, they check each other, with the result that their public conduct is the same *as if they had no such evil intentions* [*als ob keine solche böse Gesinnungen hätten*]."[12] That the reconciliation necessary for equality is written in the subjunctive is an important issue, to which I will return later. For now, I would like to point out that Kant's formulation here establishes an intriguing parallel between the imperatives of the state and the imperatives of marriage: both check the conflicting inclinations of acquisitive individuals. Yet we still need to investigate in more detail Kant's justifications for viewing the condition of being a (sexual) Object as antithetical to being human, and how precisely this is overcome in a just moral and political order.

In his 1785 Groundwork of the Metaphysics of Morals (Grundlegung zur Metaphysik der Sitten), Kant famously proclaims that "the human being and in general every rational being exists as an end in itself, not merely as a means to be used by this or that will at its discretion."[13] Because the value of any Object is utterly conditional on and determined by the inclinations to which it corresponds, Objects in themselves cannot have an absolute value. An Object is so only to the extent that it is an Object for something else, such as human desire. When this something else ceases to regard the thing as an Object, it ceases to exist as an Object. In order for something to have an absolute value, Kant argues, its very existence must be unconditional, must be in itself an end. Such an end is "one such that no other end, to which they [rational beings] would serve merely as means, can be put in its place, since without it nothing of absolute value [Wert] would be found anywhere; but if all value is conditional and therefore contingent, then no supreme practical principle for reason could be found anywhere."[14] The incontingency of value grounds practical reason; absolute value and reason go hand in hand. The absolute value of humans as persons Kant designates as their "dignity" (Würde). Dignity is a value that accrues to humans as rational beings as ends in themselves because they have the "capacity for choice" (Willkür) conditioned by pure reason (reine Vernunft) alone. That is, the human capacity for choice is rational, and because it is rational and not conditioned by inclinations (such as sexual inclination), it is therefore free.

This argument underlies the justification for his later The Metaphysics of Morals: "If, therefore, a system of a priori cognition from concepts alone is called metaphysics, a practical philosophy, which has not nature but freedom of choice [freie Willkür] for its object, will presuppose and require a metaphysics of morals, that is, it is itself a duty to have such a metaphysics. . . ."[15] In this justification for a metaphysics of morals, Kant elaborates more fully the distinction between a capacity for choice determined by pure reason alone—free choice—and a capacity for choice determined by inclination—animal choice (tierische Willkür). The ability to choose independently of inclinations marks humans as qualitatively different beings: "Freedom of choice is this independence [Unabhängigkeit] from being determined by sensible impulses [sinnliche Antriebe]; this is the negative concept of freedom" (Metaphysics 375). Because humanity "itself is a dignity," a human being "raises himself [*sich erhebt*] above all other beings in the world that are not human beings and yet can be used, and so over all *things*" (*Metaphysics* 579). The action of raising oneself (*sich erheben*) aligns with the translation of private vices into public virtues that Habermas points to as the precondition for the citizen subject in the classical bourgeois public sphere. As with the dichotomy between private and public, the dichotomy between the animal and the rational aspects of human beings sets up two different economies of value. In the one, humans are on a level of equivalence with beasts and are driven by inclination alone. In the other, human beings become fully adequate to their humanity by raising themselves onto a level in which inclinations are subordinated to *rational* free choice. In this economy there is the possibility of a fully human equivalence based on the dignity of each.

In his discussion of servility, Kant encapsulates his argument with the following economic metaphors and value distinctions:

> In the system of nature, a human being (*homo phaenomenon, animal rationale*) is a being of slight importance and shares with the rest of the animals, as offspring of the earth, an ordinary value [*gemeinen Wert*] (*pretium vulgare*). Although a human being has, in his understanding [*Verstand*], something more than they and can set himself ends, even this gives him only an *extrinsic* value [*äußere Wert*] for his usefulness (*pretium usus*); that is to say, it gives one man a higher value than another, that is, a *price* of a commodity in exchange [*Verkehr*] with these animals as things, though he still has a lower value [*niedrigen Wert*] than the universal medium of exchange, money [*das allgemeine Tauschmittel, das Geld*], the value of which can therefore be called preeminent (*pretium eminens*). (*Metaphysics* 557)

To rescue humans from a natural economy of value in which they possess only a *supplemental* value over animals, Kant regards human dignity—the capacity for rational freedom—as the sign of *a separate economy of value altogether*, of which human equality is the beneficent effect: "But a human being regarded as a *person*, that is, as the subject of a morally practical reason, is exalted [*erhaben*] above any price; for as a person (*homo noumenon*) he is not to be valued merely as a means to the ends of others or even to his own ends, but as an end in himself, that is, he possesses a *dignity* (an absolute inner value) by which he exacts *respect* [*Achtung*] for himself from all other rational beings in the world. He can measure himself with every other being of this kind and value himself [*sich schätzen*] on a footing of equality [*Gleichheit*] with them" (*Metaphysics* 557; original emphasis). When considered as free rational beings, humans become their own universal equivalent through their inherent dignity. Each is the measure of him- or herself. Because this is true for every human, each may be considered of equal value, an equivalence that would imply the equality of all.

However, the move from each person recognizing his or her rational freedom and thus his or her dignity, to each person recognizing this in others as equals is problematic. What uniquely defines humans *as* humans — innate dignity, rational capacity for free choice, and thus by extension the acquisition of Objects, or property — is precisely what would make an equality of human beings with conflicting acquisitive capacities difficult to achieve. As mentioned in "Toward Perpetual Peace," this is the problem of the just state. It is also, interestingly, the problem of sex. Recall Kant's intriguing metaphor when speaking of nature's economy of value. Within this economy, humans have only a slightly greater "price," as between two commodities, than animals do. Yet both are "commodities," are *formally* equivalent insofar as both, as natural beings, are led by their inclinations rather than reason, even if they are, as separate species, substantively different. If humans retain their animal nature, if they are in fact "incomplete" without sexual inclination, this leads us to ask how an inclination may be elevated such that humans are no longer "commodities" within an animal economy but are rather themselves universal equivalents, the possessors of their own measure of worth. As Kant notes in *Lectures*, "there must be a basis for restraining our freedom in the use we make of our inclinations so that they conform to the principles of morality" (*Lectures* 165/207). How, in other words, can there be an equality of "sexual commerce" without degradation, without equivalence to nonrational beings? The sexual issue at hand is isomorphic to the issue of a just state: How can humanity's freedom to choose and own be made to conform to a human economy of value, in which all humans as freely choosing agents are equal and equivalent to each other?

Not surprisingly, Kant's answer is contractual, cross-sexual, monogamous marriage. The companionate and equitable union between a man and a woman in marriage, and in marriage only, fulfills the completely *human* potential for sex as the expressive medium for love.[16] "The sole condition [*Bedingung*] on which we are free to make use of our sexual inclination," Kant argues, "depends upon [*gründet sich*] the right to dispose over [*dispo-*

nieren über] the person as a whole. This right of another to dispose over the whole person concerns the entire welfare and happiness and generally all the circumstances of that person. . . . This happens only in marriage" (*Lectures* 166–67/209–10). This sort of marriage achieves the harmonious and equitable distribution of pleasures and duties within the economy mandated by this contract. This is the supreme tautology of marriage; it becomes what it ensures: "Matrimony means an agreement [*Vertrag*] between two persons in which they grant [*restituieren*] each other reciprocally equal rights and each enter into the conditions, such that each of them surrenders [*übergibt*] the whole of their person to the other with a complete right of disposal over it. We can now apprehend by reason how a *commercium sexuale* might be possible [*möglich sei*] without degrading humanity and violating morality" (*Lectures* 167/210). Enclosing sexual expression within the contractual terms of marriage ensures the equitable distribution of rights, stabilizes the exchange value of sexual interest, and wards off the danger that sex will degrade human propriety. Moreover, Kant argues here that only by granting each other an equitable disposal to the whole of his or her person can sexual inclination, the rendering of free rational subjects into Objects, be mitigated. Rather than considering a person merely as a sex, marriage allows each partner to be the property of one another. The entire person is surrendered, and in this way sexual objectification is annulled.

In *The Metaphysics of Morals*, however, such a complete dependence on another is considered immoral. To be the property of another is to negate absolutely one's innate human dignity, an abrogation of one's capacity for free choice. Yet in marriage—the condition in which sexual inclination may be "translated" or "raised" into virtue—each becomes the property of the other, and thus *neither* becomes an Object: "[I]f I give my entire person completely to another and win [*gewinne*] the person of the other in return, thus I win myself back and have reoccupied [*habe reokkupiert*] myself; I have given myself up as the property [*Eigentum*] of another, but in turn I take that other as my property, and so win myself back again because I win the person whose property I have become. In this way the two persons become a unity of will [*Einheit des Willens*]" (*Lectures* 167/210). Marriage thus involves an exchange of property that not only renders each item of exchange equivalent, but also allows each person to retain property ownership and lifts each out of an economy of animal inclinations.

Kant argues here that marriage effects a kind of transfiguration—an idealization through debasement. Within Kant's corpus marriage would seem to be utterly unique in this regard. Except when the law has been broken, there are no other morally acceptable circumstances in which a person may become another's property. Moreover, there are no other morally acceptable circumstances in which a person rendered into property can, on the very terms of becoming property, reclaim his or her dignity as a human. How is it, then, that marriage can effect this reclamation, the transfiguration of human Objects into free rational subjects?

We can begin to answer this question by looking at Kant's comments on another kind of sexualized contract: concubinage. Kant dismisses concubinage because even though the agreement could be mutual, each party would be using only a part of the other, not their "whole person." In concubinage, one does indeed have a contract (Pactum), but according to the terms of this contract, one does not have rights over the entire person, but rather over only a part. However, Kant also maintains that "it is not possible to have the disposal over only a part of a person without having at the same time a right of disposal over the whole person, for each part of a person is integrally bound up with the whole" (Lectures 166/209). Kant argues that in reality, when one has disposal over only a part of the person, one also has disposal over the whole person, because he or she is an indivisible unity. The contradiction between the contract and the reality of the union thus renders concubinage illegitimate and immoral; the contract does not fully recognize the actual relationship. Because one enjoys the entire person in concubinage and yet this enjoyment of the whole person is not recognized by the contract—that is, is not established as a right—concubinage therefore renders a person into a thing.

The transfiguration of vice into virtue, property into person with regard to sexual inclination thus requires a contract that fully establishes the equality of persons based on their shared rationality, dignity, capacity for free choice, and ability to own. One may de facto have a whole person at one's disposal through sexual encounters—indeed by definition one does—but one must have it de jure in order to avoid objectifying that person and degrading his or her humanity. Proper erotic expression must have, via the contract, an irreducibly social component. While freedom may be an innate characteristic of humans qua humans, the equality they share based on this characteristic can come into being only through law, or Right. Their absolute inner value is by definition in and for themselves. Freedom may be innate to each individual, but this does not in itself guarantee an equality across and among individuals—that is, it does not guarantee equality as a transitive sociopolitical phenomenon. There remains the question, then, by what principle this innate human value, which is in and for oneself only, may be understood *distributively* in relation to other humans. For this self-enclosed value to acquire a distributive quality, it must enter the realm of moral duty, contract, and Right. The equivalence of persons within a humanistic economy of value is secured *only* through the assurances of law.

Assuring the distributive quality of a human's inner value as a free, rational agent is particularly pressing with regard to sex. Sexual inclination, Kant argues, is a necessary animal aspect of humans. Yet it also renders its Objects—other persons, or indeed oneself—into property. Significantly, this animal aspect of humans coincides with their rational capacity to choose, which justifies (or rather naturalizes) the ownership of property. Kant famously made this explicit in his 1793 essay, "On the Common Saying: That May Be Correct in Theory, But It Is of No Use in Practice," one of his "popular" essays in which he defends his moral doctrines in *Groundwork* and extends from them the germs of his doctrine of right found in *The Metaphysics of Morals*: "Everyone in his capacity as a human being, a being subjected by his own reason to certain duties, is accordingly a *businessman* [*Geschäftsmann*]." [17] Kant establishes an isomorphism between the appetitive animal of sexual inclination whose Objects become property and the human *qua* human whose dignity and capacity for free choice enshrines the ownership of property: the bourgeois businessman. Yet the owning of another as property within sexual relations cannot be tolerated, because this would deny another human a similar capacity. Kant underscores this point by limiting the use one can have of one's own sexual capacities. These limitations are significantly linked by the issue of property: "A human being cannot dispose over himself because he is not a thing. A human being is not his own property. This is a contradiction. For in so far as he is a person he is a Subject [*Subjekt*] who can own property and other things. Were he however his own property, he would be a thing over which he could have ownership. But a person cannot be a property and so cannot be a thing which can be owned, for it is impossible to be a person and a thing, the proprietor and the property" (*Lectures* 165/207). Because humans are by definition beings who own, Kant reasons, they cannot *be* owned themselves. To become (sexual) property would be to become less than human.

The question of property and sex returns in *The Metaphysics of Morals* when Kant discusses the nature of the marriage contract. Here Kant reiterates his argument in *Lectures* that only within marriage can sexual commerce enter into a human economy of value. Within marriage there is an "equality of possession" not only with regard to the persons involved but also with regard to their material possessions (*Metaphysics* 428). More importantly, however, the *reclamation* of oneself as a person, one who can own property and not be owned as property, within marriage depends on the curiously *subjunctive* relation of each other as property: in marriage, "while one person is acquired *as if it were a thing* [als Sache erworben wird], the one who is acquired acquires the other in turn; for in this way each reclaims itself [gewinnt sie wiederum sich selbst] and restores its personality" (*Metaphysics* 427). While grammatically Kant uses the passive tense here, there is also an implied subjunctive that is decisive. As a verbal tense or mood the subjunctive is used to signal both the counterfactual state of that which is signified, and its dissimulation as actual. Recall that in "Toward Perpetual Peace" the conflict between freedom and equality in civil society, or rather the struggle between private inclinations, is checked by the contractual laws of the state, with the result that citizens' public conduct can proceed "*as if they had no such evil intentions.*" In other words, the human capacity to render everything into an Object, or property—including other humans—is retained; however, it is retained within a context that pretends to annul this capacity. The contractual terms of the state merely provide a beneficent social cover for the untrammeled accumulation of property. Civic equality is fundamentally contingent on an emphatic "as if."

Kant's comments on marriage, however, provide just the reverse state of affairs. The subjunctive aspect of marriage signals that it is sexual objectification, *not* its annulment, that is rendered, or rather transfigured, as counterfactual through the reciprocal exchange of property. Each person does not acquire each other *as* a thing but *as if* each were a thing, since the reciprocity Kant sees in this contractual arrangement nullifies the objectification of each person. Objectification is counterfactual through (sexual) property exchange *only* on the condition of marriage; but the contracted parties also retain an at least imaginary relation to each other as Objects, as if each were "a thing." Thus, there is an irreducible conditional and deferral in this type of contract. To reclaim oneself as human through becoming the (sexual) property of one's spouse, one's status as (sexual) property is dissimulated by the reciprocity and rights of the marriage contract. That is, sexual objectification is annulled and transfigured—we might say sublated—by the marriage contract. However, the human *as* property owner is retained, is precisely that which is reclaimed in this subjunctive transfiguration of sexual objectification. It is the very pretense of property ownership, of sexual objectification, that marriage *must* dissimulate. The terms of this contract—equal value through equal possession—determine the conditions under which the vice of sexual inclination may be translated into a virtue.[18]

We can now return to the problem of postulating a distributive quality to human dignity within sexual commerce, a quality that would assure equivalence within a human economy of value. Within the marriage contract, what assures the equal distribution of human value is a subjunctive rendering of sexual possession: Each person is acquired by the other equally as a thing, thus assuring that each has a reciprocal acquisition of property. At least within marriage, *the principle of an equivalent relation between humans is cast subjunctively to insure the predication of the subject as property owner.*

I call attention to the importance of the subjunctive in this and other passages because they indicate a fundamental difficulty in Kant's ability to conceptualize a humanist economy of value whereby persons are equivalent. This difficulty stems from two things: first, the predication of the Kantian subject as property owner; and second, the dependence of the Kantian subject's dignity on a nondistributive moral value. *Lectures on Ethics*, as well as Kant's other texts, make clear that the humanity of a person is predicated on the ability to own and not to be owned. One cannot be a person and an Object; a person is one who, because he or she is an end in him- or herself, has the capacity to acquire and own property. Moreover, it is only with some difficulty that Kant is able to postulate the equivalence of humans based on his understanding of the human as a being that is an end in him- or herself. To achieve equality without sacrificing freedom (to own), humans must enter into contractual relations that distribute their inherent value universally. Yet the equality thus achieved cannot compromise human dignity and its postulate of property ownership. In "Toward Perpetual Peace" the universality of equality could also be figured only subjunctively. In relation to both the just state and the marriage contract, Kant essentially dissimulates the relation between the atomistic individual as property owner and the universal, social equality of the citizen.

This cuts to the heart of what many have seen as the problem with Kant's categorical imperative. This imperative requires that a moral law be universal only if it can be comprehended *as if it were* universally applicable. As Kant argues, it would be impossible to prove empirically for each and every person in each and every case that this would be so. However, simply because we may recognize our own rationality and thus our capacity for free choice does not necessitate that we recognize others as equal in this regard. The universal distribution of equality can only receive a subjunctive and thus a dissimulating assurance. What necessitates this subjunctive dissimulation is the absolute value accorded to property ownership, the "logical" extension from the conception of humans as free rational subjects. In this sense we may take Kant's arguments about sex as paradigmatic of difficulties resonating throughout his architectonic. Pepita Haezrahi has pointed to these difficulties with regard to the categorical imperative and the assumed (but not fully proven) distributive quality of the capacity to choose freely on which human equality would be based. Kant assumes that

> the same complex of circumstances and conditions which assure me of the certainty of my own freedom and moral responsibility, assures other rational beings of *their* freedom and *their* responsibility. Yet, as we must stress, no point in this argument necessarily implies an assurance for men of each other's freedom and moral capacity. In other words, the inductive assumption, or even an established fact that each rational being regards himself as possessed of dignity, on the same ground and for the same reasons that all other rational beings regard each himself as possessed of dignity, does not involve a logical necessity for rational beings to regard *each other* as possessed of dignity. This, however, is the decisive test for a general recognition by rational beings of the universal application of the dignity of man.[19]

The "universal validity in the distributive sense is not an essential qualification" of the concept of human dignity. Because this concept is figured as beginning and ending within the autonomous moral subject, one cannot automatically deduce from it that all men *qua* men possess dignity. Therefore, the "synthetic concept 'the objective universality of the dignity of man' is not a self-evident concept, i.e., immediately perceived by reason."[20]

At this point it is worth recapitulating what can be drawn from the foregoing analysis. First, the distributive principle within the human economy of value in Kant's formulations—what makes universal exchange, equivalence, and thus social and political equality possible—can be written only in the subjunctive. Human dignity can be the universal equivalent in this economy only counterfactually, only if we act as if it were so. Second, the necessity of a subjunctively inflected universality and equality stems not only from the logical, procedural aspects of Kant's formulations but also, and perhaps more importantly, from the predication of the Kantian subject, in both its "animal" and "human" aspects, as property owner. And third, Kant's discussion of sexual inclination and marriage is both paradigmatic of his particular resolution between freedom and equality, *and* unique insofar as sexual inclination is the only private vice that in itself threatens to deprive others of their humanity by rendering them into property.

Crimina Carnis

If the universal equality of citizens can be conceptualized and guaranteed only subjunctively, and if in turn the translation of erotic vice into a public virtue must itself be a subjunctive, dissimulating transfiguration of sex into a property contract, what are the implications for conceptualizing a right to same-sex sex? To put this in contemporary terms, how can queers *as sexual subjects* be incorporated into definitions of citizenship? Is marriage the only mode in which queer eroticism can be recognized as socially legitimate and equal before the law?

To address this question, I want to turn to Kant's lecture on so-called crimes against the flesh (*crimina carnis*). These crimes consist of all "unnatural" uses of a human's sexual capacities, unnatural here defined as any use of one's sexual organs—presumed, it would seem, to be the genitalia of men and women—that is not matrimonial cross-sex sexual intercourse (penis in vagina, vagina around penis, with seminal emission uninterrupted).[21] These crimes are divided into two types. The first, *crimina carnis secundum naturam*, are those that are contrary to reason, such as adultery, concubinage, and incest. The second, *crimina carnis contra naturam*, are those crimes against the flesh that are "contrary to natural instinct." They include masturbation, cross-species sex involving humans ("sodomy"), and same-sex sex. "All *crimina carnis contra naturam*," Kant argues, "degrade human nature to a level below that of animal nature and make a human being unworthy of his humanity" (*Lectures* 170/214). Importantly, only humans are capable of these vices, "for an animal is incapable of all such *crimina carnis contra naturam*" (*Lectures* 164/206). Crimes against nature are excluded from the animal economy of value. In this formulation, only humans would engage in these activities. They are uniquely human, yet they are excluded as well from a human economy of value. One who engages in them "no longer deserves to be a person from the point of view of duties towards himself. Such conduct is the most disgraceful and the most degrading of which a human being is capable" (*Lectures* 163/205). "These vices make us ashamed that we are human beings and, therefore, capable of them" precisely because *only* humans, and not animals, indulge in them, are in fact *capable* of doing so. They degrade not because they make humans into beasts, but because they reveal a constituent yet shameful feature of what turns out to be uniquely human.

Both types of *crimina carnis*, however, go against the grain of Kant's sexual humanism, insofar as each at least minimally understands the value of the particular pleasures offered by indeterminate erotic expression. Indeterminate erotic expression need not have an end other than itself. Reproduction, patrimony, spiritual love, social position, the transfer of property, life-long interpersonal commitment—all are ancillary, often unnecessary, to the economy of pleasures distributed within and across bodies during such erotic expression. In this respect, indeterminate erotic expression is its own reward, freed from a totalized reduction to a (purely supplemental) social or ideological telos. Insofar as the sexual humanism outlined by Kant depends on the bourgeois predication of the subject as property owner, however, I would suggest that a sexual humanism that similarly conceptualizes indeterminate erotic expression as objectifying will remain bound to marriage as its ultimate ideal.[22]

What we might term, a posteriori, a heteronormative rhetoric—peppered with no small amount of prudery—certainly animates Kant's contradictory formulations about the (in)human status of same-sex sex. However, neither their contradictoriness, nor their at times bizarre idiosyncrasy, are necessarily what is most interesting about them. We should notice that Kant places same-sex sex within a simultaneously inhuman *and* human economy of value, yet same-sex sex is quite far removed from free rational beings equal in their dignity. Is it possible to translate the private vice of homoeroticism into a public virtue, such that those subjects defined in relation to it could be guaranteed equality and rights as free rational beings?

If within sexual humanism marriage is the *only* standard by which this translation can occur, on what *other* terms might those persons defined in relation to homoeroticism be politically "humanized"? Or is the question rather, how might their "inhumanity" become a different principle of value that would not necessarily abnegate the sociopolitical freedom and equality that rights promise?

To get at this question, let me summarize the points I have tried to make thus far. Underlying Kant's formulations is the predication of the subject as property owner, both in terms of inclinations and in terms of the capacity for free choice. Kant thus naturalizes and moralizes the desire (*Begehrung*) to own property; desire *is* ownership. At least within the animal economy of value, therefore, there is a historically specific, quasi-materialist subject predication: the subject who desires, and thus the subject who owns (property). It is the dissimulation of this predication of the human as property owner, both in terms of animal inclinations and free rational choice, that leads to the "necessary" positing of a human economy of value with an idealist subject: the free rational citizen. The problem of organizing a rationally conceived, republican form of government built on the inherent rights and equality of free rational beings is at one level isomorphic with the problem of translating sex as a private vice into a public virtue. Erotic desire, as both an animal inclination *and* an expression of the properly human capacity to own and "objectify," reveals the extreme pressure put on universal moral laws, like rights, by predicating the human on property ownership. This pressure is also the classic one between individual freedom and social equality.[23] For sex as a private vice to be translated into a public virtue according to the dictates of Kant's model of the state and civil society, it must be transfigured within the marriage contract. The "ownership" of sexual "property" must be transfigured into a relation of equal property owners. In this formula, the predication of the subject as property owner is retained, but only insofar as the principle of equality is itself predicated by property ownership; each party is equal *only to the extent that each owns property.* This retention makes explicit the hidden norm guiding the universality of civic equivalence in this model: the historically particular elaboration of the bourgeois property owner as the ultimate moral-political standard by which all others (homo- or heteroerotically interested) who strive for equivalence will be measured. Thus, the universal equivalent in a human economy of value—human dignity—is both contoured and constrained by property ownership and its extension into (a heteronormative) sexual humanism. With regard to sex, to achieve the universality of civic equality thus entails, at least in part, becoming a monogamous, married property owner. Within Kant's model of a bourgeois sexual humanism, these are the only terms by which the private vice of homoeroticism could conceivably be translated into public virtue.

Citizen Slut

Here I would like to draw a polemical parallel between the dictates of Kant's thought on sex, rights, and civic equality and the recent dominance of marriage rights within contemporary lesbian and gay politics in the United States. To begin, at least two historical phenomena not related to Kant can explain this dominance. First and most obviously, marriage as it is now conceived in the United States excludes same-sex couples, recent judicial rulings in the state of Hawaii notwithstanding. Second, the pathologizing of indeterminate erotic expression, particularly as practiced by gay men, with the advent of HIV and AIDS has found its way into lesbian and gay politics itself. AIDS has become the alibi for denigrating promiscuity, indeed most any form of sex outside of what are termed long-term committed relationships.[24]

To illustrate the terms by which this alibi operates, I will descend from the sublime to the ridiculous for a moment and point to an infamous 1997 article in which the gay activist and playwright Larry Kramer bemoans the omnipresence of sex, particularly promiscuous sex, in contemporary gay male literature and lesbian and gay studies. Kramer claims that the gay academic "obsession" with sex distorts the true cultural accomplishments of gay folk like Michelangelo, Da Vinci, Schubert, George Washington, Abraham Lincoln . . . and so on. More perniciously, he claims that this "obsession" is complicit with the "fact" that gay men "brought AIDS upon ourselves by a way of living that welcomed it."[25] Significantly, the second half of Kramer's confused diatribe champions the cause for lesbian and gay marriage and the "1,049 rights" that would accompany it. The link Kramer's article establishes between valorizing marriage, as both civic propriety and prophylactic against HIV transmission, and the denigration of indeterminate erotic expression, has recently become extraordinarily commonplace in national lesbian and gay publicity venues. This link is succinctly articulated by a letter to the editor of the *Advocate* supporting Kramer's article: "When I hear of friends still joining in orgies at their local bathhouse, I have to wonder why we as a culture still feel that anonymous sex is a positive treat. I want those 1,049 rights Kramer mentioned that our straight counterparts take for granted. But perhaps society won't take us seriously until we take our commitments a bit more seriously. We need to honor ourselves and our relationships and our innate humanness, beyond just our sex, before we can expect the world at large to return the favor."[26] As this quotation makes clear, the argument for same-sex marriages, for "honoring" our relationships and realizing our "innate humanness," is not restricted to the simple removal of a legal exclusion. It also entails recoding a "private vice" by entering it into a sexually conservative (and logically tortured) humanist economy of value. As in Kant's texts, indeterminate erotic expression is excluded from the human, and as such it has no place in a social or civic order founded on such an economy. Indeed, the link between sexual conservatism and civic equality underlies most contemporary lesbian and gay arguments against indeterminate erotic expression. Columnist and author Bruce Bawer has argued that to emphasize the distinctiveness of queer sexual experiences and affiliations, indeed the centrality of erotic expression to queer self-definitions, is to "collaborate in the widespread, dehumanizing view that gay sex is invariably mechanical, impersonal, even bestial, while straight sex is an integral part of the complex web of human feeling, connectedness, and commitment before God."[27] Until we queers clean up our act, so to speak, Bawer warns that heterosexuals will justifiably see us as "a somewhat lower order of being whose personal lives can't possibly be morally equivalent to their own. And thereupon hang our rights."[28] In this view, civic equality requires that indeterminate erotic expression be repudiated.

This view of sexual propriety and equal rights now largely dominates national lesbian and gay political and media organizations. It is little wonder, then, that the struggle for queer freedom and equal rights has focused so intensely on marriage. The rationale for this focus goes far beyond removing legal barriers. Significantly, the unacknowledged yet effective linchpin connecting a humanist sexual morality to the necessity of marriage is the conceptualization of the subject as property owner, both "naturally" and "rationally." It underlies the understanding of indeterminate erotic expression as degrading because objectifying, and thus underlies in general the valorization of marriage as the contractual relation insuring that subjects-as-property-owners do not render each other *into* property. However, the idealization or transfiguration of sex in marriage—what often goes by the name of love—obscures the subject-as-property-owner *as the very ground* for this idealization and what in fact, according to Kant anyway, this idealization seeks at least in part to secure. This is not to say that there are no affective dimensions to sex—far from it. But it is to disrupt the idea that sex *must* be subordinated to what turns out to be, in effect, the affective extension of property rights (appropriately termed "propriety"). We can now pose the question with which I began this chapter in another way: Can there be a right to sex or a sexual citizen other than through marriage?

Any possibility for such a right or such a citizen would require displacing acquisition as the defining ground of the human. This displacement can begin with questioning the narrow moral standards of value that, within Kant's system, must be seen subjunctively as if they were universally valid. By moralizing enfranchisement in this way, Kant can conceive of equality as only reaching asymptotically toward its realization; one can imagine achieving it, can perhaps even approach it, but the achievement itself will remain deferred, out of reach. Yet at the same time we must pretend as if equality were actual. This asymptotic or subjunctive aspect of equality— the eternal "as if"—legitimates the dissimulated gap between the ideal of rights and its only ever approximate historical realization. This gap represents both the limitation and the promise of equality. Because the conferral of equality remains through its subjunctive figuring only ever an approximation, and contains its own dissimulation, we must question the subjunctive terms by which such (fictive) equality is conferred. In Kant's system, and by extension within modern humanist sexual morality, sexual equality is conferred *only so that* the subject-as-property-owner can be retained. If the promise of equality demands a different predication of the subject, this demand in turn must imagine distributive principles for the equality of citizens other than the dignity of bourgeois Man.

This demand also raises the following questions: Should social equality, and by extension, enfranchisement in the fullest sense, be grounded in universalist moral-political principles of the human, or in the communal norms that provide a distinct sense of self and group belonging? Should equality be abstract and formal, to allow greater autonomy, or more substantive, so as to recognize differences? Intervening in debates over such questions in political philosophy, Habermas decidedly supports a Kantian universalism. However, in his recuperation of a nonobjectifying and interactive rationality, he looks to Hegel, a primary inspiration for contemporary communitarians. As a founding moment in his turn to a discourse ethics that retains the universalism of Kantian moral-political theory, Habermas's move thus necessitates coming to terms with Hegel's critique of Kant in the *Phenomenology of Spirit*. This was necessary because Hegel's critique raises the problem of "whether issues of justice can be isolated from particular contexts of the good life." [29] The clash between Kant's and Hegel's differing conceptions of equality raises for Habermas a relevant utopian aspect of discourse ethics: "To the extent that we become aware of the intersubjective constitution of freedom, the possessive-individualist illusion of autonomy as self-ownership disintegrates." [30] Does Hegel's critique suggest going beyond "autonomy as self-ownership," such that the proprietary and heteronormative sexual humanism disabling rights can also be effectively displaced?

Because the subject of Kant's moral and political theory is self-enclosed, atomistic, in and for itself only, Hegel argued that Kant could only postulate a "contradictory universality." [31] Because universal equality opposes the self-enclosed individual, but is also a universality modeled *on* this individual, the "individual has, by the principle [*Begriff*] of his action, determined the more precise way in which the actual universality, to which he has attached himself, turns against him." [32] Because this universality can only be an imagined pretense, Hegel argues, this subject formulates laws negating its own freedom for an equality it must only pretend to justify. The universal equality imagined by Kant's system, therefore, is only an "empty universality," one that contradicts the "equally *individual* laws of their [the individuals'] hearts." [33] What Hegel's critique importantly reveals is the ease with which Kant's formalist universality can render moral *hypotheticals* into moral *injunctions*. That is, it reveals the ease with which wondering whether others *would* conform to a particular moral law can transform into the demand that they *should*. Despite these important reservations to Kant's universalist moral theory, however, the appeal to communal norms can hardly be said to safeguard indeterminate erotic expression. Even as Hegel critiqued Kant's thoroughly contractual understanding of marriage as "shameful," he retains Kant's moral prohibition of sex outside of cross-sexual monogamous marriage by subsuming it into the idealized features of a communal "ethical life" (Sittlichkeit).[34] Indeterminate erotic expression, it would seem, can be philosophically damned by both a moral universalism, as with Kant, or an appeal to communal ethos, as in Hegel. The question remains whether or not the values of the public sphere can imagine a different economy of value for sex, in which indeterminate erotic expression could be a recognizable feature, rather than the repudiated shadow, of the citizen.

FOUR   Inseminating the Orient,

Disseminating Identity

Before, I had delighted in that very fixity which afforded my mind its precision: all the facts of history had seemed to be museum pieces, or better still, specimens in an herbarium whose final desiccation helped me forget that once, rich with sap, they had lived under the sun. But now, if I could still take some pleasure in history, it was from imagining it in the present—Michel, in André Gide's THE IMMORALIST

The dispossession of homoeroticism from the normative outlines of Western citizenship certainly provided the constraints under which its revaluation would take shape. Yet as I argued in the previous chapter with respect to Kant, more than erotic norms are at work in the dispossession, and thus also the revaluation, of homoeroticism. The historical reliance on proprietary standards exceeding the sexual in attempts to revalue homoeroticism can be seen in nineteenth-century texts by Englishmen who sought same-sex adventures in the Greek Orient. Their participation in re-orienting Greece as a Western nation and ideal in the nineteenth century helped to make visible the erotic possibilities these lands seemed to offer. Greece and its heritage for the West became a crucial site in the nineteenth-century cultural public sphere for attempts to legitimate male homoerotic desire as a matter of private *and* public interest. The ability to represent homoerotic desire within this cultural public sphere, however, was circumscribed by the very bourgeois norms of propriety to which Victorian homophiles appealed, and for which Greece seemed a potentially and enablingly homoerotic symbol. The result was a severe narrowing of what male homophilic interest could entail. Surely this narrowing followed the ontological and epistemological dictates of the closet as these structured erotic definitions and possibilities. Yet legitimating appeals to Greece reveal that the closet was itself etched by other forms of dispossession. That is, for male homophilic interest to legitimate itself on the terms of the cultural public sphere necessitated a quid pro quo: in exchange for occupying the class and imperial norms defining what Greece meant to the English, male homoerotic desire was legitimated as a peculiarly athletic, ideally chaste affair.

The legacy of this exchange can be seen in the *Grecian Guild Pictorial*, a U.S. periodical of thinly veiled male homosexual erotica published during the late 1950s and early 1960s. Above its table of contents one finds the following passage from Percy Shelley's preface to his 1821 poem *Hellas*: "We are all Greeks. Our laws, our literature, our religion, our arts have their roots in Greece." For the Grecian Guild, the term "Greeks" signified a purposefully ambiguous set of associations, allowing male homoeroticism to coexist alongside a mainstream, presumptively heterosexual humanism. To laws, literature, religion, and the arts, the Grecian Guild silently adds sex. It is sex itself that, to modern minds, marks the ambiguity: the "we" includes at once everyone in the West, and at the same time only those who would say, with a knowing wink, that they are indeed "Greeks."

Shelley himself attempted to come to terms with this ambiguity, one which threatened to place what was and mostly still is seen as an odious erotic inclination at the heart of western Europe's cultural genealogy. In his "A Discourse on the Manners of the Ancient Greeks Relative to the Subject of Love" (written in 1818, but not published in its entirety until 1949), Shelley could not conceive that the pursuit of ideal truth and beauty in fifth-century Athens (B.C.E.) could have anything to do with the practice of pederasty alluded to in what were and are considered the foundational texts of Western civilization. This incongruity was so marked for Shelley that he postulated wet daydreams as the true source and meaning behind such allusions to male same-sex sexual relations: "If we consider the facility with which certain phenomena connected with sleep, at the age of puberty, associate themselves with those images which are the objects of our waking desires; and even that in some persons of an exalted state of sensibility a similar process may take place in reverie, it will not be difficult to conceive the almost *involuntary consequences* of a state of abandonment in the society of a person of surpassing attractions, *when the sexual connection cannot exist*, to be such as to preclude the necessity of so operose and diabolical a machination as that usually described." [1] That ancient Greek men seemed to differ in some of their erotic inclinations and practices from nineteenth-century

Englishmen could not, however, negate the more important cultural, political, and moral identity Shelley believed existed between ancient Greece and modern Europe. The presumed "Westernness" of ancient Greece seems to motivate Shelley's rather creative explanation of troublingly erotic relations between men in Plato's texts. Immediately following his universalizing statement in the preface to *Hellas* quoted by the Grecian Guild, Shelley argues that had it not been for the legacy of ancient Greek civilization, Europe might have become brutishly ignorant from the militarism of Rome "or, what is worse, might have arrived at such a stagnant and miserable state of social institution as China and Japan possess."[2]

Given Shelley's positioning of Greece as the saving grace of Western civilization, a positioning implicitly contained within the Grecian Guild's citation, what is the significance of the Shelley quotation adorning the Grecian Guild's closeted male homoerotica? Shelley wrote *Hellas* in 1821 at the beginning of the Greek war for independence from the Ottoman empire; his poem was part of a discursive armory of western European texts in the early nineteenth century that sought to "decolonize" Greece from the Ottomans, and disengage Greek lands from the "Orient" in general. It allegorizes a politically radical strain of European cultural philhellenism that since the late eighteenth century had sought to articulate Greece as a distinctively, fundamentally Western nation, race, and cultural ideal. By the 1950s, the Grecian Guild could presume the idealized occidental connotation of "Greek" as a thin veil for the term's erotic connotations that Shelley had sought to "clarify." Their use of Shelley's philhellenic statement suggests the extent to which geopolitical and erotic boundaries can mutually map their respective territories, though such boundaries, as with the Grecian Guild, may be drawn with invisible ink. Moreover, it suggests that the nineteenth-century connection between "Western" and "homoerotic" in the signifier "Greece" was successful precisely to the extent that this connection could later be so effortlessly presumed.

In this chapter, I want to explore the confluence of geopolitical and erotic territorializations of "us" and "them" in a few nineteenth-century British texts that speculate on the simultaneously national and sexual significance of Greece. The very intimacies these texts enact between erotic and geopolitical boundaries, I would suggest, were rendered opaque precisely in what they helped to make possible: late-nineteenth-century English articulations of a characterological, transhistorical, paradigmatically male, and culturally normative homoeroticism.[3] In laying claim to a racial and national signification of Greece, homoerotically interested English-men attempted to legitimize their interest through the already established value of a European Hellenic cultural tradition. The intimacies between the erotic and the geopolitical acquired their charge through narratives about Greece's past, narratives that in turn were made possible by the contemporary exigencies surrounding their construction. This dialectic be-tween past and present is informative not only for what it might tell us about nineteenth-century England's encounter with "the Levant," but also, and more importantly, what light it can shed on the enduring trace of this dialectic in the present. If, as I want to argue, the articulation of a culturally normative, characterologically enclosed male homoeroticism in late-nineteenth-century England obscures the geopolitical dynamics that helped make this articulation possible, then it may very well be that such dynamics continue to legitimate a normative male homosexual identity through their very obscurity.[4]

Degenerate Descendants

A part of the Ottoman empire since the fifteenth century, Greek lands be-came a matter of aesthetic, national, and sexual speculation and discursive debate in the late eighteenth and nineteenth centuries in Europe. Richard Chandler (1738–1810), one of the few Britons who undertook the jour-ney to "Hellas" before the Napoleonic Wars disrupted the usual tours of France and Italy and made travel to Greek lands more popular, wrote in his 1775 *Travels in Asia Minor* that the "Ephesians are now a few Greek peas-ants, living in extreme wretchedness, dependence, and insensibility; the representatives of an illustrious people, and inhabiting the wreck of their greatness . . ."[5] As Terence Spencer observes, such disparaging compari-sons were commonplace before 1800: "In 1700 the Greeks were an object of curiosity as the degenerate descendants of the glorious creators of lit-erature and the arts." By 1800, however, it increasingly became "a matter of eager speculation and controversy whether the Greeks inherited any of the virtues of their ancestors, whether their language could be purified, and whether they would owe their liberation to the kindly, but interested, arms of Russia, France, or England, or to their own exertions."[6] Even after 1800, when the groups of what Lord Byron termed "Levant lunatics" arrived in

Ottoman Greece in greater numbers, many British travelers compared the modern Greeks unfavorably with the Attic heroes they had read about at Eton, Oxford, or Cambridge. William Martin Leake, who wrote one of a number of popular travel books on the eastern Mediterranean in the early nineteenth century, dryly observed that the "modern Greek dialect bears the same comparison with its parent language, as the poverty and debasement of the present generation to the refinement and opulence of their ancestors."[7] "Few desperate scholars and artists," noted John Cam Hobhouse, Lord Byron's traveling companion to Ottoman Greece in 1809–10, "ventured to trust themselves among the barbarians to contemplate the ruins."[8]

Contemplating the ruins were what many western Europeans had come to Greek lands to do, inspired by the aesthetic impulses of European philhellenism. Philhellenism fueled the disparaging evaluations of Ottoman Greeks and their society, providing a standard of aesthetic idealization and heroic athleticism against which Ottoman Greeks were judged. Yet philhellenism also encouraged idealizations of Greek lands as the repository of a buried Western tradition: Greece, wrote an anonymous author in the *Eclectic Review* in 1812, was "one of the selected countries composing that world in the imagination, which is the scene of enthusiastically affecting historical recollections."[9] Such a convergence of affect and history in descriptions and idealizations of Greece by homoerotically interested men was intimately entwined within discursive mappings of geopolitical terrain. Greece was enthusiastically reimagined as a generalized Western cultural ideal that could carry within it the promise of male homoerotic meditation and/or practice, which were often vilified as the corrupt, vicious, and effeminate tastes and practices of the "Orient."[10] In his essay "Offences Against Reputation," written in the 1780s but not published until 1838, Jeremy Bentham expresses a relatively common orientalist axiom that the Islamic Orient was the true inheritor of ancient Greek pederasty: "Among other traits which discover the manners of the ancient Greeks, we learn, from what Xenophon relates regarding himself, that crimes against nature could be esteemed but a joke. Even now, wherever the Mahometan religion prevails, such practices seem to be attended with but little disrepute."[11]

This attitude about the Orient could be both titillating and alarming to the Britons, such as Lord Byron, John Cam Hobhouse, John Addington Symonds, Edward Carpenter, and E. M. Forster who, for over a century, looked eastward for homoerotic possibilities. While Byron privately celebrated as a peculiarly Turkish practice what Symonds would later call "Greek love," even as he publicly supported Greek independence from Turkish "tyranny," later writers such as Symonds deployed the nineteenth-century Westernization of Greece, including its status as a newly formed nation, to de-Orientalize the "Turkish" vice and rearticulate it as a particularly Greek, resolutely vital, virile, and integral part of a Western cultural heritage. As Eve Kosofsky Sedgwick has noted, "the Romantic rediscovery of ancient Greece cleared out—as much as recreated—for the nineteenth century a prestigious, historically underfurnished imaginative space in which relation to and among human bodies might be newly a subject of utopian speculation."[12] How might we characterize the complex interweaving of racial, gender, sexual, and geopolitical conflicts in the formation of both a Western and a homophilic eastern Mediterranean nation, the convergence in and on Greece of "enthusiastically affecting historical recollections"?

Any attempt to characterize this interweaving necessarily inhabits a similar terrain of erotic and geopolitical intimacies. The construction of an enthusiastic scene of imaginative historical recollection partly informs what we now call identity politics. In terms of sexual identity, such politics have been seen as structuring intellectual and cultural work in two ways: an "essentialist" project of "homosexuals throughout history," or an "anti-essentialist" deconstruction of a transhistorical (paradigmatically male) homosexual Subject on behalf of a more historically nuanced narrative of emergence through political struggle and discursive redefinitions. The latter is often cast as taking the teeth out of the former. By analyzing identity in terms of historical situation and ideological construction, the force of sameness in identity is rendered merely a phantasm of a more constitutive politics of difference. Inescapably, however, the structuring question of identity grants this phantasm a haunting ground in the very historical recollections that would exorcise it, a phantasm that may be termed a trace of the present. This enduring trace of present politics renders the essentialist/antiessentialist dichotomy somewhat moot, since an "antiessentialist" project cannot simply wish away or disavow its own positioning in relation to contemporary struggles. Recent work in the history of sexuality, Sedgwick has argued, has often tended inadvertently "to refamiliarize, renaturalize, damagingly reify" the categories it deconstructs historically by implicitly assuring such categories contemporary coherence based on their alterity in relation to the past.[13] I will not attempt to erase the trace of present concerns for the sake of a misguided sense of "historical objectivity," which would only insure a return of the repressed. Rather, I want to mobilize it to examine what contemporary complicities embedded in the contestive consolidation of a Western male homosexual identity may be read through affective historical recollection.

The Psychic Tourist

Two essays by Freud can help us to understand the workings of an affective historical recollection, less for their paradigmatic privilege for understanding sexuality (or indeed history) than for their own historical and ideological participation in the intersection between consolidating sexual and geopolitical identities. I want to suggest that the psychoanalytic reading of subjective history as an erotically charged homology of human history is symptomatic of reading Greece (here via the Oedipus complex) as the privileged repository of "Westernness." One might say that such a reading of Greece is an instance of fantasy reconstructing history. In his 1908 essay "The Relation of the Poet to Day-Dreaming," Freud casts fantasy as a point of temporal convergence, where past, present, and future meet and reorganize along the contours dictated by desire:

> The relation of phantasies to time is altogether of great importance. One may say that a phantasy at one and the same moment hovers between three periods of time—the three periods of our ideation. The activity of phantasy in the mind is linked up with some current impression, occasioned by some event in the present, *which had the power to rouse an intense desire.* From there it *wanders* back to the memory of an early experience, generally belonging to infancy, in which this wish was fulfilled. Then it creates for itself a situation which is to emerge in the future, representing the *fulfillment* of the wish—this is the day-dream or phantasy, which now carries in it *traces* both of the occasion which engendered it and of some past memory. So past, present and future are threaded, as it were, on the string of the wish that runs through them all.[14]

Freud's narrative of historical reimagining occurs only on the level of the subject's history. Desire wanders, like a psychic tourist, over the landscape of the subject's past experiences, reconstructing a future out of a selectively re-presented trace of a utopian past of wish-fulfillment. Yet Freud's narratives, we should remember, emerged out of and often conflicted with the moment in European history when sexual identities were "discovered" as transhistorical, scientific "truths." Their truth-function effectively displaced their emergence from social struggles and historically contingent readings of human behavior. As Meaghan Morris has observed, "Identity meditations . . . offer a site *of* ideological conflict and *for* discursive transformations—opportunities for rewriting the rules to different purposes and in other interests." [15] The ability of fantasy to reimagine subjective history indexes the displacements of ideological conflicts and discursive transformations that help to consolidate the very concept of an "essential" identity. Fantasies construct a seamless historical continuum between past wish-fulfillments, present desires, and a utopian future. They displace the complexities of a subject's past, uproot and deploy the trace of a past wish-fulfillment, and construct an idealized "tradition" of erotic satisfaction built out of contemporary libidinal investments. An essential identity obtains in fantasy between a subject's past and present, an identity based on the fulfillment of desire.[16]

While for Freud the movement of fantasy displaces the material circumstances of subjective history, this movement also characterizes the idealized Western tradition informing psychoanalysis. Fantasies displace the specific context of a subject's history in a way similar to that in which the historically specific geopolitical dynamics underwriting Greece-as-West are displaced by the ontogenetic/philogenetic conflation embedded in, for example, the concept of the Oedipus complex. The movement of fantasy is symptomatic not only of the subject's rewriting of its own history, but also of the psychoanalytic construction of sexual identity-formation.

In a much later piece Freud situates such historical displacements and reconstructions at a precise geographical location: Athens. In his 1937 essay "A Disturbance of Memory on the Acropolis," Freud describes the process by which a subject's *relation* to the real becomes subjective *reality* through the psychic wandering of desire. In this open letter to Romain Rolland, Freud tells the story of his first trip to Greece with his brother, a trip they had not originally planned. While on their way to Corfu, a friend in Trieste told the Freud brothers that it would be much easier to travel to Athens. Despite some misgivings, they made the journey, and soon found themselves atop the Acropolis. Freud recollects exclaiming to his brother, " 'So all this really *does* exist, just as we learnt at school!' "[17] Yet apparently Freud had never really doubted the existence of the Acropolis at all, only the possibility of his ever seeing it. For some reason, the materiality of the Acropolis within his field of vision spawned a "disturbance of memory and a falsification of the past."[18] His incredulity was "doubly displaced in its actual expression: first, it was shifted back into the past, and secondly it was transposed from my relation to the Acropolis on to the very existence of the Acropolis."[19] What motivated this double displacement, effecting a new relation between both subjective history and present reality? Freud reads into this double displacement a guilty pleasure stemming from competition with his father, from having accomplished something beyond his father's grasp: ". . . a sense of guilt was attached to the satisfaction of having got so far: there was something about it that was wrong, that was from earliest times forbidden."[20] In a sense Freud has journeyed to the present trace, the Acropolis, of an archeological past, ancient Greece, to "restore" an ontogenetic Oedipal conflict to its geographical home. This restoration, effected by a guilty pleasure, is inseparable from the global imaginings of the tourist: "When first one catches sight of the sea, crosses the ocean and experiences as realities cities and lands which for so long had been distant, *unattainable things of desire*—one feels oneself like a hero who has performed deeds of improbable greatness."[21] The return to Greece is read as a confirmation of the significance of this return itself: the psychoanalytic tourist reads his encounter with Greek ruins through the lens of a desire originating in the ruins themselves. For Freud they echo and confirm the enduring legacy of Oedipus as the originary dynamic of Western desire.

Hyacinths and Parasols

Rather than situating the "guilty pleasure" that motivates historical reimaginings within a mythic family romance, we might better situate it in the material circumstances of nineteenth-century European injunctions against male same-sex sexual practices that partly motivated the turn to the East by European men who valued homoeroticism. The late eighteenth and early nineteenth centuries in Britain, for example, saw a large increase in the number of prosecutions and hangings for sodomy between men.[22] Even after capital punishment no longer applied to sodomy convictions, public disapprobation and legal prosecution continued, the most famous example being Oscar Wilde's conviction for "gross indecency" in 1895. The climate on the European continent was similarly draconian. This provided a compelling reason for many bourgeois and aristocratic men who sought to engage in same-sex sexual activity and/or erotic meditation to look eastward to what was seen as the more sexually permissive Orient. It is out of such persecution and geopolitical imagining that "Greece," as a valued cultural ideal, became entangled in the consolidation and legitimation of a Western male homosexual identity.

This entanglement can be read in many types of discursive production, ranging from private letters and pamphlets to the most public arenas of publication. In what follows, I will focus on just a few of the many discourses that value-coded Greece as the signifier of both a cultural *and* an erotic ideal. Such value-codings in the late eighteenth and early nineteenth centuries often maintained an ambiguous geopolitical resonance for the male homoerotic potential of Greece. Later in the nineteenth century, however, J. A. Symonds, a key figure in the articulation of a distinct and normatively valued male same-sex sexual identity in Britain, took great pains to reconstruct Greece as a Western nation and race. The difference between the two approaches, I want to suggest, indicates a number of shifts in the complex dynamics among class, gender, and sexual stratifications, and their relation to geopolitical terrains. In Britain specifically, these shifts can be glimpsed by the difference in approach between two nineteenth-century writers: Lord Byron, whose public persona combined contradictory elements of residual aristocratic codes of amorous adventure and emergent codes of (ambiguously) radical political agendas; and Symonds, who deployed late-Victorian codes of race, national identity, and middle-class manliness in an attempt to integrate male homoeroticism into a Western cultural economy of value. The emergence of Greece as an independent nation-state in 1829 in some sense marks the pivotal junction between the two approaches, providing later writers with a point of departure not available to Byron. While Byron's popularity provided Greek nationalists with a ready European constituency of support during their war of independence, Symonds built on the Westernizing efforts of Greek nationalists and Europeans to articulate a particularly Greek form of male same-sex sexual and erotic relations as crucially, vitally, and valuably Western.

For both Byron and Symonds, European philhellenism provided a potent discursive terrain through which to understand Greece in relation to male homoeroticism. The German art historian and aesthetician Johann Joachim Winckelmann is usually credited with articulating the major impulses of philhellenism in the late eighteenth century. Winckelmann's pronouncements on the superiority of classical art constructed a reverential aesthetic against which his contemporaries often reacted: "There is but one way for the moderns to become great," he wrote in 1755, "I mean by imitating the ancients." [23] Winckelmann's neoclassical aesthetic revolved around an intense affective reimagining of ancient Greek artistic tradition, a tradition traced along the contours of sculpted male bodies. For Winckelmann, ancient Greece became the site of an untrammeled celebration of a universalized male beauty, an eroticized utopia that became the prescriptive standard of future artistic practice. Ancient Greek sculptures of male bodies, in particular, signified a lost past of an aesthetically ideal and athletically exciting male same-sex eroticism:

> The most beautiful body of ours would perhaps be as much inferior to the most beautiful Greek one, as Iphicles was to his brother Hercules. The forms of the Greeks, prepared to beauty, by the influence of the mildest and purest sky, became perfectly elegant by their early exercises. Take a Spartan youth, sprung from heroes, undistorted by swaddling-clothes; whose bed, from his seventh year, was the earth, familiar with wrestling and swimming from his infancy; and compare him with one of our young Sybarits [sic], and then decide which of the two would be deemed worthy, by an artist, to serve for the model of a Theseus, and Achilles, or even a Bacchus. The latter would produce a Theseus fed on roses, the former a Theseus fed on flesh, to borrow the expression of Euphranor.[24]

The "supreme beauty" of Greek art, Winckelmann claimed, "is rather male than female." [25] Yet the above passage indicates a particular kind of male beauty. The comparison between the ancient Spartan and the modern Sybarite differentiates the value of types of male bodies, behaviors, and ideas as a way to signify the degeneration from an ancient athletic male homoeroticism to a more vicious modern licentiousness. "Sybarite" generally denotes a sensualist, but was a common term for men engaged in same-sex sexual activity, usually connoting a corrupt and "effeminate" love of luxury and sensual gratification.[26] The term literally refers to an inhabitant of the southern Italian area of Sybaris, indicating the geographical, and racial, connotation superadded to the value-coding of types of male homoeroticism. Winckelmann's aesthetic calls for a contemporary regeneration of both a cultural and erotic ideal, based on an affective reconstruction of an artistic tradition and built out of a complex interweaving of racial, gender, and geopolitical codes, preferring the virile contours of masculine "flesh" to the perfumed delicacy of the "rose."

There is also an element of pastoral idealization underwriting Winckelmann's aesthetic eroticization of ancient Greece, an idealization that at times extracts a homology between Homeric heroes and "uncivilized" hunters: "Behold the swift Indian outstripping in pursuit of the hart: how briskly his juices circulate! how easy his whole frame! Thus *Homer* draws his heroes." [27] By constructing an idealized ancient Greece full of noble and yet cultured savages, Winckelmann ironically helped to inspire the rhetoric of degeneration used to compare Ottoman Greeks to their heroic ancestors. As more European antiquarians and tourists made their way to the Peloponesus, they began to compare the sculptures of Venus and Apollo to local populations. The rhetoric of decline used to compare the two maintained a strict divide between past civilization and modern barbarity.

Yet this divide is not unambiguously present in Winckelmann. On the one hand, all forms of male homoeroticism in "uncivilized," naturally heroic communities seem to be isomorphic; on the other, such communities are divided by the particular *way* such eroticism is seen to be experienced and expressed, a divide often value-coded by geopolitical and gender dichotomies. Either male homoeroticism somehow transcended geopolitical boundaries, or it could be categorized according to orientalist assumptions about the differences between Europe and its others. Because Greek lands in the nineteenth century were in the process of being disengaged discursively and politically from the Orient, this categorical contradiction between a sexual isomorphism and a geopolitical difference had to be negotiated by later writers who, unlike Winckelmann, actually traveled to Ottoman lands to get firsthand experience of "the glory that was Greece."

Lord Byron, who first visited Ottoman lands in 1809–10, negotiated with this contradiction by maintaining a divide between public literary idealizations of Greece-as-West and private celebrations of an erotically charged Greece-as-Orient. Byron combined his knowledge of ancient Greek and Roman texts, which formed the staple of male aristocratic education in England until the early twentieth century, with his own discursive incursions into late-eighteenth- and early-nineteenth-century orientalism. Much of the orientalist discourses of which he boasted great knowledge maintained an indistinction between Greece and the Orient in terms of "corrupted" sexual practices.[28] François Pouqueville, an agent of Napoleon whose *Travels in Morea, Albania, and Other Parts of the Ottoman Empire* (translated in 1806) Byron quotes in his notes to *Childe Harold's Pilgrimage*, groups modern Albania and Greece together as sexually barbaric: "[I]t seems as if a passion disowned by the first laws of our nature is one of the ordinary concomitants of barbarism. The Albanian is no less dissolute in this respect than the other inhabitants of modern Greece. . . ."[29] As Louis Crompton notes, Byron also read Nicolas Sonnini's 1799 *Travels in Upper and Lower Egypt* (originally published in French), which, like many of Bentham's writings on "crimes against nature," claims the Orient as the modern inheritor of ancient vices: "The passion contrary to nature which the Thracian dames avenged by the massacre of Orpheus, who had rendered himself odious by gratifying it, the inconceivable appetite which dishonoured the Greeks and Persians of antiquity, constitute[s] the delight, or, to use a juster term, the infamy of the Egyptians."[30] Byron often duplicates a sexual isomorphism between ancient Greece and the modern Ottoman Orient in his private correspondences. When first setting out for his oriental grand tour in 1809, Byron described to his friend Charles Skinner Matthews, who shared Byron's erotic interest in young men, his expectations of having same-sex sexual encounters in the East. In the English port of Falmouth, Byron claims he and his companions were "surrounded by Hyacinths & other flowers of the most fragrant [na]ture, & I have some intention of culling a handsome Bouquet to compare with the exotics we expect to meet in Asia" (LJ 1:207). In ancient Greek legend, Hyacinth was a young man loved by Apollo; Byron's letter deploys a Greek legend as a shared code to allude both to an English and to expected "Asian" erotic experiences.[31]

The sexual isomorphism in Byron's letter, however, obtains only in terms of his individual experiences. That is, for Byron the restrictiveness of English society was far removed from "Asia" in terms of accepted sexual practices, even if he was able to pluck a "Hyacinth" in Falmouth. The traditional aristocratic grand tour, whose customary routes were disrupted by the Napoleonic Wars, gave Byron the opportunity to leave behind the possibility of British persecution (but not, as Jonathan Dollimore points out, to leave behind the privilege that enabled such tours in the first place).[32] The crucial mediating term for Byron between Western persecution and Eastern permissiveness was Greece. In his highly public poetry Byron could deploy philhellenism to render Greece a fallen Western "nation," while in private correspondence to like-minded men he could celebrate a distinctly oriental "Greek love." In an 1810 letter to Henry Drury, Byron explains that the only essential differences between East and West are their fashions and vices, which placed Greece within the purview of the Orient: "I see not much difference between ourselves & the Turks, save that we have foreskins and they none, that they have long dresses and we short, and that we talk much and they little. — In England the vices in fashion are whoring & drinking, in Turkey, Sodomy & smoking, we prefer a girl and a bottle, they a pipe and a pathic. . . . I like the Greeks, who are plausible rascals, with all the Turkish vices without their courage" (LJ 1:238).[33] The vice the Grecian Guild a century and a half later would silently recode under the term "Greek" is situated by Byron in Turkey, becoming itself the true heir to ancient Greek pederasty.

While Byron, following Bentham, Pouqeville, and Sonnini, privately described the Ottoman Orient as the heir to ancient Greece's erotic legacy, in public he resolutely defined modern Greece as the debased origin of Western civilization, brutishly enslaved by the Ottoman Turks. He articulated Greece as a fundamentally Western society, in bloodline if not in appearance, worthy of idealization and even volunteer military duty in their war for independence in the 1820s, a war in which Byron died. *Childe Harold's Pilgrimage*, for example, whose publication in 1812 catapulted Byron into cultural fame and "contributed to the rise in Europe and the United States of a vigorous literary philhellenism," figures Greece as a "sad relic of departed worth! / Immortal, though no more; though fallen, great!" (2.73).[34] Childe Harold chastises both Greeks and Europeans for not fighting against the "slavish sickle" of Turkish tyranny: "Ah! Greece! they love thee least who owe thee most— / Their birth, their blood, and that sublime record / Of hero sires, who shame thy now degenerate horde!" (2.83). Inaction keeps the Greeks "Trembling beneath the scourge of Turkish hand; / From birth till death enslaved in word, in deed, unmann'd" (2.74). The racial ("blood") and political ("birth") identity between modern Europe and ancient Greece is subtly value-coded by gendered terms—the ungrateful Europeans will not come to the aid of their "hero sires," leaving them to degenerate "unmann'd" under an oriental despotism. Byron deploys a similar rhetoric of gender degeneracy to characterize the ancient Persian despot Sardanapalus in his "closet" drama of the same name. Here a contemporary orientalist rhetoric reconstructs the erotic excesses of Sardanapalus as the cause of his downfall: this "man-queen" indulges his "effeminate heart" in "palling pleasures" with "women, and beings less than women . . ." (1.9.24, 31). What seems par for the course in ancient Persia becomes in modern Greece the symptoms of a contaminating oriental profligacy. The struggle to articulate and realize a distinctly Western national identity for modern Greece was presented by Byron to the British public as a struggle between a virile, manly Occident and an effeminate, debilitatingly voluptuous Orient.

With the publication of Byron's private writings, we are able to reconstruct an ambiguous valence in his discursive construction of a Greek geopolitical genealogy and national identity. Sardanapalus the "man-queen" is dressed up in codes that would elicit public disapprobation but which, in the context of Byron's tropological shaping of the eastern Mediterranean in his letters, we might imagine would elicit among his friends a knowing giggle. Byron himself boasted of sporting with "women and beings less than women" in Ottoman Greece. In an 1810 letter to Hobhouse, Byron describes traveling to Patras with a Greek youth, Eustathias Georgiou, who rode with them "Clothed very sprucely in Greek Garments, with those ambrosial curls hanging down his amiable back, and to my utter astonishment and the great abomination of Fletcher, a *parasol* in his hand to save his complexion from the heat" (LJ 2:6; original emphasis). In spite of the parasol, Byron writes, "we traveled very much enamoured"; later Byron gave Eustathias a "green shade instead of that effeminate parasol," and the two "*redintegrated* [sic]" their "affections at a great rate" (LJ 2:7; original emphasis). The "effeminate" parasol protecting the Greek youth seems to signify for Byron not so much the "Turkish occupation of Greek soil," as Jerome Christensen has argued, as it signifies the very semiotic shade offered his private celebratory integration of Greece into the eroticized topography of the Orient, a sunscreen from the public glare of his nationalist integration of Greece into a Western cultural genealogy.[35] The divide between public and private in Byron's texts on Greece, and Byron-as-text, is a divide driven by Western persecution, orientalist assumptions, and a displaced nationalist noblesse oblige. This divide and its discursive baggage is located in the enablingly ambiguous semiotic potential of Greece, able at this moment to signify both the originary site of a Western humanist imaginary awaiting national liberation, and a contemporary site of particularly *oriental* erotic possibilities for amorous aristocrats. While the West inherited ancient Greek "civilization," the Orient inherited its unacceptable erotic proclivities. This genealogical split provided the British public with a selectively illustrious history underlying an insurgent Greek nationalism, a history and nationalism that were thus presented as in many ways their own. At the same time, this genealogical split provided Byron and his coterie with geopolitical and erotic relations that were not on speaking terms in public, but "redintegrated" in private. Byron, then, could have his Greece and eat it too.

If "Greece" was for Byron a somewhat schizophrenic category, we might attribute it less to calculation or the closet than to the cultural terrain, in terms of value-coding erotic practices and inclinations, on which he adventured. Byron seems less interested in constructing an *erotic* tradition for Greece than in articulating a cultural, national one. Because Greece had as yet not been disengaged from the Orient as an independent and fully Western nation-state, and because male same-sex erotic relations were as yet more of a sin—and crime—than a constitutional defect whose characterological veracity was inescapable, indulging in "Turkish vices" seems more of a fringe benefit than a primary instigation for Byron's discursive, as well as military, struggle to define Greece as the West's forgotten forefather.

Greek Love

"Redintegrating" what came to be perceived as Greece's erotic, cultural, national, and racial legacy for the West into a full-blown historical and cultural tradition relied on a number of decisive cultural and political shifts in both Britain and Greek lands in the nineteenth century. One such shift was the political alignment of a newly independent Greek nation with western Europe. The Greek war of independence in 1821–29 represented for many western Europeans a chance to realize politically the philhellenic articulation of Greece as the originary "nation" of the West. As Gregory Jusdanis has shown, Greece's conflict received disproportionate attention in

Europe, compared to the nationalist struggles of Serbians, Bulgarians, and Armenians, because of the special place accorded it within a Western cultural genealogy. "The ideological connection between ancient and modern Greece," Jusdanis notes, "made the Greek tragedy European."[36] Given the relatively common disparaging comparisons between ancient and modern Greece in European travel books in the late eighteenth and early nineteenth centuries, European interest in the Greek war stemmed more from idealizations of a Hellenic past and a wish to re-Hellenize Hellas, than from a sense that modern Greece was *already* Western. Still, the "Easternness" of Greece disappointed many of the volunteer soldiers: "For them Greece possessed an identity only in relationship to its past. The philhellenes expected to fight alongside the descendants of Leonidas's warriors, not peasants with oriental manners and dress." The Greek war was "portrayed not only as a fight for democracy and freedom from oppression but also as a struggle between Europe and Asia. . . . The Greek intellectuals understood this very well and thus tried to portray Greeks as Europeans."[37] The emergence of Greece as a western European nation-state, Jusdanis shows, was thus deeply implicated in the ideological contours of European orientalism.

The formation of a Greek nation earlier in the century gave later nineteenth-century apologists for male homoeroticism greater leeway in publicly presenting such relations as properly, valuably Western, but only at the expense of the enablingly ambiguous geopolitical and erotic positioning of Greece by writers like Byron. Where Byron maintained a geopolitical ambiguity for Greece, an ambiguity mapped by erotic boundaries, hovering between public distinctions and private isomorphisms, J. A. Symonds began to give a resolutely Western texture to ancient Greek pederasty in the 1870s and 1880s. This is not to say that the erotic isomorphism one finds in Winckelmann and Byron completely disappeared. In the "Terminal Essay" appended to his 1878 translation of the *Arabian Nights*, Richard Burton argues that there is a "Sotadic Zone" that spreads itself across the globe, encompassing "meridional France, the Iberian Peninsula, Italy and Greece," "Africa from Morrocco to Egypt," "Asia Minor, Mesopotamia and Chaldaea, Afghanistan, Sind, the Punjab and Kashmir," "China, Japan and Turkistan," the "south Sea Islands and the New World." The "execrabilis familia pathicorum," the "Vice" of boy-love, is "popular and endemic" in the Sotadic Zone, "held at the worst to be a mere peccadillo, whilst the races to the North and South of the limits here defined practise it only sporadically amid the opprobrium of their fellows who, as a rule, are *physically incapable* of performing the operation and look upon it with the liveliest disgust."[38] While Burton energetically upholds his claim that "Pederasty" is "geographical and climatic, not racial," the claim that the "races" to the north and south of this zone are physically incapable of "the operation" mitigates his argument for a purely environmental causation.

The crucial difference between Burton and Symonds, however, lies not just in their seemingly different localizations of male homoerotic practices, but also in how Symonds presents ancient "Greek love" as resolutely distinct from any of its neighbors in the so-called Sotadic Zone. This articulation depends not only on the geopolitical shift from an Ottoman Greece to an independent, and Westernized, Greek nation, but also on a shift from an aristocratic to a middle-class coding of homoerotic possibilities. Byron's amorous adventures—both public cross-sex and private same-sex encounters—inhabited a tradition of aristocratic libertinage and seduction, vividly portrayed in eighteenth-century fiction such as Samuel Richardson's *Pamela* (1740) and *Clarissa* (1747–48), and in early-nineteenth-century stage melodramas. Byron's "insemination" of the Orient was contiguous with the cultural dissemination of his public persona as a dangerous Don Juan. Later nineteenth-century European bourgeois ideals of manliness, however, were counterposed to the sexual license and licentiousness often associated with male aristocratic predators. An erotically purified philhellenism, as George Mosse has argued, played a key role in articulating the features of bourgeois manliness: "But above all, manliness was based upon the Greek revival which accompanied and complemented the onslaught of respectability and the rise of modern nationalism."[39] Ironically, Winckelmann's celebration of an erotically charged Greek male ideal was "integrated into the scheme of bourgeois values associated with restraint, chastity, and purity." "The Greek ideal," Mosse writes, "was stripped of any lingering eroticism, while its harmony, proportion, and transcendent beauty were stressed." In this way Hellenism could bring together bourgeois gender and nationalist ideals: "The idea of masculinity, including its borrowed Greek standards of male beauty, was drafted by European nationalisms into service as national symbol or stereotype."[40]

Symonds called upon such late-Victorian middle-class conceptualizations of proper masculinity as part of his effort to achieve abeyance in the public, legal, and medical condemnations of male homoeroticism, and include it within the very core of Western culture. As Jeffrey Weeks observes, his "aim was to establish, by using the Greek analogy, that homosexuality could be accepted as part of the social mores."[41] In "A Problem in Greek Ethics," written in 1873, privately published in 1883, and later incorporated, without his name, in Havelock Ellis's sexological opus *Sexual Inversion* in 1897, Symonds reconfigures ancient Greek pederasty in terms that would be recognizable as, or at least semiotically contiguous to, manly virtues. These virtues have been categorized by David Newsome as including "the duty of patriotism; the moral and physical beauty of athleticism; the salutary effects of Spartan habits and discipline; the cultivation of all that is masculine and the expulsion of all that is effeminate, unEnglish and excessively intellectual."[42] Pederasty in ancient Athens, Symonds argues, "was closely associated with liberty, manly sports, severe studies, enthusiasm, self-sacrifice, self-control, and deeds of daring, by those who cared for those things."[43] This particular form of pederasty, distinct from the "baser" form it could take, Symonds defines as "Greek love," a "passionate and enthusiastic attachment subsisting between man and youth, recognised by society and protected by opinion, which, though it was not free from sensuality, did not degenerate into mere licentiousness" (17).

"Licentiousness" operates here as a dense signifier for the convergence of that which is not only antipathic to middle-class manliness, but also to *English* middle-class manliness. For Symonds the difference between "sensuality" and "licentiousness" is a boundary between Europe and the Orient, a boundary drawn with the pen of English middle-class masculine norms. Symonds counterposes the healthfully masculine homoeroticism of Doric camaraderie to the "effeminacies, brutalities and gross sensualities which can be noticed alike in imperfectly civilised and in luxuriously corrupt communities" that also practiced male same-sex sexual activities, communities that included "the Scythian impotent effeminates, the North American Bardashes, the Tsecats of Madagascar, the Cordaches of the Canadian Indians, and similar classes among Californian Indians, natives of Venezuela, and so forth . . ." (30–31). "The nobler type of masculine love developed by the Greeks," Symonds maintains, ". . . is that which more than anything else distinguishes the Greeks from the barbarians of their own time, from the Romans, and from modern men in all that appertains to the emotions" (17). Even in his recognition that a lower, merely lustful form of pederasty existed in ancient Greece, Symonds speculates that "paiderastia in its crudest form was transmitted to the Greeks from the East" (14). He admits the impossibility of proving his assertion; yet in any case, "whatever the Greeks received from adjacent nations, they distinguished with the qualities of their own personality. Paiderastia in Hellas assumed Hellenic characteristics and cannot be confounded with any merely Asiatic form of luxury" (14).

Symonds deploys Greece-as-West to distinguish between, and thus evaluatively divide, the seemingly identical sexual practices of "civilized" Grecians and "barbarian" communities, thus shoring up the radical Westernness of a particularly "Greek" (i.e., virile, spiritual, and vaguely physical) male homoeroticism. The Westernness of Greece re-places the particular features of ancient Greek male homoeroticism into Europe's cultural inheritance. Greece's Westernness accrues a particularly powerful rhetorical emphasis in the terms deployed throughout Symonds's study: describing ancient Greece as a "nation" and a "race" with a "consciousness" and "spirit" distinct from the "Orient" surrounding it. In this way Symonds maintained an affirming convergence of national, racial, and sexual identity.

This is not to say that Symonds's particular deployment of such late-Victorian middle-class conceptualizations of proper masculinity, national consciousness, and racial demarcations suddenly and perceptively shifted both condemnatory and affirming understandings of male homoeroticism. Oscar Wilde's trial and conviction in 1895 provided ample ammunition for demonizations of an increasingly visible homosexual subculture as effeminate and aristocratic in style, if not in substance. Sedgwick convincingly argues that the "middle-class-oriented but ideologically 'democratic,' virilizing, classicizing, idealistic, self-styled political version of male homosexuality . . . seems with the protracted public enactment of the [Wilde] trials to have lost its consensus and its moment." "The durable stereotype that came to prevail," Sedgwick continues, "has been close to Symonds only as Symonds resembled Wilde: a connoisseur, an interpreter of aristocratic culture to the middle class, a socialist insofar as socialism would simply expand the venue of leisure, privilege, and high culture." [44] What I have wanted to suggest, however, is that Byron and Symonds, if in nothing else than their different handlings of Greece as a potent signifier, indicate particular structurings of erotic value that cannot be disentangled from geopolitical value. While the Grecian Guild's invocation of Greece follows a similar public/private divide as Byron, its knowing assumption about what the precise *content* of the private would *be* follows more closely the publicly available continuities between the West and the homosexual articulated by Symonds. The moment of recognition—"There I am"—enacted in the Grecian Guild's invocation of Greece may enable an insight into a privatized identity, but perhaps only through congealing its geopolitical intimacies into a blinding opacity.

Tropics of Identity

Perusing the many national lesbian and gay magazines—hailed as signs that lesbians and gay men in the United States have been increasingly successful, albeit unevenly, in what many see as the positive goal of visibility within the public sphere—one is struck by the overwhelming advertising presence of the travel and tourism industry. Lesbians and gay men, it would seem, like to travel. At least, those who would give them economic visibility would like to think that they do—or better, would like to spur them to flex their mythically high average income in an exotically erotic locale. Advertisements for Atlantis at Club Med Resorts, for example, entice gay men with a photo of three muscled beauties atop a horizontally sloping palm tree, sunbathing under the caption "Vacation. Unparalleled." Three Atlantis resorts are listed: Huatalco, "Unspoiled tropical luxury"; Playa Blanca, "Our outrageous non-stop fiesta"; and Punta Cana, "Caribbean excitement." Yet another advertisement, in the January/February 1994 issue of 10 *Percent*, announces "The Gay and Lesbian World Travel Expo," which promises one-day seminars for both travel agencies and interested consumers. Entrepreneurs are offered the opportunity to learn more about "reaching the gay travel market." Potential tourists are lured by the following list of imperatives: "Get wild in Africa, Ski Winterfest '94, wine-taste in Italy, pilgrimage to Israel, shop in Hong Kong, party hearty at the Sydney Mardi Gras, evolve in the Galapagos Islands." As if to emphasize the potential for such activities to transform self-representation into a profound sense of entitlement, indeed a transformation of identity literally into propriety, the latest "international gay travel magazine" is called, simply, *Our World*.

I mention these advertisements, magazines, and the corporate marketing activities they signal not simply to point to their rhetorical construction of the exotic as an erotically charged tour package, although this is certainly important (an ad for First Travel, Inc., emphasizes this quite explicitly: "A different type of cruising for the gay and lesbian traveller"). Rather, I use them to signal that the elaboration (in terms of discursive production as well as of labor in general) of lesbians and gay men, quite often by lesbian and gay businesses, as a valuable market niche for the tourist industry marks both a continuation and a rearticulation of the exoticizing, vaguely erotic adventure that, as I have attempted to show, undergirds a nineteenth-century legitimation and inclusion of male homoerotic self-representations in terms of a normative cultural tradition. Today it is the tourist industry that subtends class-marked gay *and* lesbian self-representations with erotically exotic romps across the globe. The entanglements between commercial tourism and lesbian and gay public recognition indicate the irreducible complexities of self-representation, particularly for groups historically marginalized from the means of representing themselves "as such" within the public sphere. Crucially, the legitimating effects of value-coding cultural traditions as affirmatively homoerotic cannot be exhaustively understood by the opposition homophobia/affirmation guiding forms of queer publicity. That is, we cannot think of these effects as if they amounted to nothing more than the legitimate and authentic inclusion of homoeroticism in the public sphere. I would suggest, then, that because the present offers potent occasions for queer self-representation, it also offers, must offer, occasions for making the determinate conditions, such as the dynamics structuring the public traditions to which queers would seek entrée, the focus of critical attention.

FIVE Shelley's Heart

They are the mere body-snatchers of literature. —Oscar Wilde, "The Critic as Artist"

The entanglements between an imperialist axiology and nineteenth-century male homoerotic meditation in Britain point to the secretion of value within the traditions by which such meditation would legitimate itself. Legitimating homoeroticism in the public sphere thus engages with orders of value beyond the reversing of a moralizing demonization. This chapter will continue this line of thought by examining the secretion of cultural value with regard to homoerotically charged recuperations of the poet Percy Bysshe Shelley. As a point of entry for this examination, recall that Shelley's broadly humanistic statement adorning the Grecian Guild's masthead (discussed at the beginning of chapter 4) authorizes an enabling *double entendre*. Preceding pages of bulging blue boys athletically poised in G-strings and loin cloths, the Guild's quotation of Shelley endows the term "Greeks" with an ambiguous set of associations, allowing male homo-eroticism to coexist alongside a mainstream, presumptively heterosexual humanism. Here the contextual ambiguity of "Greeks" circulates both a minority, homoerotic valence and an ostensibly universal, sexually sani-tized one.[1] That the Grecian Guild chose a quotation from Shelley to autho-rize their coded use of "Greeks" might seem capricious, at best obliquely campy. After all, Shelley was married twice, fathered children, and him-self objected to what he saw as the odious practice of male same-sex sex in ancient Athens in his "A Discourse on the Manners of the Ancient Greeks Relative to the Subject of Love" (written in 1818, but not published in its entirety until 1949). Either the Grecian Guild quoted Shelley because they thought they knew something about him that perhaps others did not, or they used him precisely because they were assured of what others thought they knew.

At the same time that Shelley's statement normalizes the Grecian Guild's dubiously "normal" publication, this publication in turn lends a homo-erotic charge to Shelley's statement. Quoting Shelley in the masthead of closeted male homoerotica subtly manages to implicate Shelley himself in the context he is called upon to authorize; like the Grecian Guild, Shelley would seem to invoke "Greeks" with a knowing wink. Indeed, twenty years earlier Edward Carpenter and George Barnefield had explicitly argued that the poet had been a sexual invert, the categorization out of which crystal-lized the modern understanding of homosexuality.[2] Yet the Grecian Guild could have arguably quoted any valued cultural figure as to the enduring, foundational legacy of ancient Greece for modern Western culture (why not Alexander Pope? Matthew Arnold? Rock Hudson?). We might wonder, then, why Shelley?

While it might seem that this is only a question of perverse intentions, it is also and perhaps more importantly a question about the relationship between history and value. The Grecian Guild relied on the previous val-orization of Shelley at the same time that they rearticulated it for their own purposes. While their provocative citation of Shelley confirms the argu-ment that cultural value is subject to the vagaries of historically specific articulations, it also points to this argument's incompletion.[3] That is, this argument cannot explain the endurance and effect of cultural value even as it may be redirected beyond the limits of its generative circumstances. It would seem that the condition of possibility for rearticulating value would be its very solidity. The Grecian Guild presumably would never have even heard of Shelley, nor be assured of the normative cultural cover he could lend their publication, had the poet not survived in the usual way poets do—in editions of their poems.

Textual editions of Shelley, as the material forms of his cultural value, provided the source for the Guild's asexual humanist cover. The subcul-tural appropriation of this literary figure depended on textual editions as material bearers of cultural value within the public sphere. The Guild's sig-nification of Shelley as homoerotically suspect, however, also bears a con-tiguity to the historical *content* of such textual forms. That is, the process by which Shelley came to be valued was irreducibly entangled in nineteenth-century sexual politics: the question of Shelley's cultural value and his erotic value were in many ways one and the same. Authoritative editions of Shelley's corpus emerged out of this irreducible entanglement, and continue to bear its traces. I want to suggest that such editions, by which Shelley's canonicity has become salient, continually emit *precisely to the extent that they conceal* the politics of sexual perversity that structured Shelley's originary evaluation as important. This is achieved by the *normativity of* these canonical value-forms; the supposedly disinterested scholarship that seems to lend an innocent, ahistorical, and neutral aspect to such forms grew out of an intense fetishism of the poet (or "Shelley-love" as it was called in the nineteenth century) insofar as this fetishism had been homoerotically charged. Because they could absolve this fetishism of any overt homoerotic interest, the "scientific" apparatuses of the authoritative Shelley text encoded the displacement of erotic veneration onto normative cultural interest.[4] To the extent that authoritative editions continue to define fetishistic interest in Shelley, the originary historical content of these texts has not been entirely exhausted.

Through the following analysis of these dynamics of canonization in the Victorian cultural public sphere, this chapter will suggest a closer cautionary look at attempts to appropriate cultural figures in the formation of something like a "gay canon." Such attempts need to attend not only to the putative "gay content" of the texts at hand, but also to the forms and their histories by which cultural figures maintain their value. At least for Shelley, the historical circumstances in which his cultural value was painstakingly elaborated continue to have a residual effectivity insofar as they seem as if they have none at all.[5]

Hearts and Bones

The body of critical work on Shelley had been possessed by love of the poet ever since his death. This love found a particularly charged and enabling fetish object in Shelley's literal and figurative heart, the metaphoric site of his valorization. His physical organ was stolen by Shelley's friend Edward Trelawny from the poet's cremated corpse, argued over by Leigh Hunt and Mary Shelley, and finally installed as part of a shrine at Sir Percy Florence and Lady Jane Shelley's home, Boscombe Manor.[6] "Shrunken, half-burned, and falling into dust," Shelley's heart, Sylva Norman has observed, "was to take its independent course on earth, unburied for nearly seventy years. . . .

Its treatment has been slightly absurd, a trifle vulgar, wholly sentimental—which is not to be wondered at, since, after leaving Shelley's body, it was handled by no one free from fanaticism, exaltation, misery, or some such *abnormal feeling* towards Shelley."[7] While Shelley's scorched organ provided a material symbol of the poet's own depth of feeling, his figurative heart became the object of the "abnormal feeling" toward him that others felt: the passionate identification between Shelley's body and corpus, the loving union of aesthetic and affective value. His heart, Lady Jane Shelley claimed in her 1859 anthology *Shelley Memorials*, "could not be consumed by fire," nor had age yet ravaged his "ethereal body."[8] Like the Grecian Guild's evocation of ancient Greece, however, the slippery connotative possibilities of the term "heart" both revealed *and* concealed the erotic investments it could circulate.

In nineteenth-century England the term "heart" vacillated ambiguously between signifying what many saw as the "noble" sentiments of certain strains of Protestant morality, the rhetoric of romantic love, and the fervent stirrings of sexual desire. As a metaphor it still carries, and often bridges, the idealization of both compassion and eroticism. "Heart," according to the *Oxford English Dictionary*, can mean the "emotional nature, as distinguished from the intellectual nature," as well as "the seat of the mental or intellectual faculties." It can also signify courage, conscience, the soul, vitality, as well as "Mind" in its widest meaning, including "the functions of feeling, volition, and intellect." The more Victorian literary criticism and scholarship invested in Shelley's heart, however, the more two distinct valences of this metaphor intersected: "heart" as the originary location of erotic desire, and "heart" as "the seat of one's inmost thoughts and secret feelings" (OED). The compulsion to uncover the hidden springs of Shelley's heart, his inmost thoughts and secret feelings, echoes late-nineteenth-century articulations of sexuality as a characterological truth, as an ontology not necessarily coextensive with activity.[9] Commentators created the cultural text called Shelley by bringing together the same ingredients that made up these articulations: bodily surfaces as signs of inner truth; secondary sexual characteristics as signs of sexual difference; and sexual difference as the reigning paradigm for understanding erotic proclivities. More importantly, Shelley commentary could not avoid becoming infected by its own object of knowledge. As the discourse of Shelley-lovers created an image of the poet that would seem increasingly perverse to the

Victorian reading public, Shelley-love itself became a suspect feeling. As an anonymous reviewer commented in 1861, "It almost seems as if the waywardness, lawlessness, and impulsiveness, half weak, half fiery, of the poet's own nature, infected all who had to do with Shelley, or the memory of Shelley." [10]

How might we more precisely characterize this "abnormal feeling towards Shelley"? To begin with, professions of love for the poet often deployed his heart as an idealized metaphor for his character. Harry (né Henry) Buxton Forman, an important Victorian editor of Shelley and man of letters, claimed that "Shelley in other circumstances might have been the Saviour of the World." [11] Charles and Mary Cowden Clarke wrote that "[a] more crystalline heart than Shelley's has rarely throbbed in human bosom." [12] "He was one of the most extraordinary men that ever walked the earth," claimed Richard Henry Stoddard, "so extraordinary, I think, that Shakespeare alone could have plucked out the heart of his mystery." [13] For Victorian Shelley-lovers, plucking out the heart of Shelley's mystery often entailed delving into their own mysterious feelings. William Michael Rossetti argued that "to be a Shelley enthusiast has been the privilege of many a man in his youth, and he may esteem himself happy who cherishes the same feeling unblunted into the regions of middle or advanced age." [14] Rossetti himself received a letter from a "Mr." E. Lynn Linton (probably the author Eliza Lynn Linton, either misidentified or self-disguised) in January 1870, thanking him for his memoir, and telling him that "[a]ll my life I have been ridiculed for my love of Shelley, and told how his poetry has been my ruin; and now you come forward not only to defend but even to eulogize his lovers. . . ." [15] Adolescent idolatry and misunderstood persecution: these topoi used to represent Shelley-love constellate it within the same sphere as other pubescent feelings. This constellation indicates a contiguity between the predication of Shelley-love and modern Western sexuality in general—as a "feeling" generated in puberty and continuing "unblunted into the regions of middle or advanced age." Articulating an identity for Shelley on which his canonicity could be based thus involved a concomitant articulation of Shelley-love itself. The close identification between the figure and his fans, however, would eventually prove to be rather troubling.

In his 1870 memoir of Shelley, Rossetti recalls being told that "while out walking with a friend in Italy, Shelley was taken for a woman in man's clothes. But this feminine aspect," Rossetti warns us, "is liable to be understood in too positive a sense, especially by persons who accept the portraits in good faith." [16] Rossetti is responding to the heavily reinforced image of Shelley as a kind of androgyne (interestingly as a masculine woman, not a feminine man), an image constructed not only by those whom Robert Browning, in an 1852 essay, called his "original lovers" but also by his "foolish haters." [17] Why does Rossetti express anxiety over accepting feminized descriptions of Shelley "in good faith"? The answer can be found in the distance between somewhat "innocent" interpretations of feminized virtues in a man, characteristic of earlier nineteenth-century middle-class religious and moral ideals of an androgynous "manliness," and interpretations of such a feminized masculinity in the later part of the century as male effeminacy, associated with a host of degenerative and immoral perversities.[18]

The earlier, more "innocent" ideal of manliness circulated an androgynous mixture of (masculine) spiritual autonomy and (feminine) sentiment and purity, based loosely on interpretations of Christ by both middle-class Protestants and radical thinkers in England as embodying the virtues of both sexes. This ideal of manliness, Claudia Nelson has argued, was "thoroughly androgynous and thoroughly asexual: a shorthand for 'humanliness,' it sometimes applied to girls as well as boys." Patience, continence, compassion, and self-control were central to manliness, so that, like chastity, "true manliness may come more easily to the woman than to the man." In this sense "androgyny (if not feminization) could appear necessary to humanity's perfection." [19] However, a vocal assertion of a more virile and aggressive middle-class masculinity in mid-century signaled an intensification of the conflict between competing, class-inflected models of proper male subjectivity in the later Victorian period. After mid-century, the androgynous ideal for male subjectivity came under attack and suspicion, perhaps most famously by Charles Kingsley in his efforts to reinvigorate masculinity as "Christian manliness" (often maligned as "muscular Christianity"). This strain of middle-class manliness departs from earlier ideals. J. A. Mangan and James Walvin locate this shift roughly between 1850 and

1870, and characterize it as a movement from a "concern with a transition from Christian immaturity to maturity," to a "neo-Spartan virility." [20] Jeffrey Weeks isolates this shift in the 1860s, when a new virile and aggressive ideal of masculinity replaced the "spiritual autonomy and intellectual maturity" previously exalted by, among others, Thomas Arnold.[21] "[T]he angel in the house," Claudia Nelson argues, "was gradually reinterpreted as the degenerate in the closet. . . . To approximate femininity was no longer fashionable, and this had much to do with the fear of homosexuality. . . ."[22]

A powerful wedge that divided feminized androgyny from aggressive virility as competing masculine ideals during the later nineteenth century was an increasingly specified fear and loathing of male homoeroticism. The cultural practice of Shelley criticism and commentary became entangled with the power of this fear and loathing to reorient the public semiotics of gender and sexual behavior during this period, such that the idealization of the poet as an androgynous mixture of masculine and feminine virtues established by mid-century could be turned around by more hostile critics later on as a sign of the poet's inner degeneracy. Shelley's body thus became a kind of semiotic battleground; a war of readings in the cultural public sphere was waged to dispute or ensure the poet's cultural value in terms of middle-class gender norms. Because these norms were highly contested during the latter half of the century, Shelley criticism and biography during this same period reveals at once a willingness to accept his feminized idealization, and an uneasiness with what came to be associated with such male femininity.

The establishment of a feminized Shelley was in large measure a response to his image while alive as a depraved, dissolute atheist. The opinion of the respectable and cultured had placed Shelley's "heart" squarely in the domain of sex and desire. Most of the English middle and upper classes who knew of him viewed him as an atheist adulterer, seducing young women in the name of principles that only masked baser sentiments. R. R. Madden comments in his 1833 *Infirmities of Genius* that "[t]en years ago the indiscretions of Shelley rendered his name an unmentionable one to ears polite; but there is a reaction in public opinion, and whatever were his follies, his virtues are beginning to be known, and his poetry to be justly appreciated." [23] To purify his sullied reputation, Shelley's friends and admirers attempted to shift his "heart" out of the domain of lawless desire and into the realm of a sexless ideal of compassion, sympathy, and brotherhood.

To do so required presenting a feminized image of Shelley, an image that might allay anxieties about his lawless activities, but only at the expense of generating future concern about his queer peculiarities.

An Aesthetic Case History

Shelley's body became the central text read by Victorians in order to unravel his mystery. In his 1850 *Autobiography* Leigh Hunt highlights Shelley's "very sensitive and graceful mouth and chin" and his "naturally fair and delicate" complexion.[24] Shelley's close friend Thomas Jefferson Hogg claims in his 1858 *Life of Percy Bysshe Shelley* that "[h]is complexion was delicate and almost feminine, of the purest red and white. . . ."[25] Ernest Dowden, in his 1886 biography, consolidates a generation of Shelley images that had presented him as a young boy on the edge of adolescence: he was "slight of figure, with a well-set head, on which abundant locks, now of rich brown hue, curled naturally; his complexion was fair and ruddy like a girl's." He had "luminous, large blue eyes" that revealed "at one time a dreamy softness, at another a fixed wild beauty, or under the influence of excitement became restlessly brilliant"; "the expression of his countenance," Dowden remarks, " 'was one of exceeding sweetness and innocence,' full of animation when his interest had been aroused."[26]

Victorian commentators on Shelley were obsessed with the poet's early development. For example, the social critic W. R. Greg noted in 1873 that Shelley's youthful distaste for sports in particular was a significant symptom of his femininity: "Poor Shelley—gentle, tender, ethereal, and aspiring, sober and abstemious, a pale student, an abstract and highly metaphysical thinker, delicate as a woman in his organization, sensitive as a woman in his sympathies, loathing all that was low with a woman's shrinking, detesting all field-sports as barbarous and brutal."[27] Because of the supposedly feminine cast of his bodily and mental constitution, Shelley was regularly portrayed as unfit for the rigors of his early education outside the classroom. Rossetti notes that the "frail, shrinking, girlish Shelley . . . joined in no boyish sports from shyness and delicacy," yet emphasized that the future poet "was not made to be bullied in sheepish acquiescence. He rose in unquenched indignation against the fagging system," the practice in English public school culture of enslaving younger students to older ones.[28] As one reviewer put it, "he would not be a fag."[29]

Shelley's neglect of sports would have a significant resonance with the later Victorian middle-class reading public. As Jeffrey Richards suggests, the late-Victorian cult of athleticism grew out of and in some ways replaced the "muscular Christianity" of Hughes and Kingsley, and became especially resonant for the defense of the British empire.[30] Because sports were so bound to middle-class gender categorizations at the time, one's affinity for or aversion to athletics and games could become a sign of an essential femininity or masculinity. In this respect, Shelley's dispositions during adolescence were seen retrospectively, like symptoms, as kernels of characterological truth. However, reading Shelley's adolescence in retrospect sheds light not so much on his puberty as it does on how puberty was read by his commentators. Thomas De Quincey precisely captures this process of reading and textualization with typically fantastic Gothicism: "When one thinks of the early misery which [Shelley] suffered, and of the insolent infidelity which, being yet so young, he wooed with a lover's passion, then the darkness of midnight begins to form a deep, impenetrable background, upon which the phantasmagoria of all that is to come may arrange itself in troubled phosphoric streams, and in sweeping processions of woe."[31]

In many ways Shelley's pubescent body formed the "deep, impenetrable background" upon which was arrayed his truth. His adolescent irregularities dominate accounts of his life, so much so that they describe a body and temperament arrested at the threshold between child and adult, innocence and desire, androgyny and the decisive differentiation of secondary sexual characteristics. For example, a remarkable amount of effort went into delineating the nature of his voice, reputedly high, weak, and shrill. Shelley's friend and cousin Thomas Medwin, in his 1847 biography, originates this characteristic in his youth: his voice at Sion House was "soft and low, but broken in its tones,—when anything much interested him, harsh and unmodulated; and this peculiarity he never lost."[32] For J. A. Symonds Shelley's voice signified the essential truth of the poet's character: "This peculiar voice, varying from moment to moment and affecting different sensibilities in divers ways, corresponds to the high-strung passion of his life, his fine-drawn and ethereal fancies, and the clear vibrations of his palpitating verse. Such a voice, far-reaching, penetrating, and unearthly, befitted one who lived in rarest ether on the topmost heights of human thought."[33]

Arrested, androgynous adolescence became the norm for imaging Shelley's body and character. De Quincey, borrowing a phrase from the Rev. George Gilfillan, called Shelley "the eternal child"; Trelawny wrote that Shelley "had seen no more of the working-day world than a girl at a boarding-school. . . ." "What Shelley was at first he remained to the last," claimed Coventry Patmore, "a beautiful, effeminate, arrogant boy. . . ." Peter George Patmore recalls Hazlitt speculating, with pre-Freudian pre-science, that Shelley's peculiarities arose from the Shelley family romance: "[H]is features had an unnatural sharpness, and an unhealthy paleness, like a flower that has been kept from the light of day; his eyes had an almost superhuman brightness, and his voice a preternatural elevation of pitch and shrillness of tone;—all which peculiarities probably arose from some accidental circumstances connected with his early nurture and bringing up." Medwin mentions that upon entering Sion House Shelley exchanged "for the caresses of his sisters an association with boys" who would reject him for his "girlishness." As the anonymous reviewer of Hogg's *Life* comments, "His education, in short, began at the wrong end." [34]

As if to ward off any perverse implications of Shelley's "unnatural" and "unhealthy" constitution stemming from an irregular upbringing, narratives of Shelley frequently deny him the masculine libido of the post-adolescent that nineteenth-century commentators in England would have thought natural and normal in a young man. De Quincey commented in 1845 that Shelley had a "purity from all fleshliness of appetite." James Anthony Froude claimed in 1883 that "Shelley, however free his theories, was a person on whose imagination a licentious image had never left a stain." [35] In his 1909 study of British romantic writers, Arthur Symons recognized the potential perversity that Shelley's femininity could suggest, and countered this danger with Shelley's sexlessness: "To Shelley the word love meant sympathy, and that word, in that sense, contains his whole life and creed. . . . It is a love which is almost sexless, the love of an enthusiastic youth, or of his own hermaphrodite. He was so much of a sentimentalist that he could conceive of incest [in *The Cenci*] without repugnance, and be so innocently attracted by so many things which, to one more *normally sexual*, would have indicated perversity. Shelley is not perverse, but he is fascinated by every problem of evil, which draws him to contemplate it with a child's enquiring wonder of horror." [36] "Shelley could touch pitch," Symons claims, "and be undefiled."

Rather than making him perverse, it would seem that Shelley's femininity endowed him with the Victorian ideal of feminine "passionlessness." "His love for women," Symons maintains, "seems never to have been sensuous, or at least to have been mostly a matter of sympathies and affinities; if *other things followed*, it seemed to him natural that they should, and he encouraged them with a kind of unconsciousness." The love figured in Shelley's poem *Epipsychidion* is "sisterly," and thus reveals "the deepest thing that Shelley had to say," letting out "the secret of his feminine or twy-fold soul."[37]

The Angel in the Closet

Not everyone could extend De Quincey's and Symons's interpretive generosity with such ease. Matthew Arnold, for one, palpably presents the ambivalence that Shelley's femininity could inspire. In perhaps the most famous Victorian estimate of the poet, Arnold comments at the end of an 1881 essay on Byron that Shelley was "a beautiful and ineffectual angel, beating in the void his luminous wings in vain."[38] Arnold's characterization calls on an ideal figure that had already become well known: the angel-wife idealized by Ruskin and Patmore. Seven years after casting Shelley as a beautiful and ineffectual angel, however, Arnold had occasion to mourn the loss of this image. In his 1888 review of Ernest Dowden's authorized two-volume *Life of Percy Bysshe Shelley*, Arnold expresses deep regret that the image of Shelley as "the soul of affection" had been tarnished by Dowden's account of the poet's alleged mistreatment of his first wife, Harriet. "It is a sore trial for our love of Shelley," Arnold laments.[39] Yet he argues strenuously that despite the reemergence of the free-love Shelley, the poet's old angelic image still remained. While repeating anecdotes provided by Dowden of Shelley's "feminine refinement" and "high and tender seriousness," Arnold quotes one last testament that significantly authorizes all the others by virtue of the ostensibly unimpeachable source. "Feminine enthusiasm" for the poet "may be deemed suspicious," Arnold claims after quoting a particularly effusive and loving portrait of Shelley by a certain Miss Rose, "but a Captain Kennedy must surely be able to keep his head."[40] This military epitome of masculinity, who after meeting Shelley characterized him as "beautifully fair," "exquisitely fine," with a "great delicacy of constitution" and a gait that was "decidedly not military" — in short, a characterization of a man "different from other men" — could not be impugned as a source, not even if he himself displayed a most feminine enthusiasm for the poet. Arnold ends his recuperation of the angelic Shelley with Captain Kennedy's virile stamp of approval.

That Arnold felt the need to use Captain Kennedy's authorizing masculinity registers, I would argue, the need to detach homoerotic overtones not only from Shelley's feminization, but also from the "feminine enthusiasm" many believed characterized Shelley-love itself. The critical attraction must seem as pure as the idealized images. By presenting Shelley himself as diseased and degenerate, critics such as Carlyle, Ruskin, and especially Kingsley had laid the foundations earlier in the century for reading Shelley-love as guilty by association. Contrasting Shelley to what he termed the "naked force" of Frederick the Great (who ironically had a reputed taste for boys), Carlyle called the poet "weak in genius, weak in character (for these two always go together); a poor, thin, spasmodic, hectic, shrill and pallid being." Shelley filled the earth, Carlyle believed, with "inarticulate wail," subjecting the English public to his "hysterical" rather than "strong or robust" temperament.[41] Carlyle's condemnation infected John Ruskin, who adds this footnote to his 1846 essay "The Imagination Contemplative," where he compares a passage from Scott's Lady of the Lake to Shelley's Alastor: "Let it not be supposed that I mean to compare the sickly dreaming of Shelley over clouds and waves, with the masculine and magnificent grasp of men and things which we find in Scott. . . ."[42] Ruskin's rhetoric displays the way sexual difference could be used to delineate aesthetic distinctions. Yet the opposition between masculine and feminine was not always enough to praise masculinity and condemn femininity; Ruskin himself certainly had a notion of feminine virtue. The vehemence of the condemnation lies not only in deviance from norms of masculinity, but also in the association of such deviance with sexual nonconformity.

The pernicious, parasitic attachment of gender norms to understandings of erotic tastes, especially as it affected Shelley's image, is a hallmark of Charles Kingsley's 1853 essay "Thoughts on Shelley and Byron" (published anonymously). Kingsley was concerned that Shelley's femininity, together with his growing popularity among the Victorian literati, were symptomatic of an age on the road to degeneracy, decadence, and political decay: "The private tipping of eau-de-cologne, say the London physicians, has increased mightily of late; and so has the reading of Shelley."[43] Oddly enough, Kingsley contrasts the "effeminate" Shelley with the "sturdy" Byron, aristocrats both, as compass points for the possible directions English society might take: "The age is an effeminate one; and it can well afford to pardon the lewdness of the genteel and sensitive vegetarian [Shelley], while it has no mercy for that of the sturdy peer [Byron], proud of his bull-neck and his boxing, who kept bears and bulldogs, drilled Greek ruffians at Missolonghi, and 'had no objection to a pot of beer;' and who might, if he had reformed, have made a gallant English gentleman; while Shelley, if once his intense self-opinion had deserted him, would have probably ended in Rome, as an Oratorian or a Passionist." [44] Byron might indeed have "drilled" Greek ruffians, but apparently Shelley did not have such powers of penetration.

Kingsley's invocation of Rome situates Shelley within the religious controversy between Kingsley's "virile" Protestantism and what he saw as the "effeminacies" of the Anglo-Catholic movement, exemplified by John Henry (later Cardinal) Newman and the religious brotherhoods and quasi-monastic communities associated with the Tractarians, such as the Oratorians and the Passionists. As David Hilliard has pointed out, "At the end of the nineteenth century the conflict between Protestant and Anglo-Catholicism within the Church of England was still regularly depicted by Protestant propagandists as a struggle between masculine and feminine styles of religion." [45] Coding this religious controversy by gender, however, did not involve a simple binarism between masculine and feminine. For Kingsley the "femininity" of Anglo-Catholicism was unnatural and unhealthy precisely because it was "effeminacy," a word often used by Kingsley to refer to male homoeroticism. "Kingsley is never explicit about homosexuality," Norman Vance points out, "in common with most of his contemporaries, but he leaves it open to the reader to suspect that the 'maundering, die-away effeminacy' of the 'Manichees' [Newman and the Tractarians] who repress the instinct to marry and be conventionally manly may include this element of unspoken and unspeakable sin. Unnatural vice, unnatural at least by the standards of the 1850s, would be an appropriately awful consequence of unnatural contempt for one's ordinary physical nature [exemplified by the celibacy of the Tractarians]." [46] According to Kingsley, Shelley really would have preferred an effeminate and unnatural celibacy, passionate only in the glorious sight of Christ's Passion, to Byron's drilling, bullnecks, and beer.

By 1859, as one reviewer put it, Shelley's reputation had been "hunted down by an obloquy more bitter and unsparing than that which persecuted even Lord Byron himself. Good men have insisted upon confounding the errors of his head with a deep-seated depravity of heart, without making any allowance for the eccentricities of genius, or for the want of experience common to youth."[47] Thornton Hunt, Leigh Hunt's son, responded to this obloquy four years later. The younger Hunt attempted to allay anxieties about Shelley's alleged femininity, to set his image straight, so to speak. Through a combination of bodily re-creation and tales of heroic derring-do, Hunt wanted to indicate "the amount of 'grit' that lay under the outward appearance of weakness and excitable nerves."[48] Shelley, he claims, regularly and energetically hiked across Hampstead Heath with the young Thornton, and on one occasion carried a fatigued woman all the way to the Hunt household. Moreover, Hunt suggests that Shelley tampered with "venal pleasures" while at college. It may not have done much for his health, as Hunt points out, but the suggestion of dissipation could dispel the image of Shelley as a libido-less, and thus unnatural, angel. Hunt also returns to Shelley's body the telling signs of secondary sexual characteristics denied him by others. Hunt emphasizes the "girth" of Shelley's thorax, as well as a chest that had grown "3 or 4 inches" during Shelley's first residence in Italy. "The outline of the features and face," Hunt observes, "possessed a firmness and hardness entirely inconsistent with a feminine character. . . . The beard also, although the reverse of strong, was clearly marked, especially about the chin. Thus, although the general aspect was peculiarly slight, youthful, and delicate, yet, when you looked 'to the points' of the animal, you saw well enough the indications of a masculine vigour, in many respects far above the average." Shelley's "masculine vigour" permeated every tender fiber of Shelley's body and every expression that crossed his face, all of which "bespoke a manly, and even a commanding character." Even Shelley's infamous voice, Hunt argues, was not *really* a falsetto, but rather a "high natural counter-tenor."[49]

Hunt may be splitting hairs, but his efforts register an anxiety about the implications of a feminized Shelley. More importantly, Hunt's positive citation of Shelley's alleged "venal pleasures" while in college indicates that this feminization implied more damaging forms of depravity than Shelley's adultery: better to have a healthy masculine appetite than a diseased effeminacy. Hunt's tactics to masculinize Shelley attempted to shift the poet into a proper domain of middle-class male gender norms and cross-sex sexual behavior that began to consolidate by mid-century. But as John Addington Symonds's denigration of effeminacy and celebration of homoerotic virility in his 1878 "A Problem in Greek Ethics" shows, normative masculinity could *also* be appropriated by homosexual apologists; the Grecian Guild clearly inherited this butch idiom. If sexual perversity could be linked both to gender deviance *and* disengaged from it, a line pursued by Symonds and the virile homoerotica of the Grecian Guild, how could the cultural value of Shelley be discharged of such messy irregularities and confusions? How could the creation of Shelley as a publicly valuable cultural and canonical ego-ideal displace the constant threat, whether he was masculine *or* feminine, of a homoerotic identification? How could Shelley-love be pursued without tainting its textual erotics with perversity?

An 1841 speech by the barrister T. N. Talfourd on behalf of the publisher Edward T. Moxon, who was fighting a suit filed to halt the publication of Shelley's supposedly indecent writings, can provide a clue. The suspect passages of Shelley's poems, Talfourd argues, "like details and pictures in works of astronomy and surgery, are either innocent or criminal, according to the accompaniments which surround them, and the class to whom they are addressed." Such context makes a difference, he continues, because if "really intended for the eye of the scientific student, they are *most innocent;* but if so published as to manifest *another intention,* they will not be protected from legal censure by the flimsy guise of science. By a similar test let this publication be judged." [50] The "scientific" interests of the editor, scholar, or student, according to Talfourd, provide a kind of Teflon that deflects any impure prurience associated with Shelley-love. As a review of Rossetti's 1870 *Poetical Works* notes, the Shelley editor needs "an interest in his author passing the ordinary love of editors." [51] Such extraordinary love would need to peer at Shelley with the "eye of the scientific student" if it were to avoid entanglement in Shelley's own supposed perversities. Shelley-love would need editorial methodologies that could effectively transform Shelley's inordinate erotic value into what could publicly pass as normative cultural value.

The Textual Fetish

In February 1872, Ford Maddox Brown held a small party to which William Michael Rossetti brought an unusual party favor. Rossetti had just procured

a piece of Shelley's skull from an aging Trelawny, and unveiled his possession to his intimate, fascinated group of friends. "It was curious to observe
the different feelings with which the sight of the fragment of Shelley's skull
was received by different people. Mathilde Blind changed countenance in a
moment: her eyes suffused, and she put the fragment fervently to her lips.
Next to her, [William Bell] Scott seems the most impressed—also [John
Westland] Marston, [Ford Maddox] Brown and his family, and some others
in varying degrees. Swinburne, to my surprise, paid next to no attention
to the matter. [Dante] Gabriel [Rossetti] passed it off jokingly, but was
interested nevertheless." [52]

Mathilde Blind's response seems to correspond rather loosely to an an-
thropological definition of fetishism: the valuation of an object as the material repository of a deity's presence. In the later nineteenth century the
epistemology of fetishism was also used to label a particularly perverse
form of erotic valuation (not to mention Marx's famous use of fetishism
to describe the work of commodification). [53] In Freud's recasting of fetishism in the *Three Essays on the Theory of Sexuality* and the 1927 essay "Fetishism," for example, the perversion's defining characteristic is a double and
contradictory attitude: the fetishist believes that what an object represents
"lives" in that object, yet the very fact that it must be re-presented by a substitute object implicitly acknowledges the original's absence. This contradictory attitude approximates the fantasy involved in re-creating the presence of an author through imagining a fully present intention organizing
an authoritative text. A review of Lady Jane Shelley's 1859 *Shelley Memorials* states quite unambiguously an axiom of nineteenth-century Shelley
criticism: "The poetry of Shelley corresponds to his life. It contains many
passages of nobleness and beauty; it abounds in grace, delicacy, and refinement; and yet it is essentially *faulty, unnatural, and incongruous.*" [54] Like
the Freudian fetishist, this axiom denies (and thus paradoxically acknowledges) Shelley's absence through a metaphysically enduring presence in his
poems.

Beyond being epistemological analogs, the valuations built into Shelley's
authoritative texts and those in Freud's understandings of sexual fetishism both bear witness to the particular contorting power of heteronormativity, as well as the conditions it can create for enabling displacements
and appropriations. The compensatory presence of Shelley in editions of
his works also accomplishes what Freud believed sexual fetishism accom-

163

plished. Freud famously describes fetishism both in the *Three Essays* and in his 1927 essay as a "compromise" that enables the fetishist to avoid becoming homosexual, while allowing him to forgo confronting the traumatic "truth" of the castration threat. Thus fetishism occupies a liminality with respect both to deviance and normality: it "borders on the pathological," yet it also has a "point of contact with the normal." [55] According to Freud, fetishism allows for a disjunction between fantasy and activity, and thus operates as a kind of defense mechanism that testifies to the need to make heterosexuality palatable, and homosexuality workable. It points to the fetishist's attempts to maintain the value of homoeroticism in the face of its social devaluation. It is a liminal deviance that allows one to pass as normal and at the same maintain one's homoerotic fantasies.

A case history he mentions in the 1927 essay bears testimony to this enabling aversion, yet is read by Freud only in terms of sexual difference, uncomplicated by a difference of object-choice. He tells of a man who fetishized "an athletic support-belt which could also be worn as bathing drawers": "This piece of clothing covered up the genitals entirely and concealed the distinction between them. Analysis showed that it signified that women were castrated and that they were not castrated, and it also allowed the hypothesis that men were castrated, for all these possibilities could equally well be concealed under the belt—the earliest rudiment of which in his childhood had been the fig-leaf on a statue." [56] Freud's case history subtly reveals an enabling, opaque displacement: the fetishized jock strap allows the fetishist to reconfigure the gender of object-choice in *fantasy*, in and through an ostensibly heteronormative erotic scenario. This particular case illustrates fetishism as an instance of having your cake and eating it too—without anyone knowing.

Other sexologists affirmed this peculiarly enabling erotic refraction, the fetish's ability to allow the fetishist to pass. Krafft-Ebing argues in *Psychopathia Sexualis* that "it often happens that the fetichist diminishes his excitability to *normal* stimuli by his perversion, or, at least, is capable of coitus only by means of concentration of his fancy upon his fetich." [57] Similarly, Havelock Ellis describes a case history, from Goron's *Les Parias de l'Amour*, of a man who fell in love with the shadow of a woman changing clothes in a window. He returned to the spot every evening to gaze longingly at the shadow, or at the spot where it would hopefully appear: "Yet—and herein lies the fetichism—he made no attempt to see the woman or to find out who she was; the shadow sufficed; he had no need of the reality."[58] Perhaps with this case in mind and thus revealing the terms of its fantastic structuring, Jacques Lacan describes such a fetishistic voyeur in his essay "The Partial Drive and its Circuit": "What the voyeur is looking for and finds is merely a shadow, a shadow behind the curtain. There he will phantasize any magic of presence, the most graceful of girls, for example, even if on the other side there is only a hairy athlete."[59]

It would sound as if my rhetorical use of Lacan's joke attempts to transform his "even if" into an "especially because," from a conditional hyperbole to an emphatic causality. But I want to underline that this "even if" carries the weight of a powerfully enabling ambiguity: according to late-nineteenth- and early-twentieth-century sexological thought, the fetishist avoids homosexuality *not* through repression, but through a compromise that generates a subjunctive indecipherability. However, the fetishism involved in canonizing Shelley did not render the poet's *own* perversities indecipherable, but rather those of his lovers. That is, the authoritative text *integrated* Shelley-love into the ostensibly nonerotic practice of humanistic scholarship, such that this could be indulged *as if* it were "normal." What makes the text authoritative is precisely a naturalistic inclusion of every textual irregularity, every sign of the poet's genius made present by the text. As the reviewer of Shelley *Memorials* acknowledged, Shelley's texts have as much grace and delicacy, unnaturalness and incongruity, as Shelley himself. "No poetry is more sincere than Shelley's," Arthur Symons claimed, "because his style is a radiant drapery clinging closely to the body which it covers."[60]

The editorial apparatus could unflinchingly present Shelley's body/corpus, his "emasculated," "corrupt," or indeed "perverse" texts because the authoritative text fetishistically refracts Shelley's "perversities" into scholarly questions of punctuation, spelling, and style, determined in turn by the very presence they authorize. Translating Shelley's bodily and mental perversities into questions of "corrupt" texts, "deviant" readings, and Shelley's own "perverse" orthography provided Shelley-lovers with a normative cover for their increasingly suspect interest in the poet. In this way their vice, and indeed Shelley's own, could become editorial virtues. The "critical autopsy" of Shelley (characterized approvingly by Harry Buxton Forman as "these days of eager and ceaseless disinterment") did not just create convenient and useful tools for disinterested scholarship. The sexually charged debates about Shelley in the nineteenth century demonstrate most potently that the presumably neutral mechanisms of editing Shelley were so only to the extent that they had something to neutralize.[61]

The two most important Shelley editors in the late nineteenth century, William Michael Rossetti and Henry Buxton Forman, successfully accomplished this passionate project. In the memoir introducing his two-volume *The Complete Poetical Works of Percy Bysshe Shelley* (1870, revised in three volumes 1878), Rossetti argues that in Shelley "a truly glorious poetic genius was united with, or was one manifestation of, the most transcendent beauty of character, —flecked, indeed, here and there by semi-endearing perversities, or by some manifest practical aberration. However this may be, he commends into love and homage every emotion of the soul and every perception of the mind."[62] Rossetti followed this invitation to love, clothing his devotion with the commands of scholarship. In his revised preface to the 1878 reissue, Rossetti skillfully translates the love of Shelley's body into the restitution of his text as a proper substitute: "From all critics and all cooperators I hope to have learned something: the only object worth editing for being that of securing the utmost purity and rationality of text, and so helping to diffuse a knowledge—which is also a *love*—of the glorious poet's work."[63] Donald Reiman has correctly pointed out that for Rossetti the standards of purity and rationality demand an editorial creativity in reconstructing poetic intention—what Rossetti termed "conjectural emendation," and what a reviewer of Rossetti's edition called "the rectification of annoying grammatical negligences."[64] This involves correcting, for example, "absolutely wrong" grammar, meter, and rhyme. Rather than hiding the true Shelley, however, Rossetti believed such creativity would better restore him, paradoxically making much clearer Shelley's peculiarities and development. Thus, even though Rossetti acknowledges that Shelley's juvenilia is "not only poorish sort of stuff, but absolute and heinous rubbish," nothing better than "rant and resonance, twaddle and tinsel," it still "interests me as being Shelley's, and ought in my opinion to interest everybody to whom the later developments of that astonishing mind are dear."[65] By positioning an austere aesthetic judgment alongside a high-pitched love and devotion, Shelley-love's "feminine enthusiasm" could be fetishistically reworked into cultural authority and production, enabling a safe retention of the text's erotic pull.

Forman, in his four-volume *The Poetical Works of Percy Bysshe Shelley* (1876–77), follows Rossetti's voyeuristic lead while raising the status of maintaining Shelley's textual perversities to an unimpeachable editorial principle. He claims intention as his ultimate standard, but grants that this often raises more questions than it answers. Like Rossetti, Forman presents Shelley's irregularities of writing as the very signs of intention, predicated on a previously established image of Shelley's perverse subjectivity: "The lesson we have to learn is that it was inherent in the very nature of Shelley's mind that certain unevenness[es], inconsistencies, and divergences of practice should find place in his work, and that, instead of suspecting corruption where these occur, we should feel satisfied of incorruption, and do all in our power to preserve the fruit of his spirit intact,—not try to make it the fruit of some other and lesser spirit." [66] Thus Shelley's own fastidiousness, Forman claims, created the "marvelously corrupt state of the original edition of *Laon and Cythna*," largely because "the minute history of Shelley's mind . . . is unfolded to us in the peculiarities and inconsistencies of his orthography, etc. . . ." [67] Here Forman follows the by then established practice of directly identifying Shelley's texts with the poet himself. Measuring editorial practice by faithfulness to Shelley's intention, moreover, is a principle derived from devotion to the poet. Previous editors had corrected and covered over Shelley's textual perversities, Forman claims, out of a "want of veneration" and "a failure to perceive that one man is *not* as good as another, and that Shelley's eccentricities, even his errors if errors there be, must be far more interesting to intelligent humanity at large than the punctilious correctness of intelligent mediocrity." [68] Editing Shelley could normalize Shelley-love by actually requiring the presence of the poet's perversity, thus subsuming desire into the demands of scholarship. Forman effectively transfigures a "perverse" subjectivity into a textuality governed by truth, a truth enabling, satisfying, and normalizing the desire for the poet.

Forman and Rossetti sought to make fully present, because "interesting," Shelley's orgasmic "intellectual passion and . . . depth of ideal sympathy that in moments of excitement fused all the powers of his mind into a continuous stream of creative energy, and gave the stamp of something like inspiration to all the highest productions of his muse." [69] Editing Shelley's metaphorically orgasmic poems, however, could itself entrance without anyone coming to the wrong conclusion. Forman could thus successfully claim that "We who love Shelley and his poetry can afford to take him as he is. . . ." [70] Embedding Shelley-love in the value-form of the authoritative text enabled, precisely to the extent that it normatively disguised, the homoerotic dynamics underwriting his canonical worship. By doing so, the sexual politics predicating the establishment of Shelley's cultural value became the silent yet effective partner in the enterprise of Shelley scholarship. Authoritative Shelley texts have become, to borrow from Marx, homoerotic hieroglyphs that continually bear witness to the normalizing entanglements between erotic and aesthetic valuation in the Victorian cultural public sphere. To the extent that gay recuperations of cultural figures may unwittingly inhabit these entanglements, recuperation as a practice of value will continue to secrete, in both senses of the word, its conditions of possibility.

Beyond Tolerance

The bourgeois, however, is tolerant. His love of people as they are stems from his hatred of what they might be. —Theodor Adorno, MINIMA MORALIA

In his 1798 *The Contest of the Faculties*, Kant decries the false republicanism of the British Parliament. To say that the House of Lords and the House of Commons limit the power of the British monarchy, Kant argues, is to dissimulate their true nature. Casting members of Parliament as "representatives of the people" flies in the face of what "everyone knows perfectly well" — that "the monarch's influence on these representatives is so great and so certain that nothing is resolved by the Houses except what he wills and purposes through his minister."[1] If Parliament was no more than a rubber stamp for the royal will, how was it dissimulated as an organ of popular sovereignty? The exception, Kant argues, proves the rule. Every so often the king "proposes resolutions in connection with which he knows that he will be contradicted, and even arranges it that way (for example, with regard to slave-trade) in order to provide a fictitious proof of the freedom of Parliament" (163). This approach "has something delusive about it so that the true constitution, faithful to law, is no longer sought at all; for a person imagines he has found it in an example already at hand, and a false publicity [*lügendhafte Publicität*] deceives the people with the illusion of a limited monarchy in power by a law which issues from them, while their representatives, won over by bribery, have secretly subjected them to an absolute monarchy" (163).

Kant's criticism here occurs in the context of delineating the obstacles to world progress, specifically those relating to publicity. Interestingly, Kant warns against investing too much faith in the ability or the interest of the state in protecting popular sovereignty or advancing enlightenment. The state alone cannot be entrusted with an enlightened representativeness because its only desire is to rule. Rather, it is only through publicity that legitimate grievances can be heard; thus any restriction of publicity "impedes the progress of a people toward improvement, even in that which applies to the least of its claims, namely its simple, natural right" (161). Moreover, only through an unimpeded publicity can philosophers, who as "enlighteners [Aufklärer]" are "persons dangerous to the state" (161), advance the claims of the people and thus encourage an enlightened representativeness.

Kant's criticism of a mendacious publicity cautions against more than outright censorship. It cautions against both a naïve trust in the state's interest in fully representing its constituencies, and a publicity that acts as no more than a legitimating prop for powerful interests. What Kant skillfully describes here is the extent to which the pretense of a free publicity can dissimulate its protection of entrenched interests and thus its own disconnection from both "enlighteners" and "the people." Even one of the most ardent supporters of the ideal of publicity was well aware that this ideal could be dissembled as legitimately subjunctive, thus thwarting its role as a vehicle for social enfranchisement.

The preceding chapters have sought to problematize this subjunctive aspect of the public sphere, specifically as it impacts queer representation. Queer representation, I have argued, can expose the limits of publicity as a paradigm through which varieties of experience are translated into a social, cultural, and political legitimacy—or rather, publicity in its dominant conceptualization and materialization. For alongside a critique of the public sphere in contradiction with democratic enfranchisement, the preceding explorations have also sought to emphasize the need not for a simplistic rejection of publicity dynamics as they are currently constituted, but rather for progressive ethical and political reworkings of them. This need occupies a central place in leftist critique that abjures a romantic alterity at the same time that it strives for a minimally utopian self-determination.

It is worth emphasizing that this need opens up within, rather than outside of, practices of value. Value determination pinpoints the processes by which the public sphere betrays its own promise, and by which it dissimulates this betrayal. Yet practices of value also constitute the vital resources that emerge from oppositional counterpublic spheres. Formed alongside of and often from within a dominant publicity, these counterpublic spheres can produce queer practices and experiences that exceed a restrictively normalized lesbian and gay identity. Their excesses provide vital resources for reimagining how democratic sociality and civic belonging might be shaped, not the least because their valuations may follow a different set of standards and judgments. Thus while it is important that these resources emerge out of oppositional spheres, it is surely as important for them to extend into and inform the character of a more general publicness.

For them to do so requires an ethical and political judgment attuned to the utopian possibilities of self-determination and social participation. Whether aesthetic, moral, or political, judgment hinges the mediation between the universal and the particular, the abstract and the concrete, norms and their materializations. In this sense it is a practice of value that brings together public and private, morality and ethics, social life and individual experience. Submitted to critique, judgment would seem to present an exacting and alien process. Yet it can also present a strength, for it is a mode that saturates those powerfully vital sites of belonging and self-making that queers can inhabit at any moment and in any place. What indeed we risk in pushing for a conformist political agenda is precisely that resource by which we could contribute to a larger project of democratized enfranchisement.

For oppositional queer resources to inform a more general publicness requires moving beyond the lie of liberal pluralism—the lie that a supposedly neutral state apparatus and a capitalized media can fully accommodate competing political visions and ways of life. This lie animates the conformism by which mainstream lesbian and gay politics imagines enfranchisement. The inclusion of lesbians and gay men in the public sphere, so it goes, both represents and contributes to a greater (if uneven) tolerance for homosexuals. This account of inclusion and its effects is in a sense correct. The classic bourgeois public sphere, conceived by an emergent middle class championing freedom of association and conscience, ideally guarantees a minimal privacy that at the same time operates as a paradoxical formula for social cohesion. In this regard politics becomes more an administrative than a moral affair. Political will formation, to use Habermas's terminology, acquires a managerial function in relation to competing and often incompatible cultural traditions, political views, and ways of life. Thus the claim that inclusion both signals and generates tolerance is also mistaken, if for no other reason than its own failure to recognize tolerance for what it is: the transformation of political aspiration into a managed inequity. Tolerance is the ruse by which respect for differences covers over a legitimated disrespect.

Tolerance is thus a false hope because it engenders a false sense of democratic sociality and belonging. And perhaps more importantly, as Adorno indicates in the epigraph, tolerance utterly neglects, indeed implicitly rejects, the utopian energies of self-determination insofar as these energies aim for more than an administrative maintenance of antagonism. The antagonisms animating modern social movements and political struggles rise up at the failure of the universal—which is to say, at the failure to recognize the socially transformative force the universal both contains and more often than not distorts. Such failure cannot be a legitimated feature of administering the universal. To move beyond this limiting vision of social and political self-governance demands an ethically attuned judgment that holds accountable a public sphere promising with one hand and retracting with the other. Such judgment must come not simply from those organizations and outlets that throw all their faith into forms of social life already legitimated by the state, but rather from counterpublic spheres that imagine enfranchisement and social belonging as more than an administrative conformity. In this sense we might rewrite Kant's pessimism about the capability of people to be enlightened. He cautions against expecting too much from one's fellow citizens because this will lead only to disappointment. Given his astute criticism of a dissimulative publicity, however, we should rather caution against hoping for too much from the state or dominant forms of publicity as appropriate venues for fully respecting queer life, "lest we fall prey with good reason to the mockery of the politician who would willingly take the hope of man as the dreaming of a distraught mind" (167).

NOTES

INTRODUCTION *Homoeroticism and the Public Sphere*

1   Because identity terms can condense powerful affective and political investments, a note
    on terminology here is appropriate. When I use the terms *lesbian and gay*, I mean to in-
    dicate their official circulation, as in the National Gay and Lesbian Task Force, or *Out*,
    which bills itself as "America's best-selling gay and lesbian magazine." These are de-
    scriptors of an officially sanctioned identity. When I use the term *queer*, I mean to mix
    both description and advocacy. The latter includes a certain utopian instability of ref-
    erence, along with an intended movement away from the officialness (and increasing
    officiousness) of *lesbian and gay*, in affiliation with a more progressively radical direction
    for erotic nonconformity. By bringing *homoeroticism* within the referential orbit of *queer*, I
    thus do not mean to suggest that *homoeroticism* in any way exhausts, even as it anchors,
    queer's designative possibilities.

2   For more on the translation of *Öffentlichkeit* into English, see the "Translator's Note" to
    Jürgen Habermas, *The Structural Transformation of the Public Sphere: An Inquiry into a Cate-
    gory of Bourgeois Society*, trans. Thomas Burger with Frederick Lawrence (Cambridge, MA:
    MIT P, 1991), xv–xvi. Habermas himself has recently clarified "publicness" as a relational
    quality; see his *Between Facts and Norms: Contributions to a Discourse Theory of Law and Democ-
    racy*, trans. William Rehg (Cambridge, MA: MIT P, 1996), 360–68. Oskar Negt and Alex-
    ander Kluge are particularly instructive on publicity as an ambiguated relation between
    material sites and normative qualities: "The public sphere denotes specific *institutions*,
    agencies, practices (e.g., those connected with law enforcement, the press, public opin-
    ion, the public, public sphere work, streets, and public squares); however, it is also a
    general social *horizon of experience* in which everything that is actually or ostensibly rele-
    vant for all members of society is integrated" (*Public Sphere and Experience: Toward an Analysis
    of the Bourgeois and Proletarian Public Sphere*, trans. Peter Labanyi, Jamie Owen Daniel, and
    Assenka Oksiloff [Minneapolis: U of Minnesota P, 1993], 1–2; original emphases).

3   Jürgen Habermas, *Structural Transformation* 28. In subsequent citations from this work, I
    have occasionally modified the translation when warranted by context or emphasis.

4   Ibid. 50.

5 Ibid. 52.
6 Ibid. 85. For an extended discussion of these historical foundations for the bourgeois public sphere, see *Structural Transformation* 43–56, 102–17, and *The Theory of Communicative Action, Volume 2: Lifeworld and System: A Critique of Functionalist Reason*, trans. Thomas McCarthy (Boston: Beacon P, 1987), 328–29. Catherine Hall and Leonore Davidoff have similarly argued for the social historical importance of the English middle-class family in the conceptualization of public virtue in the late eighteenth and early nineteenth century; see *Family Fortunes: Men and Women of the English Middle Class, 1780–1950* (Chicago: U of Chicago P, 1987).
7 Habermas, *Between Facts and Norms* 374.
8 Lauren Berlant and Michael Warner, "Sex in Public," *Critical Inquiry* 24 (winter 1998): 548 n. 2. Berlant has also persuasively argued that contemporary public representations, mostly via national media culture, tend to "sexualize" citizenship and a national imaginary, at the same time that sexuality is presented as a private issue; see *The Queen of America Goes to Washington City: Essays on Sex and Citizenship* (Durham: Duke UP, 1997).
9 By "bourgeois publicity" I mean to indicate those norms guiding public discourse, its operations, and its organizational settings that owe allegiance to the historical triumph of bourgeois values and capitalist social formations. While in some respect these values and formations may indeed be discontinuous with each other, I would argue that there are still vital points of contact, even as class has been rethought and reorganized in some significant ways by late capitalism; see Negt and Kluge, *Public Sphere and Experience* xliv.

As will hopefully become apparent, the subjunctive mood, or what in logic is called "contrafactual conditionals," has a problematic relation to truth claims, even as subjunctive statements tend to clothe themselves precisely *as* truth claims. As W. V. Quine has noted, this presents significant difficulties for logic: "Whatever the proper analysis of the contrafactual conditional may be, we may be sure in advance that it cannot be truth-functional; for obviously ordinary usage demands that some contrafactual conditionals with false antecedents and false consequents be true and that other contrafactual conditionals with false antecedents and false consequents be false. . . . It may be wondered, indeed, whether any really coherent theory of the contrafactual conditional of ordinary usage is possible at all. . . . The problem of contrafactual conditionals is in any case a perplexing one, and it belongs not to pure logic but to the theory of meaning or possibly the philosophy of science" (*Methods of Logic*, 4th ed. [1950; Cambridge, MA: Harvard UP, 1982], 23). Quine's exclusion of contrafactual conditionals—conditionals written in the subjunctive mood—from pure logic should indicate that the problematic truth-functions of the subjunctive is one of its most intriguing and significant characteristics. See also Habermas's discussion of the tension between "meaning and truth" with regard to counterfactual validity claims in *Postmetaphysical Thinking: Philosophical Essays*, trans. William Mark Hohengarten (Cambridge, MA: MIT P, 1992), 57–87, and in *Between Facts and Norms* 9–17. What I term the subjunctive rendering of publicity ideals is a complex issue for Habermas; I have therefore deferred more detailed discussion of its place in Habermas's thought until chapter 2.
10 Habermas, *Between Facts and Norms* 374; original emphasis. Habermas's invocation of Fou-

cault here, I would argue, is built on a distorted reading. With regard to sexuality in particular, Foucault details the normalizing and disciplinary effects that *include*, not exclude, sexual deviance within public professional discourses in the nineteenth century.

11 Negt and Kluge, *Public Sphere and Experience* 10. Michael Warner has condensed quite well similar difficulties many have had with the bourgeois conceptualization of the public sphere, as well as Habermas's immanent critique of it in *Structural Transformation*. Warner notes that the bourgeois public sphere "has been structured from the outset by a logic of abstraction that provides a privilege for unmarked identities: the male, the white, the middle class, the normal" ("The Mass Public and the Mass Subject," in *Habermas and the Public Sphere*, ed. Craig Calhoun [Cambridge, MA: MIT P, 1992], 383). Abstraction per se, however, may be a necessary but not sufficient cause for the continuing dominance of unmarked privileges. The abstraction of person into citizen via civic equality may present an alibi for repudiating certain aspects of personhood, but this does not mean that equality itself, as a political abstraction, should be discarded. Rather, the issue is how the abstraction necessary for something like civic equality is articulated and managed. A counterfactual, *subjunctive* management of the abstraction to equality risks becoming socially unresponsive because the disjunction between actual forms of social life and legitimate public discourse can be dissembled and ideologically justified.

12 Negt and Kluge, *Public Sphere and Experience* 10; original emphasis.

13 Ibid.

14 Ibid.; original emphasis, translation modified.

15 Ibid. xlvi.

16 It may sound as if I am arguing here for a Hegelian notion of history striving to be commensurate with its idealization. I only aim to mark, however, the extent to which the public sphere itself embodies this notion that idealizations guide historical development.

17 On the conformist dynamic in bourgeois publicity, see Negt and Kluge, *Public Sphere and Experience* 58–60.

18 Amy Gluckman and Betsy Reed, eds., *Homo Economics: Capitalism, Community, and Lesbian and Gay Life* (New York: Routledge, 1997), xxvi.

19 Habermas has thus been most vulnerable for his argument that a confusion between commercial and publicity practices, along with increasing encroachments of the state on an ideally autonomous public sphere, indicate the "degeneration" of classic bourgeois publicity (see *Structural Transformation* 159–235). This publicity, as both conceptualized and materialized, had always been and remains irreducibly bound to economic interests. As Benjamin Lee has argued, the idea that the bourgeois public sphere "disintegrated" with the rise of consumer culture and increasing intrusions by the state is an important problem in Habermas's account. This account tends in fact to reproduce the bourgeois idealization of public sphere norms: "In the early bourgeois public sphere, the disembodied, rational public imaginary gave unity to the nation-state through its ideal of citizenship. In modern capitalist societies the media representation of the body politic now includes those who were provisionally disenfranchised; the disembodied rational public imaginary is only one moment in an expanded public sphere. What Habermas had to ex-

175

clude to give unity to his account of the bourgeois public sphere has become, with the development of an expanded consumer economy, internal to it" ("Textuality, Mediation, and Public Discourse," in Calhoun, *Habermas and the Public Sphere* 407).

I would add here that critics who fault lesbian and gay economic visibility for excluding non-middle-class queers make an important point. However, by implicitly assuming that all one would need is the inclusion of excluded aspects of queer life in economic visibility leaves unanswered the more pressing question of what economic representation entails and what functions it can have. For analyses of the relations between queers and capitalism, see Danae Clark, "Commodity Lesbianism," in *The Lesbian and Gay Studies Reader*, ed. Henry Abelove, David M. Halperin, and Michèle Aina Barale (New York: Routledge, 1994), 186–201; Eric Clarke and Mathew Henson, "Hot Damme! Reflections on Gay Publicity," in *Boys: Masculinities in Contemporary Culture*, ed. Paul Smith (New York: Westview-Harper Collins, 1996), 131–50; David T. Evans, *Sexual Citizenship: The Material Construction of Sexualities* (London: Routledge, 1993), 89–113; the essays collected in *Homo Economics*; Rosemary Hennessy, "Queer Visibility and Commodity Culture," *Cultural Critique* 29 (winter 1994–95): 31–76; and Urvashi Vaid, *Virtual Equality: The Mainstreaming of Gay and Lesbian Liberation* (New York: Doubleday, 1995). Daniel Harris, in *The Rise and Fall of Gay Culture* (New York: Hyperion, 1997), has also critiqued the commercial determination of queer value for destroying what he sees as the distinct achievements of a specifically gay culture. However, this critique is too elegiac to be of much use.

20   My thoughts on value here and throughout this book rely fundamentally on the analyses of value found in Karl Marx's *Grundrisse* and volume one of *Capital*; of particular importance to my study is his discussion of the movement from the relative form of value to the equivalent form (see *Capital: A Critique of Political Economy*, volume 1, trans. Ben Fowkes [London: Penguin, 1990], 138–53). Also of importance is the German sociologist and philosopher Georg Simmel's reflections on value in *The Philosophy of Money* (1900). Like Marx, Simmel underscores that value has no basis in ontology, even if it seems to take on ontologized forms: "That there is a value at all, however, is a primary phenomenon. All value inferences only make known the conditions under which values are realized, yet without being produced by these conditions, just as theoretical proofs only prepare the conditions that favour the sense of affirmation or existence. The question as to what value is, like the question as to what being is, is unanswerable" (*The Philosophy of Money*, 2nd ed., ed. David Frisby, trans. Tom Bottomore and David Frisby [London: Routledge, 1990], 62; I have slightly modified the translation). In a May 1898 letter to his friend Heinrich Rickert, Simmel locates the analytic difficulties presented by the objectified forms that value takes on: "I have reached a dead end in my work—in the theory of value!—and can progress neither forwards nor backwards. The concept of value seems to me to contain not merely the same *regressus in infinitum* as that of causality, but also in addition a *circulus vitiosus* because, if one follows the connections far enough, one always finds that the value of A is grounded in that of B, or that of B only in that of A. I would be already be quite satisfied with this and explain it as a basic form of representation, that cannot in fact be removed by logic—if it were not for the fact, just as real, that absolute and objective values lay claim to recognition" (quoted in *The Philosophy of Money* 518). Both

Marx and Simmel emphasize that the abstractions and objectifying *effects* of value relations are thus no less real than the very relations they obscure, and cannot be reduced to mere illusion. Gayatri Chakravorty Spivak has provided some of the most productive and sophisticated contemporary explorations of value, to which my study here is also greatly indebted; see in particular "Scattered Speculations on the Question of Value," *In Other Worlds: Essays in Cultural Criticism* (New York: Routledge, 1988), 154–75, and "Marginality in the Teaching Machine," *Outside in the Teaching Machine* (New York: Routledge, 1993), 53–76. As my comments here on the continuing analytic and political importance of value might indicate, I view Habermas's rejection of Marx's analysis of value as unwarranted. The themes of commodification and reification one finds in twentieth-century Marxist thought, to which Habermas objects as limiting, do not exhaust the analytic potential of value in *Capital*; see Habermas, *Legitimation Crisis*, trans. Thomas McCarthy (Boston: Beacon P, 1975), 50–53; and *The Theory of Communicative Action*, Volume 2, 332–43.

21 As Cindy Patton has suggested, the ontological taken-for-grantedness of identities obscures the fact "that what is at stake is not the content of identities but the modes for staging politics through identity" ("Tremble, Hetero Swine!" in *Fear of a Queer Planet: Queer Politics and Social Theory*, ed. Michael Warner [Minneapolis: U of Minnesota P, 1993], 145). The exclusive and limiting focus of the Gay and Lesbian Alliance Against Defamation on "positive" images of lesbians and gay men in mainstream media illustrates this point. What turns out to be a "positive" image is more often than not utterly cleansed of anything resembling radical sexual dissent, not to mention cleansed of anything other than the white, middle class, and suburban. Anna Marie Smith has gone so far as to term the conservatism found in mainstream lesbian and gay publications and organizations "the new homophobia": "The new homophobia in a sense promises inclusion in return for our transformation from the 'dangerous queer' into the figure of the 'good homosexual' who is closeted, disease-free and monogamous, white, middle-class and right-wing" ("The Good Homosexual and the Dangerous Queer: Resisting the 'New Homophobia,' " in *New Sexual Agendas*, ed. Lynne Segal [New York: NYU P, 1997], 221). Smith's essay is one among many recent publications that challenge the conservatism of mainstream lesbian and gay politics in the United States. While I cannot hope to produce an exhaustive list of dissenting publications on the current dynamics of lesbian and gay inclusion, some that have been pivotal for the way I have formulated my concerns include Berlant and Warner's "Sex in Public"; Pat Califia's *Public Sex: The Culture of Radical Sex* (Pittsburgh: Cleis P, 1994); John Champagne, *The Ethics of Marginality: A New Approach to Gay Studies* (Minneapolis: U of Minnesota P, 1995); Dangerous Bedfellows, eds., *Policing Public Sex: Queer Politics and the Future of* AIDS *Activism* (Boston: South End P, 1996); Lisa Duggan and Nan D. Hunter, *Sex Wars: Sexual Dissent and Political Culture* (New York: Routledge, 1995); Philip Brian Harper, "Gay Male Identities, Personal Privacy, and Relations of Public Exchange: Notes on Directions for Queer Critique," *Social Text* 52/53 (fall/winter 1997): 4–29; Cindy Patton, *Fatal Advice: How Safe-Sex Education Went Wrong* (Durham: Duke UP, 1996); Mark Simpson, ed., *Anti-Gay* (London: Cassell, 1996); Linda Singer, *Erotic Welfare: Sexual Theory and Politics in the Age of Epidemic*, ed. Judith Butler and Maureen McGrogan (New York: Routledge, 1993); and the excellent essays collected in the inaugural pamphlet pre-

pared by the New York City activist group SexPanic! (*Sex Panic!* [New York: SexPanic!, 1997]). More generally, my discussion of the historical and structural contours of contemporary lesbian and gay conformity has been greatly informed by Michel Foucault's diagnosis of a "society of normalization" in, among other writings, "Two Lectures," in *Power/Knowledge: Selected Interviews and Other Writings 1972–1977*, ed. Colin Gordon, trans. Colin Gordon, Leo Marshall, John Mepham, and Kate Soper (New York: Pantheon, 1980), 78–108.

22 There are a number of places where Habermas advances this argument, but I will point here to two key texts: *The Philosophical Discourse of Modernity: Twelve Lectures*, trans. Frederick Lawrence (Cambridge, MA: MIT P, 1987); and "Modernity—An Incomplete Project," in *The Anti-Aesthetic: Essays on Postmodern Culture*, ed. Hal Foster (Port Townsend: Bay P, 1983), 3–15.

23 See in particular Albert O. Hirschman, *The Passions and the Interests: Political Arguments for Capitalism before Its Triumph* (Princeton: Princeton UP, 1977).

24 This is in fact one of the major arguments advanced by Negt and Kluge in their critique of the bourgeois public sphere (see Negt and Kluge, *Public Sphere and Experience* 1–2, 75–80). In the American context, Lauren Berlant has also made a strong case that "there is no public sphere in the contemporary United States, no context of communication and debate that makes ordinary citizens feel that they have a common public culture, or influence on a state that holds itself accountable to their opinions, critical or otherwise" (*The Queen of America* 3). Nevertheless, Berlant's work has recognized that public sphere ideals represent a powerful set of normative guidelines for adjudicating issues of public interest, or rather, for guiding what constitutes public interest to begin with. As "real fictions," the norms of publicness serve as the justificatory premises of political institutions and media culture, and thus lead a charmed life as constitutively counterfactual, yet nevertheless effective, horizons of expectations.

25 To mitigate this double bind, Habermas has elaborated procedural, as opposed to substantive, norms that would delimit how democratically organized societies decide matters of public interest. There is merit in this approach, but similar problems persist in his description of their necessary counterfactuality; I will return to this issue in chapter 2.

26 I have borrowed the term "completed world" from Oskar Negt's characterization of Kant's and Hegel's architectonics, as opposed to Marx's dynamic view of history. Negt also usefully glosses the "double structure" of Marxist categories, one that recognizes the utility of describing things "as they are," *and* how this description at the same time points away from itself to how things might be—a transformation, that is, of the tense stasis that, I have suggested, characterizes the subjunctivity of the bourgeois public sphere. On the one hand, Marxist categories "designate reality in its sentient, graspable, and discoverable qualities. On the other hand, insofar as they also always indicate *better possibilities*, they point beyond the conditions reality has attained. Reality and anticipation are thus inseparable from all Marxist concepts about the determining relationships of society" ("What Is a Revival of Marxism and Why Do We Need One Today?: Centennial Lecture Commemorating the Death of Karl Marx," trans. Michael Palencia-Roth, in *Marxism and the Interpretation of Culture*, ed. Cary Nelson and Lawrence Grossberg [Urbana:

U of Illinois P, 1988], 211). Thus Marxist categories, he argues, "carry within themselves a *memento mori*," and thus exist under the historical pressure of fallibility (215).

The possibilistic and transformative force of the "negative"—the distance between an ideal and its actual, material unfolding within history, and the latent utopian potential this negative represents—borrows from Herbert Marcuse's and Theodor Adorno's conceptualizations of dialectics; see Herbert Marcuse, "A Note on Dialectic," *Reason and Revolution: Hegel and the Rise of Social Theory* (Boston: Beacon P, 1960), vii–xiv; and Theodor Adorno, *Negative Dialectics*, trans. E. B. Ashton (New York: Continuum, 1973), especially part 2. Habermas's subjunctive formulation of publicity ideals, I would argue, tends to foreclose unnecessarily the transformative potential of the negative as Marcuse, and especially Adorno, work through it.

Recently José Esteban Muñoz has productively extended the utopian thrust of Adorno's (and Ernst Bloch's) thought to increasingly threatened queer sexual milieus; see "Ghosts of Public Sex: Utopian Longings, Queer Memories," in Dangerous Bedfellows, *Policing Public Sex* 355–72. See also Phillip Brian Harper's similar discussion of public sex in "Play in the Dark: Privacy, Public Sex, and the Erotics of the Cinema Venue," *camera obscura* 30 (May 1992): 93–111.

27 The classic text on sexuality and value-coding remains Gayle Rubin's "Thinking Sex: Notes Towards a Radical Theory of the Politics of Sexuality," in *Pleasure and Danger: Exploring Female Sexuality*, ed. Carole S. Vance (Boston: Routledge & Kegan Paul, 1984), 267–319.

28 Duggan and Hunter, *Sex Wars* 15.

29 "The systematic method seeks out precise concepts and terms that are analytically articulate and capable of distinguishing between phenomena. However, the historical method of analysis, in order to grasp real historical movement, must repeatedly sublate [*muß . . . aufheben*] the apparent precision of systematic concepts, especially their tendency toward exclusion" (*Public Sphere and Experience* xliv n. 1; I have slightly modified the translation).

30 See Armstrong, *Desire and Domestic Fiction: A Political History of the Novel* (New York: Oxford UP, 1987). For the American formation of a literary public culture, see Michael Warner, *The Letters of the Republic: Publication and the Public Sphere in Eighteenth-Century America* (Cambridge, MA: Harvard UP, 1990).

31 As Eve Kosofsky Sedgwick has usefully noted, overemphasizing historical alterity (for example) can have the pernicious effect of presuming a simplistic understanding of what constitutes the present itself (see *The Epistemology of the Closet* [Berkeley: U of California P, 1990], 44–45).

32 While there are many examples of such work that could be cited here, one of the most cogent continues to be Sedgwick's *Epistemology of the Closet*. Arguably, the problematic demarcations characterizing sexual definitions could be traced back to Freud's *Three Essays on the Theory of Sexuality*.

ONE Visibility at the Limits of Inclusion

1 Bruce Handy, "He Called Me Ellen Degenerate?" *Time*, 14 April 1997: 86. During the same interview, Degeneres was asked whether her public coming out was more difficult than

coming out to her family. She explained that her family was very supportive, adding that her father "said the most hilarious thing when I told him what I was going to do on the show. He said, 'You're not going to go all flamboyant, are ya?' I was like, 'Yeah, Dad, I'm going to completely change. I'm going to start wearing leather vests. I'm going to get one of those haircuts that they all have'" (86). Jokes aside, Degeneres herself provides the repudiation of "flamboyance" deemed necessary for a propitiatory tolerance to be granted. As publicly circulated representations, her comments extend beyond their resonance with the offhand and familiar. Thus I do not take Degeneres's interview to be so much the authentic pronouncements of the star as individual, but more as one text among many in the publicity for the sitcom, and by extension the star's career. The function of star interviews as authentic pronouncements, I would argue, is a part of their function as more generalized media publicity. This function was entirely lost in the World of Wonder/Channel Four documentary *The Real Ellen Story* (dir. Fenton Bailey and Randy Barbato), which aired on PBS on March 1, 1999. This documentary presented a "behind the scenes" narrative so as to chronicle the struggles of the staff and the star herself during the year-long buildup for the coming-out episode.

My discussion of Ellen Morgan's and Ellen Degeneres's coming out was presented as part of a workshop at the Console-ing Passions: Television, Video, Feminism Conference in Montréal, May 1997. I have benefited greatly from the comments of the audience and the other participants. I am particularly grateful to the workshop's organizer, Jane Feuer, and to the co-organizer of the conference, Chantal Nadeau.

2   Alan Frutkin and Gerry Kroll, "Gays on the Tube," *Advocate*, 20 August 1996: 11.

3   "[E]qual protection theorizing should focus not, as it has until the last few years, on *categories*, but on *practices of categorization*" (Janet E. Halley, "The Construction of Heterosexuality," in *Fear of a Queer Planet: Queer Politics and Social Theory*, ed. Michael Warner [Minneapolis: U of Minnesota P, 1993], 83; original emphasis). Halley's groundbreaking work has provided powerful arguments against a substantive, which is to say traditionally moral and identitarian, representation of queers as a class seeking judicial protection from discrimination. She demonstrates convincingly that "sexual identity is produced by social interaction," and as such can and should fall within the purview of procedurally based judicial review. That is, discrimination can be viewed as fundamentally hindering politically relevant public debate about eroticism, and as such discrimination is not so much about a substantive moral decision about persons as it is about the political process itself: "The mere disclosure of one's gay, lesbian or bisexual identity ineluctably accumulates political significance, while one's mere participation in political action to alter laws affecting gays and lesbians can precipitously earn one a public homosexual identity. These legal and social prohibitions hobble everyone's discourse about gay rights, producing a process failure of constitutional magnitude" ("The Politics of the Closet: Towards Equal Protection for Gay, Lesbian and Bisexual Identity," in *Reclaiming Sodom*, ed. Jonathan Goldberg [New York: Routledge, 1994], 188). For a related discussion of legally binding practices of categorization, see Halley's essay "The Status/Conduct Distinction in the 1993 Revisions to Military Anti-Gay Policy: A Legal Archaeology," *GLQ* 3.2–3 (1996): 159–252. As Halley usefully points out in this latter essay,

the successful use of political process arguments in the 1996 Supreme Court decision *Romer v. Evans* indicates that "[m]oral objections to homosexuality are not, in current Supreme Court jurisprudence, a Medusa's head that turns fairness thinking to stone" (221). See also Nan D. Hunter's similarly useful analyses in "Life After Hardwick" and "Identity, Speech and Equality," both in Duggan and Hunter, *Sex Wars* 85–100, 123–41.

4   My discussion of a moral conception of the human invokes the attributes shared by both the philosophical and the more common understanding of morality. For an excellent discussion of the terms "morality" and "ethics" as they shape positions in contemporary political philosophy, see William Rehg, *Insight and Solidarity: The Discourse Ethics of Jürgen Habermas* (Berkeley: U of California P, 1997).

5   Habermas, *Justification and Application: Remarks on Discourse Ethics*, trans. Ciaran P. Cronin (Cambridge, MA: MIT P, 1994), 15; original emphasis. "The universalism of equal respect for all and of solidarity with everything that bears the mark of humanity," Habermas continues, "is first put to the test by radical freedom in the choice of individual life histories and particular forms of life" (14–15).

   While touching on debates between universalism and communitarianism in contemporary political philosophy, my comments here cannot fully engage with these important debates. A useful resource for understanding them is David Rasmussen, ed., *Universalism vs. Communitarianism: Contemporary Debates in Ethics* (Cambridge, MA: MIT P, 1990). While Habermas is sympathetic to the universalist position, he has also sought to decenter its overly ontological and transcendental aspects. In addition to *Justification and Application*, see his discussion of these issues in *Moral Consciousness and Communicative Action*, trans. Christian Lenhardt and Shierry Weber Nicholsen (Cambridge, MA: MIT P, 1990). Iris Marion Young's work has also been extremely important in elaborating nontranscendental, socially responsive modes for abstract political identities; see *Justice and the Politics of Difference* (Princeton: Princeton UP, 1990), and *Intersecting Voices: Dilemmas of Gender, Political Philosophy, and Policy* (Princeton: Princeton UP, 1997).

6   Following Nancy Fraser and Linda Gordon, we might say that the ideal of publicity aims to foster "social citizenship," which "evokes themes from three major traditions of political theory: liberal themes of rights and equal respect; communitarian norms of solidarity and shared responsibility; and republican ideals of participation in public life (through the use of 'public goods' and 'public services')" ("Contract versus Charity: Why Is There No Social Citizenship in the United States?" *Socialist Review* 22.3 [1992]: 46).

7   See Berlant, *The Queen of America*, esp. 1–54, 83–144. I have borrowed the characterization of the ideal moral citizen as "unencumbered" from Michael J. Sandel's "The Procedural Republic and the Unencumbered Self," *Political Theory* 12 (1984): 81–96; reprinted in *Contemporary Political Philosophy*, ed. Robert E. Goodin and Philip Pettit (Oxford: Blackwell, 1997), 247–55.

   In discussing the complexities of "post-traditional" societies, Habermas has used developmental psychology to generate a parallel between a subject's "evolutionary learning process" and the evolution of society. Despite important reservations one could make about such a parallel, Habermas makes a point of at least heuristic value: democratic citizenship requires participatory frameworks that enable critical and reflexive deliberation, rather than conformity to merely given norms. In the higher-level development of the subject, "role bearers [of given norms are] transformed into persons who can assert their identities independent of concrete rules and particular systems of norms. We are supposing here that the youth has acquired the important distinction between norms, on the one hand, and principles according to which we can generate norms, on the other — and thus the ability to judge according to principles" (*Communication and the Evolution of Society*, trans. Thomas McCarthy [Boston: Beacon P, 1979], 85). At this stage, one learns "to see the difference between merely traditional (or imposed) norms and those which are justified in principle" (87). For Habermas, this capability forms an essential component of a democratic deliberative public, at the very least because "need interpretations are no longer assumed as given, but are drawn into the discursive formation of will [Willensbildung]" (93). In terms of Habermas's developmental parallel, what I am calling the moralized citizen remains resolutely pre-adolescent. In this regard, I would problematize Habermas's use of the category "moral" to designate the democratic "discursive formation of will"; see also *Legitimation Crisis* 12–17; *The Theory of Communicative Action*, Volume 2, esp. 173–79, 336–42; and his much fuller discussion of these issues in *Moral Consciousness and Communicative Action* and *Justification and Application*.

8   On "dead citizenship, see Berlant, *The Queen of America* 55–82. While Habermas admits to excluding "subcultural differences" from his own consideration of these issues in *Legitimation Crisis* (76), he has more recently acknowledged the need to build up autonomous counterpublics to revitalize publicity practices in general; see *Between Facts and Norms*, esp. chap. 8; and "Further Reflections on the Public Sphere," in Calhoun, *Habermas and the Public Sphere* 421–61. Yet even in these texts Habermas remains vulnerable to the criticism that he does not provide adequate mechanisms by which subcultural formations and autonomous counterpublics themselves could effectively determine which interests, in the name of "public interest," become generalized. This criticism can be found in Seyla Benhabib, *Situating the Self* (New York: Routledge, 1991); Simone Chambers, "Discourse and Democratic Practices," in *The Cambridge Companion to Habermas*, ed. Stephen K. White (Cambridge: Cambridge UP, 1995), 233–59; and Iris Marion Young, *Intersecting Voices*, esp. chaps. 2 and 3. Such mechanisms would need to be worked out further if we are to understand how the imaginative resources of antihomophobic struggle could adequately destructure the limiting moral value grounding public representability.

9   This is to say something both more and less than "eroticism is amoral." The incompatibility of indeterminate erotic expression and a moral conception of the human owes much not only to the historically heteronormative contours of morality—as both a mode of judgment and a set of behavioral codes—but also to humanist sexual ethics in general. A main difficulty lies in conceptualizing desire as an adjunct to consciousness (which finds its fullest expression in Hegel's *Phenomenology of Spirit*). Because desire as an adjunct to consciousness is understood to objectify, humans as ontologized bearers of consciousness, as *subjects*, are improper *objects* of desire. Thus desire must be continually contorted into merely given moral channels that would mitigate desire's supposedly objectifying effects. (These issues are discussed in greater detail in chapter 3.)

In this regard, Leo Bersani's recent advocacy of an anticommunitarian, because thoroughly immoral and nonredemptive, notion of desire constitutes an important rejoinder to sexual humanism, but one which does not adequately escape the latter's conceptual terrain. While Bersani's critique of lesbian and gay emphases on "normality" is welcome, he elegiacally and inexplicably reasserts a substantively different gay identity based at least in part on what he sees as the identity-fracturing power of sex and desire. In this sense his analysis remains tied to the domain of substantive ontology delimiting the moral view of erotic personhood he nevertheless wishes to explode. With respect to the emphasis on normality in visibility politics, the point is not the communitarian or anti-communitarian nature of sex "itself," but rather the entry of homoeroticism, and those persons and groups who self-identify in relation to it, into an ideally democratic public sphere, and thus what effects this entry can have in reimagining erotic life beyond the constraints of moral worth. See Leo Bersani, "Is the Rectum a Grave?" in AIDS: Cultural Analysis, Cultural Activism, ed. Douglas Crimp (Cambridge, MA: MIT P, 1988), 197–222; and Bersani, Homos (Cambridge, MA: Harvard UP, 1995). For an excellent discussion of these and other issues broached by Bersani, see David M. Halperin, "More or Less Gay Specific," London Review of Books 18.10 (23 May 1996): 24–27; and Mandy Merck, "Death Camp: Feminism vs. Queer Theory," in Segal, New Sexual Agendas 232–37.

There have been earlier elaborations of a nonredemptive understanding of modern eroticism that do not necessarily fall into the ontologizing trap Bersani does: for example, Max Weber's contrast between modern eroticism and "the brotherly ethic of salvation religion" in his 1915 essay "Religious Rejections of the World and Their Directions" (From Max Weber: Essays in Sociology, ed., trans. H. H. Gerth and C. Wright Mills [New York: Oxford UP, 1958], esp. 343–50); and Theodor Adorno's 1963 essay "Sexual Taboos and Law Today" (Critical Models: Interventions and Catchwords, trans. Henry W. Pickford [New York: Columbia UP, 1998], 71–88). In this essay Adorno criticizes the "desexualization of sexuality itself" by a normalizing social "integration": "Whereas sexuality has been integrated [eingegliedert], that which cannot be integrated, the actual spiciness of sex [literally: "the actual sexual aroma"], continues to be detested by society. . . . Sexuality is disarmed as sex, as though it were a kind of sport, and whatever is different about it still causes allergic reactions" (73).

10   Bruce Bawer, A Place at the Table: The Gay Individual in American Society (New York: Simon and Schuster, 1993), 154. (I have borrowed the epithet "moral valet" from Hegel's The Phenomenology of Spirit, trans. A. V. Miller [Oxford: Oxford UP, 1977], 404.) An important precursor to Bawer's argument is Marshall Kirk and Hunter Madsen's After the Ball: How America Will Conquer Its Fear and Hatred of Gays in the '90s (New York: Doubleday, 1989). See also the collection of essays edited by Bawer called Beyond Queer: Challenging Gay Left Orthodoxy (New York: Free P, 1996).

11   In this sense Biddy Martin's recent suggestion that those who oppose the conformist trend in lesbian and gay politics and media culture "fear" the ordinary is misguided. Martin sets up a false opposition between an imaginary cultural and intellectual vanguard, and "ordinary" folk who go about their lives in much the same way as "everyone else." This opposition misses the mark at least by half. Again, the quarrel is not with such "ordinary" activities and ways of life per se, but rather their elevation into a severely

evaluative and conformist calculus that would repudiate and abject whole sectors of queer life; see Biddy Martin, "Extraordinary Homosexuals and the Fear of Being Ordinary," *differences* 6.2–3 (1994): 101–25; and "Sexualities Without Genders and Other Queer Utopias," *diacritics* 24.2–3 (1994): 104–21. See also the excellent response to Martin, to which my comments here are indebted, in Warner and Berlant, "Sex in Public" 557.

12   Bawer, *A Place at the Table* 156.

13   Ibid.

14   Bruce Bawer, "Sex Negative Me," *Beyond Queer* 173. For a similar and widely publicized connection between a moralizing heteronormativity and equal rights, see Larry Kramer, "Gay Culture, Redefined," *New York Times*, 12 December 1997: A35. Ironically, perhaps no better support for Bawer's position can be found than in the 1986 U.S. Supreme Court decision *Bowers v. Hardwick*, in which the majority upheld Georgia's sodomy statute, despite the fact that the Georgia attorney-general made it clear that the state had no interest in prosecuting cross-sex infractions covered by the law, and thus admitted that Constitutional equal protection had no place in their enforcement. In this case a heteronormative morality became *the* defining principle for distributional justice. Because Bowers had been arrested in his own home, this decision also made clear the Court's indifference to the kind of public/private distinction voiced implicitly by Degeneres and explicitly by Bawer.

15   Andrew Sullivan, "The Marriage Moment," *Advocate*, 20 Jan. 1998: 61. See also Michael Warner's extraordinary analysis of the debate over lesbian and gay marriage rights in "Normal and Normaller: Beyond Gay Marriage," *GLQ* 5.2 (1999): 119–71.

16   Ibid. 63.

17   Ibid. 67.

18   Andrew Sullivan, *Virtually Normal: An Argument about Homosexuality* (New York: Alfred A. Knopf, 1995), 170. See Philip Brian Harper's excellent critique of Sullivan in "Gay Male Identities, Personal Privacy, and Relations of Public Exchange"; Morris Kaplan's discussion of Sullivan in *Sexual Justice: Democratic Citizenship and the Politics of Desire* (New York: Routledge, 1997), 40–46; and Tony Kushner's admirable critique of both Sullivan and Bawer in "Homosexual Liberation: A Socialism of the Skin," in Gluckman and Reed, *Homo Economics* 185–92.

19   Gabriel Rotello, *Sexual Ecology: AIDS and the Destiny of Gay Men* (New York: Dutton, 1997), 256; original emphasis. Rotello here commits an error that Michel Foucault has eloquently warned against—mistaking the "search for personal ethics" for a "morality as obedience to a system of rules" ("An Aesthetics of Existence," *Foucault Live* [Interviews, 1966–84], trans. John Johnston, ed. Sylvère Lotringer [New York: Semiotext(e), 1989], 311).

20   Rotello, *Sexual Ecology* 257; emphasis added.

21   Ibid. 256.

22   As a commemorative event, Stonewall 25 was accompanied by a number of popular publications celebrating the progressive history of lesbian and gay politics; see in particular Mark Thompson, ed., *Long Road to Freedom: The Advocate History of the Gay and Lesbian Movement* (New York: St. Martin's, 1994). The preceding paragraph regarding Stonewall 25 in

New York first appeared in my review article on Eve Kosofsky Sedgwick's *Tendencies* ("All About Eve," *GLQ* 3 [1996]: 109–23).

23 See Douglas Crimp, with Adam Rolston, AIDS *Demo Graphics* (Seattle: Bay P, 1990), and Alexandra Juhasz, AIDS *TV: Identity, Community, and Alternative Video* (Durham: Duke UP, 1996).

24 Douglas Crimp, "Portraits of People with AIDS," in *Cultural Studies*, ed. Lawrence Grossberg, Cary Nelson, and Paula Treichler (New York: Routledge, 1992), 125.

25 Ibid. 126.

26 This shift was epitomized in the April 29, 1997, issue of the *Advocate*. The front cover featured their lead article on "the corporate closet," while buried on page sixteen was a two-inch news report on the tenth anniversary of ACT UP. The report did manage to mention in passing that at the anniversary demonstration in New York, seventy-two protesters were arrested. ACT UP's opposition to the conformist impulses of mainstream lesbian and gay organizations and publications had been identified in Crimp's account of ACT UP/NY's participation in the twentieth anniversary of Stonewall: "Though we are a direct-action AIDS activist group, not a gay organization, most of us are lesbian or gay, and all of us are dedicated to fighting homophobia. Indeed, we see ourselves both as direct heirs to the early radical tradition of gay liberation and as rejuvenators of the gay movement, which has in the intervening decades become an assimilationist civil rights lobby" (AIDS *Demo Graphics* 98). Rodger Streitmatter has written a highly informative history of the U.S. lesbian and gay press, and later chapters focus in particular on the ambiguously commercializing and normalizing effects of the lesbian and gay press's move to the mainstream, beginning in the early 1980s and reaching its height in the 1990s; see Rodger Streitmatter, *Unspeakable: The Rise of the Gay and Lesbian Press in America* (Boston: Faber and Faber, 1995).

27 "Lifestyle" is an intriguing term, whose analytic origins date back at least to the sociological work of Georg Simmel and Max Weber. Both understood lifestyle as a complex phenomenon associated with the reorganizations of everyday life effected by capitalism and modernity: changes in class, social groupings, and the integrated patterns of consumption, as well as the cultural implications of modernity delineated, for example, in Charles Baudelaire's essay "The Painter of Modern Life." For both thinkers, lifestyle had a perplexing relation to eroticism, a perplexity that perhaps explains the paucity of their reflections on *why* erotic nonconformity, for example, would be attached to such a decisive socioeconomic feature of modernity. Habermas, unfortunately, seems to accept this analytic impoverishment as sufficient; see for example *The Theory of Communicative Action*, Volume 2 323–24.

28 For useful discussions of these aspects of lesbian and gay marketing, see Amy Gluckman and Betsy Reed, "The Gay Marketing Moment," and Dan Baker, "A History in Ads: The Growth of the Gay and Lesbian Market," both in Gluckman and Reed, *Homo Economics* 3–10 and 11–20 (respectively).

29 Habermas, *Structural Transformation* 111.

30 Habermas, *Legitimation Crisis* 22.

31 Ibid. 24–25.

32 Negt and Kluge, *Public Sphere and Experience* 14; original emphasis. In addition to relying on Negt and Kluge's analysis, my thoughts on the connection between political and economic forms of equivalence is greatly indebted to Theodor Adorno's *Negative Dialectics*. "The exchange principle [*Tauschprinzip*]," Adorno argues, "the reduction of human labor to the abstract universal concept of average working hours, is fundamentally akin [*urverwandt*] to the principle of identification [*Identifikationsprinzip*]. Exchange is the social model of the principle, and without the principle there would be no exchange; through it non-identical individuals [*Einzelwesen*] and performances [*Leistungen*] become commensurable and identical. The spread of the principle imposes on the whole world an obligation to become identical, to become total" (*Negative Dialectics* 146; *Negative Dialektic*, *Gesammelte Schriften*, ed. Rolf Tiedemann with Gretel Adorno, Susan Buck-Morss, and Klaus Schultz, vol. 6 [Frankfurt am Main: Suhrkamp, 1973], 455). By bringing "identification" and "exchange" together in this way, Adorno calls to mind not only a metaphysical philosophical tradition preoccupied with formulating absolutist understandings of what it means to be human, but also the traditions and institutions of political liberalism that, according to Adorno, are intimately connected to Western metaphysics. These traditions and institutions presuppose that the identity of the citizen, for example, is a naturalized, self-evident sameness before the law that purports to resolve, and yet paradoxically enshrines, the competing autonomy of private individuals in civil society. Adorno's reasoning here thus configures an affiliation among Western idealist philosophy since the Enlightenment, the capitalist system of exchange and equivalence, and the historical instantiation of the bourgeois subject as a universal standard. However, Adorno understands these as *historical* connections; he cautions that thoughts cannot be simply "equated with their source" (*Negative Dialectics* 144; *Negative Dialektik* 147). Judith Butler thus inappropriately aligns Adorno with Hegel in this regard; see Butler, "Contingent Foundations: Feminism and the Question of Postmodernism," in *Feminists Theorize the Political*, ed. Judith Butler and Joan W. Scott (New York: Routledge, 1992), 5–6.

I should note that I have included the page numbers to the German edition of Adorno's work because of the conceptual and political problems with many translations of his texts, translations that tend to wrench concepts and terms out of his Marxist framework. I have therefore modified the translation of many of the passages I will cite. On these difficulties in translating Adorno, see Fredric Jameson, *Late Marxism: Adorno, or, the Persistence of the Dialectic* (London: Verso, 1996), ix–x.

33 "Missing the Boat," *Advocate*, 13 May 1997: 13. ABC had also denied airtime to a Human Rights Campaign advertisement.

34 Grant Lukenbill, *Untold Millions: Positioning Your Business for the Gay and Lesbian Consumer Revolution* (New York: Harper Collins, 1995), 2. Further page citations will be given in the text. I am indebted to my mother, Gerry Clarke, for bringing Lukenbill's book to my attention.

35 Negt and Kluge are particularly illuminating on this aspect of capitalized representation. They argue that "the consciousness and programming industry, advertising, the publicity campaigns of firms and administrative apparatuses," important elements of what they refer to as "new public spheres of production," are "nonpublicly anchored: in con-

trast to the traditional form of public sphere, they work the raw material of everyday life and they derive their penetrative force directly from the capitalist production interest. By circumventing the intermediate realm of the traditional public sphere (the seasonal public sphere of elections, the formation of public opinion), they seek direct access to the private sphere of the individual" (*Public Sphere and Experience* xlvi).

36   Ibid. xlvii.

37   Karl Marx, *Grundrisse: Foundations of the Critique of Political Economy (Rough Draft)*, trans. Martin Nicolaus (London: Penguin, 1993), 156–57; original emphases. Further page citations will be abbreviated as G and given in the text. I have made some translation modifications in the passages that follow.

38   See John D'Emilio, "Capitalism and Gay Identity," in *Powers of Desire: The Politics of Sexuality*, ed. Ann Snitow, Christine Stansell, and Sharon Thompson (New York: Monthly Review P, 1983), 100–13.

39   See Habermas's discussion of the way European political integration has followed economic integration, such that for the citizen "this translates into an ever greater gap between being passively affected and actively participating" (*Between Facts and Norms* 503).

40   Ronald A. T. Judy, "On the Question of Nigga Authenticity," *boundary 2* 21.3 (1994): 227.

41   Ibid.

42   Georg Simmel also echoes Marx's analysis of the radical social effects of a mature money economy: "It is not only because of its immanent character, but precisely because it destroys so many other kinds of relationships between people [such as the "organic unity" of the family], that money establishes relationships between elements that otherwise would have no connection whatsoever" (*The Philosophy of Money* 346).

43   Gayatri Chakravorty Spivak provides an exemplary formulation about the problem of relating the economic mode to other modes of value determination: "The binary opposition between the economic and the cultural is so deeply entrenched that the full implications of the question of Value posed in terms of the 'materialist' predication of the subject are difficult to conceptualize. One cannot foresee a teleological moment when these implications are catastrophically productive of a new evaluation. The best one can envisage is the persistent undoing of the opposition, taking into account the fact that, first, the complicity between cultural and economic value-systems is acted out in almost every decision we make; and, secondly, that economic reductionism is, indeed, a very real danger" ("Scattered Speculations," *In Other Worlds* 166). I would add here that the irreducible entanglement between visibility politics and economic representation suggests a corrective to Nancy Fraser's recent characterization of lesbian and gay politics as primarily cultural, and not economic; see "From Recognition to Redistribution: Dilemmas of Justice in a 'Post-Socialist' Age," *New Left Review* 212 (1996): 68–93. For a productive criticism of Fraser's position, see Iris Marion Young, "Unruly Categories: A Critique of Nancy Fraser's Dual Systems Theory," *New Left Review* 222 (1997): 147–60.

44   Theodor Adorno, *The Jargon of Authenticity*, trans. Knut Tarnowski and Frederic Will (Evanston: Northwestern UP, 1973), 62–63; *Jargon der Eigentlichkeit: Zur deutschen Ideologie*, in Adorno, *Gesammelte Schriften* 6:455.

45   Karl Marx, *Capital* 1:148. I have made some translation modifications. In using Marx's

187

analysis of the commodity, I do not mean to suggest that it provides the analogical key to *all* value-formations. Rather, I want to suggest that Marx's analysis, here and in the *Grundrisse*, provides a useful signpost in moving queer thought away from relying *only* on the opposition homophobia/affirmation. Some of the dangers of analogy, specifically in terms of Marx's analysis of value-formation, are cogently presented by Gayatri Chakravorty Spivak. Discussing Jean-Joseph Goux's insistence on the isomorphic relation between Marx's analysis of value-formation under capital and Freud's discussion of the formation of genital sexuality, Spivak notes that "Goux's argument is ingenious, but in the long run it seems to be an exercise in the domestication of Marx's analysis of Value. No doubt there are general morphological similarities between centralized sign-formations. But in order to see in those similarities the structural essence of the formations thus analogized, it is necessary to exclude the fields of force that make them heterogeneous, indeed discontinuous. It is to forget that Marx's critique of money is functionally different from Freud's attitude toward genitalism or Lacan's toward the phallus" ("Scattered Speculations," *In Other Worlds* 156).

46   Marx, *Capital* 1:143.

47   See Jeremy Bentham, *The Theory of Fictions*, ed. C. K. Ogden (Paterson, NJ: Littlefield, Adams, 1959). Habermas has usefully pointed out not only that identities are socially produced, but also that their attachment to individuality occurs only *through* their social production: "Identity is produced through *socialization*, that is through the fact that the growing child first of all integrates itself into a specific social system by appropriating symbolic generalities; it is later secured and developed through *individuation*, that is, precisely through a growing independence in relation to social systems" (*Communication and the Evolution of Society* 74; original emphasis).

48   See Marx's classic analysis of the stalled emancipatory potential of bourgeois civil society in his 1837 essay, "On the Jewish Question," in *Karl Marx: Selected Writings*, ed. David McLellan (Oxford: Oxford UP, 1977), 39–62.

49   Adorno, *The Jargon of Authenticity* 22; *Jargon der Eigentlichkeit* 427.

50   Adorno, *The Jargon of Authenticity* 30; *Jargon der Eigentlichkeit* 433.

51   Eve Kosofsky Sedgwick, "Queer Performativity: Henry James's *The Art of the Novel*," GLQ 1.1 (1993): 15; original emphasis.

52   Foucault indicates this point quite well when he explains his concern with "showing how social mechanisms up to the present have been able to work, how forms of repression and constraint have acted, and, *starting from there*, it seems to me, one left to the people themselves, knowing all the above, the possibility of self-determination and the choice of their own existence" (*Foucault Live* 312; emphasis added).

53   Michael Warner, "Introduction," in Warner, *Fear of a Queer Planet* xxxi n. 28.

54   Spivak, "Marginality in the Teaching Machine," *Outside in the Teaching Machine* 61.

TWO   *Autonomy and Conformity*

1   I have taken the term "practice of value" from Eun J. Suh, who has graciously allowed me to use it.

2 See Michael Kelly, ed., *Critique and Power: Recasting the Foucault/Habermas Debate* (Cambridge: MA: MIT P, 1994). Axel Honneth also presents one of the most cogent analytic comparisons of Habermas's and Foucault's work in *The Critique of Power: Reflective Stages in a Critical Social Theory*, trans. Kenneth Baynes (Cambridge, MA: MIT P, 1991), esp. part II.

3 Habermas himself has argued that the university should ideally embody and foster these capacities; see *Toward a Rational Society: Student Protest, Science, and Politics*, trans. Jeremy J. Shapiro (Boston: Beacon P, 1979).

4 My students similarly react to many of the images produced for ACT UP protests contained in *Aids Demo Graphics*, particularly the striking side-by-side images of Cardinal O'Connor and a used condom with the caption "Know Your Scumbags." Their negative reaction makes clear, at the very least, that respect for powerful religious institutions can take priority over politically relevant irony and humor in understandings of "reasonable" communication. In this sense the rational contours of communicative action are not immune from hierarchies of value orientation. One might say, following Jean-François Lyotard, that the idiom of reasonableness, or indeed persuasion, can contain restrictive standards that are not themselves "rational," and thus cannot recognize the legitimacy of claims that fall outside of these standards; see Jean-François Lyotard, *The Differend: Phrases in Dispute*, trans. Georges Van Den Abbeele (Minneapolis: U of Minnesota P, 1988).

   I should add here that there are important contextual determinants to my students' reactions, even if these determinants do not exhaust their heuristic value with regard to communicative rationality. I teach at a large state-affiliated university whose undergraduate population is largely drawn from rural Pennsylvania and the city of Pittsburgh. Neither of these contexts provide a great deal of exposure to irreverence toward religious institutions such as are more available, I would argue, in larger urban settings. Indeed, when it comes to queer issues, my university's administration vacillates between casting itself as an international research institution and as a local institution rooted in the "communal norms" of the tri-state area of western Pennsylvania. This vacillation makes undergraduate teaching about AIDS or queer issues a dangerously ambiguous project, at best. I'd like to mention here that Joy Van Fuqua's very wise advice has helped me immeasurably in parsing out what is at stake in these pedagogical encounters.

5 Jürgen Habermas, *The Past as Future*, trans. and ed. Max Pensky (Lincoln: U of Nebraska P, 1994) 97.

6 By far the most important of such critiques is Negt and Kluge's *Public Sphere and Experience*. However, I will not deal directly with this work here: first, because to do so would require a more sustained discussion than my focus here allows; and second, because much of their critique is both quoted in and presupposed throughout this book. Suffice it to say that their analysis of how the bourgeois ("traditional") public sphere is "today overlaid by *industrialized public spheres of production*, which tend to incorporate private realms, in particular the production process and the context of living" (12–13; original emphasis), could have far-reaching implications for investigations of contemporary publicity norms and practices, especially as these organize everyday experience and expectations for social justice.

   A vast amount of literature has grown up around Habermas's early work on the public sphere; Peter Uwe Hohendahl provides an excellent overview of Habermas's German critics in *The Institution of Criticism* (Ithaca: Cornell UP, 1982) 242–80. See also the essays collected in Calhoun, *Habermas and the Public Sphere*, and Nancy Fraser's critique (to which Habermas himself has been sympathetic) in *Unruly Practices: Power, Discourse, and Gender in Contemporary Social Theory* (Minneapolis: U of Minnesota P, 1989), 113–43.

7 Theodor Adorno, "Meinungsforschung und Öffentlichkeit," in Adorno, *Gesammelte Schriften* 8:533. All translations are my own.

8 Ibid.

9 Ibid.

10 Compare Adorno's position in this regard to Axel Honneth's insight that Habermas's investigation of the bourgeois public sphere and his related studies on communicative action make possible conflicting interpretations, especially regarding the opposition between publicity ideals and the "rational-purposive action" found in capitalist economic relations and the modern state: "[W]e can understand the same process of will-formation [*Bildungsprozeß*] not only as a process in which the relations of labor and domination intervene but also as a process which in turn molds the institutional conditions of these relations. Then the social conflict that it concerns no longer develops, as in the first case, between the developmental dynamic of symbolically mediated interaction and the systemic conditions prevailing at the time; rather, it *already dwells within the process of communicative action as such*" (*The Critique of Power* 247–48; emphasis added). Honneth convincingly argues that this possible interpretation stemming from Habermas's theory itself remains ambiguated in his later work on discourse ethics: at times relations of domination are understood as in conflict with the idealized presuppositions of the public sphere, while at other times they are intimately related. Honneth argues that this problematic ambiguity results from the introduction of systems theory in Habermas's work, a theory Honneth rejects. Instead, Honneth understands the "purposive-rational action" found in late capitalism and state structures as inseparable from communicative rationality and the deliberation about moral and political norms. Thus he places class struggle at the heart of moral and political "communicative" struggles for recognition: "[T]he apparently purposive-rational organizations [the economy and the state] are also codetermined by moral-practical viewpoints that must be conceived as results of communicative action" (274). This approach was possible at one stage in the development of Habermas's theory, but which, Honneth argues, his use of a systems-theoretical approach disallowed him from exploring fully.

11 Adorno reiterates this criticism in *The Jargon of Authenticity*: "The bourgeois form of rationality has always needed irrational supplements [*Zusätze*], in order to maintain itself as what it is—continuing injustice through justice. Such irrationality in the midst of the rational is the working atmosphere [*Betriebsklima*] of authenticity. The latter can support itself with the fact that over a long period of time literal as well as figurative mobility, a main element in bourgeois equality, always turned into injustice for those who could not entirely keep up. They experienced the progress of society as a verdict: a pawned-off remembrance [*angedrehte Erinnerung*] of their suffering under that progress brings authen-

ticity, along with its jargon, to a ferment. Its bubbles cause the true object of the suffering, the particular constitution of society, to vanish" (*The Jargon of Authenticity* 47–48; *Jargon der Eigentlichkeit* 444–45; translation modified).

12   Wolfgang Jäger, *Öffentlichkeit und Parlamentarismus: Eine Kritik an Jürgen Habermas* (Stuttgart: W. Kohlhammer, 1973), 29–30. All translations are my own.

13   Ibid. 43.

14   Ibid. 46.

15   Charles Tilly, "Parliamentarization of Popular Contention in Great Britain, 1758–1854," *Theory and Society* 26 (1997): 269. See also Negt and Kluge's brief analysis of the English labor movement in relation to the bourgeois public sphere in *Public Sphere and Experience* (187–200). A classic study of popular forms of claim-making before the formation of working-class political groups and trade unions remains E. P. Thompson's "The Moral Economy of the English Crowd in the Eighteenth Century," *Past and Present* 50 (1971): 76–136. On the propitiatory aspects of the 1867 Reform Bill and the Reform League's "respectability," see Harold Perkin, *Origins of Modern English Society* (London: Routledge and Kegan Paul, 1969), 401–7. However, Perkin does not understand such modes of propritiation as either ethically or politically suspect: "On the political side the trade unions were as justified, practical and pragmatic as the Anti-Corn Law League and other middle-class pressure groups had been in looking to the existing parties for redress of their grievances. In the circumstances of the age, where else could they look?" (403). While Perkin has a point, at the same time the lack of other official outlets does not necessarily absolve historical inquiry from *evaluating* the effects of such narrowed possibilities. Nancy Armstrong has usefully pointed to critiques of Perkin's study in *Desire and Domestic Fiction* (270 n. 11). With regard to the impact of mid- to late-nineteenth-century working-class associations and political lobbies on customs and habits that did not conform to middle-class notions of respectability, see F. M. L. Thompson, *The Rise of Respectable Society: A Social History of Victorian Britain, 1830–1900* (London: Harper Collins, 1988), esp. 307–61.

16   Max Weber, "The Meaning of 'Ethical Neutrality' in Sociology and Economics," *The Methodology of the Social Sciences*, trans. and ed. Edward A. Shils and Henry A. Finch (New York: Free P, 1964), 43; original emphasis. See also Weber's discussion of ideal-typical categories in chap. 1 of *Economy and Society: An Outline of Interpretive Sociology*, vol. 1, trans. Ephraim Fischoff et al., ed. Guenther Ross and Claus Wittich (Berkeley: U of California P, 1968), and "Idealtypus, Handlungsstruktur und Verhaltensinterpretation," in Weber, *Methodologische Schriften* (Frankfurt am Main: S. Fischer, 1968), 65–168.

17   "Whoever accepts the proposition that the knowledge of historical reality can or should be a 'presuppositionless' copy of 'objective' facts, will deny the value of the ideal-type. Even those who recognize that there is no 'presuppositonlessness' in the logical sense, and that even the simplest excerpt from a statute or from a documentary source can have scientific meaning only with reference to 'significance' and ultimately to evaluative ideas, will more or less regard the construction of any such historical 'utopias' as an expository device which endangers the autonomy of historical research and which is, in

191

any case, a vain sport. . . . The construction of abstract ideal-types recommends itself not as an end but as a means" (Max Weber, "Die 'Objektivität' sozialwissenschaftlicher und sozialpolitischer Erkenntnis," *Methodologische Schriften* 42; my translation).

18 Hohendahl, *The Institution of Criticism* 246.

19 Habermas, "Further Reflections on the Public Sphere" 429.

20 Ibid.

21 Ibid. 442; translation modified.

22 Habermas, *The Theory of Communicative Action, Volume 2* 329; original emphases.

23 One could argue, however, that by postulating the universal presumptions of communicative action as *facts* of everyday communication, Habermas has distilled a transhistorically cognitive and objective category from publicity as a normative ideal. To that extent, Jäger's criticism would be much more relevant. From an opposing perspective, Karl-Otto Apel has critiqued Habermas for not extending his conclusions regarding the "transcendental" presuppositions of everyday speech *far enough*. He argues that Habermas cannot ground universalist notions of validity and justification in the "lifeworld"—which is to say, in everyday speech acts occurring within specific contexts—while also neglecting to draw a strongly transcendental model from this ground. Habermas cannot, Apel argues, "maintain the *universalism* of the validity claims connected with human speech" while rejecting "the demand for an a priori valid *ultimate justification* of the philosophical validity claim made in universal-pragmatic statements about the necessary presuppositions of argumentative discourse," presuppositions such as "intelligibility, truth, sincerity, and normative rightness" (Karl-Otto Apel, "Normatively Grounding 'Critical Theory' through Recourse to the Lifeworld? A Transcendental-Pragmatic Attempt to Think with Habermas against Habermas," in *Philosophical Interventions in the Unfinished Project of Enlightenment*, ed. Axel Honneth, Thomas McCarthy, Claus Offe, and Albrecht Wellmer [Cambridge, MA: MIT P, 1992], 127–28; original emphasis). For other useful considerations and critiques of Habermas's linguistic model, see Jonathan Culler, *Framing the Sign: Criticism and Its Institutions* (Norman: U of Oklahoma P, 1988), 185–200; and Axel Honneth and Hans Joas, eds., *Communicative Action: Essays on Jürgen Habermas's The Theory of Communicative Action* (Cambridge, MA: MIT P, 1990). Characteristically, Negt and Kluge provide a trenchant critique of the exclusionary linguistic codes, including definitions of "reasonableness," built within the bourgeois public sphere; see *Public Sphere and Experience* (45–49).

24 See Habermas, *Postmetaphysical Thinking* 115–48. An important starting point for Habermas's notion of communicative action can be found in his essay "Labor and Interaction: Remark's on Hegel's Jena *Philosophy of Mind*," in Habermas, *Theory and Practice*, trans. John Viertel (Boston: Beacon P, 1973), 142–69.

25 See Habermas's discussion of these issues in *Moral Consciousness and Communicative Action* and *Justification and Application*. For an important critique of Habermas with respect to (suppressed) moral conflicts as they inform the "distribution of chances for social recognition," see Axel Honneth, *The Fragmented World of the Social: Essays in Social and Political Philosophy*, ed. Charles W. Wright (Albany: SUNY P, 1995), 205–19. Also of relevance are the important critiques of a universalist moral and political position in Michael J. Sandel's

Liberalism and the Limits of Justice, 2nd ed. (1982; Cambridge: Cambridge UP, 1998), and his "The Procedural Republic and the Unencumbered Self"; and Iris Marion Young, "Polity and Group Difference: A Critique of the Ideal of Universal Citizenship," in Goodin and Pettit, *Contemporary Political Philosophy* 256–72.

26   Habermas, *Postmetaphysical Thinking* 144.

27   Habermas, "Further Reflections on the Public Sphere" 443. For Habermas's most thorough analysis of communicative action, see both volumes of *The Theory of Communicative Action*, as well as his essays collected in *On the Pragmatics of Language*, ed. Maeve Cook (Cambridge, MA: MIT P, 1998).

28   Habermas, *Justification and Application* 164; original emphasis.

29   Habermas, *The Philosophical Discourse of Modernity* 325; original emphasis, translation modified.

30   Ibid. 40; original emphasis.

31   Jürgen Habermas, *The Inclusion of the Other: Studies in Political Theory*, ed. Ciaran Cronin and Pablo De Greiff, trans. Ciaran Cronin et al. (Cambridge, MA: MIT P, 1998), 208–9.

32   Ibid. 210.

33   Habermas, *Moral Consciousness and Communicative Action* 178.

34   Habermas, *Postmetaphysical Thinking* 138.

35   Ibid.; original emphasis.

36   Habermas, *Moral Consciousness and Communicative Action* 207; original emphasis.

37   Habermas, *Postmetaphysical Thinking* 62; emphasis added.

38   Ibid. 68; original emphasis.

39   Habermas, *The Philosophical Discourse of Modernity* 326; emphasis added.

40   Ibid.

41   The role of value determinations neglected by Habermas could usefully be explored via Kant and his understanding of judgment. Both anchoring his thought in and extending it beyond the confines of Kant's moral theory, Habermas nevertheless neglects, I would argue, the crucial mediating role of judgment between ideal and reality as thematized in the *Critique of Practical Reason* and the *Critique of Judgment*.

42   Habermas, *Justification and Application* 15; translation slightly modified.

43   Jürgen Habermas, *Autonomy and Solidarity: Interviews with Jürgen Habermas*, rev. ed., ed. Peter Dews (London: Verso, 1992), 202.

44   Habermas, *Justification and Application* 15–16.

45   Ibid. 143–44.

46   For further reflections on "reconciliation" and the sphere of justice, see Habermas's "Reconciliation through the Public Use of Reason," in Habermas, *The Inclusion of the Other* 49–74.

47   Habermas, *Autonomy and Solidarity* 223. Habermas has also usefully investigated anchoring rights in autonomy in such a way that they go beyond the thin negative freedoms of liberalism and emphasize instead equitable social participation; see *The Inclusion of the Other* 203–36.

48   See Jacques Derrida's lengthy footnote in which he effectively counters Habermas's attack in *Limited Inc* (Evanston: Northwestern UP, 1988), 156–58 n. 9.

49 Michel Foucault, "An Ethics of Pleasure," *Foucault Live* 268–69. For these reasons, Foucault disagrees fundamentally with Habermas with regard to morality: "The search for a form of morality that would be acceptable to everyone—in the sense that everyone would have to submit to it—strikes me as catastrophic" (330). "There are no universal rules," he has concluded, "which establish the types of relationships between rationality and the processes of governance" (253).

50 On this issue see Martin Jay, "The Debate over Performative Contradiction: Habermas Versus the Poststructuralists," in Honneth, McCarthy, Offe, and Wellmer, *Philosophical Interventions in the Unfinished Project of Enlightenment* 261–79.

51 Michel Foucault, *The History of Sexuality, Volume 1: An Introduction,* trans. Robert Hurley (New York: Vintage, 1980), 101.

52 Ibid. 101–2; emphasis added.

53 Georg Lukács observed a similar tendency in Kant's philosophy, and formulated this problem as a "blockage" in terms of what he called "praxis": "[T]he essence of praxis consists in annulling *that indifference of form towards content* that we found in the problem of the thing-in-itself. . . . Insofar as the principle of praxis is the prescription for changing reality, it must be tailored to the concrete material substratum of action if it is to impinge upon it to any effect" (*History and Class Consciousness: Studies in Marxist Dialectics,* trans. Rodney Livingstone [Cambridge, MA: MIT P, 1971], 126; original emphasis). The indifference of form to content has been a persistent charge against modern philosophical idealism, particularly from those traditions of thought like Marxism that have been concerned with dialectics as a methodological priority. However, the centrality of this critique also appears in a work as "eclectic" as Simmel's *The Philosophy of Money* (one can find this critique throughout the book, but he focuses on it in particular when discussing the affinities between Kantian moral theory and the effects of a money economy; these comments are peppered throughout the last section, but see in particular pp. 441–70).

It should be noted that the overall formulations and concerns of *The History of Sexuality, Volume 1* do not in themselves preclude extending Foucault's analysis to investigate historical discontinuities; my thoughts here are relatively restricted to the discourse/reverse-discourse paradigm. For an exemplary instance of using Foucault's analysis here to understand the changing historical and political entanglements of sexual discourses, see Nancy Armstrong's *Desire and Domestic Fiction.*

54 Michel Foucault, *The Archaeology of Knowledge,* trans. A. M. Sheridan Smith (New York: Pantheon, 1972), 169; original emphasis. In the later volumes of *The History of Sexuality,* Foucault ran up against the question of historical continuity versus discontinuity that I have argued plagues his formulation in volume 1. In volume 2, for example, Foucault argues that "the question that is so often raised regarding the continuity (or break) between the philosophical moralities of antiquity and Christian morality had to be reformulated. . . ." (*The History of Sexuality, Volume 2: The Use of Pleasure,* trans. Robert Hurley [New York: Vintage, 1986], 31). This question returns in the conclusion to volume 3, where Foucault warns against attributing a historical continuity among elements that may seem analogous in imperial Roman and Christian ethics: "The code elements that concern the economy of pleasures, conjugal fidelity, and relations between men may well

remain analogous, but they will derive from a profoundly altered ethics and from a different way of constituting oneself as the ethical subject of one's sexual behavior" (*The History of Sexuality, Volume 3: The Care of the Self*, trans. Robert Hurley [New York: Vintage, 1988], 240).

55 Thomas McCarthy has made a similar point with regard to Foucault's position on truth and power: "Owing in part to the continued influence of structuralist motifs in his genealogical phase, he swings to the opposite extreme of hypostatizing wholes—regimes, networks, *dispositifs*, and the like—over against parts, thus proposing to replace an abstract individualism with an equally abstract holism" (*Ideals and Illusions: On Reconstruction and Deconstruction in Contemporary Critical Theory* [Cambridge, MA: MIT P, 1991], 56). While McCarthy is much more sympathetic to Habermas's critique of Foucault than I, his critique has been influential in the way that I have framed my concerns here.

56 Eve Sedgwick's concerns regarding the uses to which Foucault's thought has been put are relevant here. She has aptly captured the stunningly banal conclusions stemming from the symmetrical conceptualization of the way supposedly opposing elements intertwine—"kinda subversive, kinda hegemonic": "It concerns me that the force of Foucault's critique of the repression hypothesis has been radically neutralized, in much subsequent engagé criticism, by numb refusals to register the pressure of and, as it were, to participate however resistantly in what can never be more or less than the oblique and queer performance of that critique. In a myriad of ways in contemporary thought—ways in which Foucault himself was hardly unimplicated—his critique of the repression hypothesis has been all but fully recuperated in new alibis *for* the repression hypothesis: in accounts of institutional, discursive, and intrapsychic prohibitions as just so many sites for generating and proliferating—what if not repression?; in neatly symmetrical celebrations of 'productive' 'multiplicities' of 'resistance'—to what if not to repression?; in all the dreary and routine forms of good dog/bad dog criticism by which, like good late capitalist consumers, we persuade ourselves that deciding what we like or don't like about what's happening is the same thing as actually intervening in its production" ("Queer Performativity" 14–15; original emphasis).

57 Two particularly sophisticated examples come to mind: Judith Butler's *Bodies That Matter: On the Discursive Limits of "Sex"* (New York: Routledge, 1993); and Lee Edelman's *Homographesis: Essays in Gay Literary and Cultural Theory* (New York: Routledge, 1994).

58 Butler, *Bodies That Matter* 53.

59 It is worth mentioning here the problematic linkage Butler makes between the deconstruction of the subject and its foundations, and the explicit political ramifications she understands this deconstruction to have. In an essay in which she defends poststructuralist critique, Butler argues that "[t]o deconstruct is not to negate or to dismiss, but to call into question and, perhaps most importantly, to open up a term, like the subject, to a reusage or redeployment that previously has not been authorized" ("Contingent Foundations" 15). These are useful formulations. I would suggest, however, that the moment of suspension alluded to here potentially disables any extension *from* the very "opening" this moment would seem to promise. The subject as a "permanent site of critique" (8) could become a troublesome permanence, insofar as it holds out the possibility of the kind

of deferral of change that remains possible in Habermas's account of the "self-critical" potential constitutive of an intersubjective rationality. In arguing for the "democratic" nature of poststructuralist critique, then, Butler's analysis begs the question of what sort of democracy this would entail, and how this democracy would understand any substantive beyond to the limits of discursive inclusion (see, for example, *Bodies That Matter* 227).

60   Foucault, *Foucault Live* 220.

61   Ibid. 143.

62   Ibid. 144.

63   Ibid. 229. See also Foucault's work contained in the recent collection *Ethics: Subjectivity and Truth*, ed. Paul Rabinow, trans. Robert Hurley et al. (New York: New P, 1997). Two studies in particular provide excellent resources for following the productive direction found in Foucault's later work: Paul Bové, *In the Wake of Theory* (Middletown, CT: Wesleyan UP, 1992), 141–75; and David M. Halperin, *Saint Foucault: Towards a Gay Hagiography* (New York: Oxford UP, 1995).

64   Habermas reveals a barely concealed annoyance that Foucault, late in his career, placed himself within the tradition of both Enlightenment thinking and the Frankfurt School; see Habermas, *The New Conservatism: Cultural Criticism and the Historians' Debate*, ed. and trans. Shierry Weber Nicholsen (Cambridge, MA: MIT P, 1989), 173–79. For Foucault's lectures on Kant, see his *The Politics of Truth*, trans. Sylvère Lotringer (New York: Semiotext[e], 1997).

THREE   *The Citizen's Sexual Shadow*

1   Anthony Giddens has presented what is perhaps the clearest argument for the ideal saturation of sexual relations by modern democratic principles in *The Transformation of Intimacy: Sexuality, Love and Eroticism in Modern Societies* (Stanford: Stanford UP, 1992). While Giddens defends the democratization of intimacy as a central promise of modernity, it is not altogether clear from his analysis precisely what would ground this promise as an ethical imperative; Giddens simply assumes that it is.

2   Habermas, *Structural Transformation* 109. See also Negt and Kluge, *Public Sphere and Experience* 10.

3   Habermas, *Structural Transformation* 111–12.

4   I should acknowledge here a limitation to the proceeding analysis: It will not discuss the racial contours of conceptualizing the citizen, indeed humanity itself, in terms of property ownership. For an excellent investigation of Kant's thinking on Africans, "blackness," and the "grammar of civility," see Ronald A. T. Judy, *(Dis)Forming the American Canon: African-Arabic Slave Narratives and the Vernacular* (Minneapolis: U of Minnesota P, 1993), esp. chaps. 3 and 4. See also Phillip Brian Harper's important discussion of racialized notions of sexual intimacy as they have impacted dominant understandings of sex, privacy, and property in "Private Affairs: Race, Sex, Property, and Persons," *GLQ* 1.2 (1994): 111–33.

5   Morris B. Kaplan has argued that sexual citizenship for lesbians and gay men is possible in terms of "situated freedoms" that go "beyond the thin conceptions of legal person-

ality and negative freedom that inform liberal theory," and that therefore we need "to insist on the concrete social dimension of the assertion of equal citizenship by lesbians and gays. Democratic citizenship is embodied in a plurality of voluntary associations and community institutions that result from the exercise of situated freedoms by specific individuals and groups" (*Sexual Justice* 13). Kaplan examines the defects of traditional liberal theory in terms of its inability to recognize "ethical self-making" and argues compellingly that "the achievement of equality for lesbian and gay citizens is part of the unfinished business of modern democracy" (3). Understandably, the primary context in which he discusses recognizing the right to intimate association is U.S. Constitutional guarantees to *privacy* (see especially pp. 217–27). To what extent this recognition can grant legitimacy to queer sexual affiliations and practices that go beyond conceptualizations of privacy and marriage, however, remains unclear. For other illuminating considerations of rights discourse and citizenship with respect to queers, see Paul Eenam Park Hagland, "International Theory and LGBT Politics: Testing the Limits of a Human Rights-Based Strategy," *GLQ* 3.4 (1997): 357–84; Mark Blasius, *Gay and Lesbian Politics: Sexuality and the Emergence of a New Ethic* (Philadelphia: Temple UP, 1994); David T. Evans, *Sexual Citizenship*; Janet E. Halley, "The Politics of the Closet" and "The Status/Conduct Distinction in the 1993 Revisions to Military Anti-Gay Policy"; the essays by Nan D. Hunter in Duggan and Hunter, *Sex Wars*; and Carl F. Stychin, *Law's Desire: Sexuality and the Limits of Justice* (London: Routledge, 1995). Also of relevance is Jean Cohen and Andrew Arato's expanded notion of rights underlying their important reconsideration of civil society. "The step from bourgeois society to a democratic civil society," they argue, "depends in some measure on a new centrality of rights guaranteeing intimacy and personal autonomy, on the one hand, and communication and association, on the other (thereby replacing the current primacy and model character of property rights). Accordingly, the project of establishing or transforming fundamental rights is one of the most important tasks for collective actors involved in the politics of civil society" (Jean Cohen and Andrew Arato, "Politics and the Reconstruction of the Concept of Civil Society," in *Cultural-Political Interventions in the Unfinished Project of Enlightenment*, ed. Axel Honneth, Thomas McCarthy, Claus Offe, and Albrecht Wellmer [Cambridge, MA: MIT P, 1992], 138). See also their jointly authored book, *Civil Society and Political Theory* (Cambridge, MA: MIT P, 1992).

6 For the differences between Kant and Wolff on "pleasure," and the differences between Kant's and Fichte's sexual theories, see Isabel V. Hull, *Sexuality, State, and Civil Society in Germany, 1700–1815* (Ithaca: Cornell UP, 1996), 300–13. This important book is in many ways a much fuller and historically informed treatment of these issues than I can provide here. Hull's work is especially useful with respect to conceptualizations of gender at the time, and the impact they had on Enlightenment conceptions of politics, the state, and civil society, a topic I have chosen not to discuss as fully as others.

7 Other manuscripts of students' notes from Kant's lectures on ethics also exist, principally one by the philosopher J. G. Herder, one by a student named Georg Ludwig Collins, and one by a lawyer friend of Kant's, Johann Friedrich Vigilantius. While Herder's and Vigilantius's manuscripts rarely refer to sexual ethics, Menzer's hybrid text and the notes

taken by Collins are nearly identical, both in general outline and substance, as well as in the sections dealing with sexual ethics. For purposes of convenience, I will refer only to Menzer's hybrid text, translated in 1930 by Louis Infield (see note 9).

The manuscript notes by Herder, Collins, Vigilantius, and Mrongovius have recently been published in English in the Cambridge Edition of the Works of Immanuel Kant as *Lectures on Ethics*, ed. Peter Heath and J. B. Schneewind, trans. Peter Heath (Cambridge: Cambridge UP, 1997). The introduction by Schneewind contains valuable information about Kant's series of lectures and the manuscript notes of them that have survived (xiii–xxvii). For more information about the manuscript notes from which these lectures were published, see also Menzer's introduction to *Eine Vorlesung Kant's über Ethik*, ed. Paul Menzer (Berlin: Pan Verlag Rolf Heise, 1924), 323–35, and Reinhard Brandt and Werner Stark, eds., *Neue Autographen und Dokumente zu Kants Leben, Schriften und Vorlesungen (Kant-Forschungen I)* (Hamburg: Felix Meiner, 1987). Brauer's manuscript, on which Menzer based his text, now seems to have disappeared. All surviving student manuscripts have been published in volume 27 of *Kant's gesammelte Schriften*, ed. Königlich Preussischen Akademie der Wissenschaften/Akademie der Wissenschaften der DDR, 29 vols. to date (Berlin: Georg Reimer, later Walter de Gruyter and Co., 1900–). Gerhard Lehmann also has a useful introduction to the manuscripts of Kant's lectures on ethics (*Kant's gesammelte Schriften* 27:1037–62). Unless otherwise noted, all emphases in quotations from Kant's works are original.

As to the unusual textual history of these lectures, and the difficulty of attributing to them authorial integrity, I would underscore here that we cannot easily append the proper name "Kant" to these lecture notes. They are, in a sense, "manuscript events," with no final stability with regard to fixed principles of adjudication. On similar difficulties with regard to a lecture by Jacques Lacan, see Jane Gallop, *Reading Lacan* (Ithaca: Cornell UP, 1985), 74–92. I am grateful to Crystal Bartolovich for this suggestion.

There are a number of issues relating to Kant's architectonic in general, and his moral philosophy in particular, that I will not touch on in this chapter, but that are nevertheless relevant to the topics discussed here. Four particular sources have been useful in the formulation of my concerns, and which deal more adequately with other relevant issues: Ronald Beiner and William James Booth, eds., *Kant and Political Philosophy: The Contemporary Legacy* (New Haven: Yale UP, 1993); Mary Gregor, "Translator's Introduction," in Immanuel Kant, *The Metaphysics of Morals*, trans. Mary Gregor (Cambridge: Cambridge UP, 1991), 1–31; Onora O'Neill, *Constructions of Reason: Explorations of Kant's Practical Philosophy* (Cambridge: Cambridge UP, 1989); J. B. Schneewind, "Autonomy, Obligation, and Virtue: An Overview of Kant's Moral Philosophy," in *The Cambridge Companion to Kant*, ed. Paul Guyer (Cambridge: Cambridge UP, 1992), 309–41; and Susan Meld Shell, *The Embodiment of Reason: Kant on Spirit, Generation, and Community* (Chicago: U of Chicago P, 1996).

8   Kant affirms this as well in appendix I to his 1795 essay, "Toward Perpetual Peace": ". . . there can be no conflict of politics, as a doctrine of right put into practice, with morals, as theoretical doctrine of right . . ." ("Toward Perpetual Peace," in Immanuel

Kant, *Practical Philosophy*, trans. and ed. Mary J. Gregor [Cambridge: Cambridge UP, 1996], 338). This edition provides page numbers to the Akademie edition of Kant's works.

9   Immanuel Kant, *Lectures on Ethics*, trans. Louis Infield (1930; reprint, New York: Harper & Row, 1963), 164; *Eine Vorlesung Kants über Ethik* 206. Subsequent page references, cited parenthetically in the text as *Lectures*, indicate first the Infield translation and then the German edition. While for the most part I have followed Infield's translation, I have made some modifications of my own.

10 The concept of "sexual objectification" has been a staple legacy of second-wave feminism, especially in the United States, and in large measure the feminist use of this concept aligns with Kant's understanding of desire as inherently objectifying, although the centrality of male privilege and power in feminist critiques of objectification are of course noticeably absent in Kant. For an excellent examination of "sexual objectification" in both feminist and Kantian ethics, and the problems that inhere in such a totalized view of sexual desire, see Martha C. Nussbaum, "Objectification," in *The Philosophy of Sex: Contemporary Readings*, ed. Alan Soble (Lanham, MD: Rowman and Littlefield, 1997), 283–321.

11 In his translation of Collins's manuscript notes, Peter Heath glosses "*commercium sexuale*" as "sexual intercourse" (see, for example, Heath and Schneewind, *Lectures on Ethics* 158). However, this translation piles one metaphoric rendering on another, while presuming "sexual intercourse" itself to have a self-evident meaning. I have preferred, therefore, to keep the term's Latin metaphor of "commerce" intact. Translating the Latin into "sexual intercourse" could have the advantage of marking how a "private vice" is translated into a publicly recognized virtue through marriage and thus into a legitimate element of the public sphere—its connection to intercourse as communication would thereby not be irrelevant. But this marking would need to be made explicit.

12 Kant, "Toward Perpetual Peace" 112.

13 Kant, *Groundwork of the Metaphysics of Morals* in Kant, *Practical Philosophy* 79.

14 Kant, *Groundwork* 79. The German word *Wert* means both "value" and "worth"; while Gregor's translation uses "worth," I have preferred to use "value." Both senses, however, should be kept in mind in these passages.

15 Kant, *The Metaphysics of Morals* in Kant, *Practical Philosophy* 371. Subsequent page references from this edition are cited parenthetically in the text as *Metaphysics*.

16 In *Lectures* Kant conceives of marriage as a union between equals, although his views on gender in other texts contradict this conceptualization; see Hull, *Sexuality, State, and Civil Society* 301–13.

17 Kant, "On the Common Saying: That May Be Correct in Theory, But It Is of No Use in Practice" in *Practical Philosophy* 289. Gregor translates *Geschäftsmann* as "man of affairs," but this is unnecessarily euphemistic.

18 Georg Lukács similarly points to Kant's ideas about marriage as a legitimized form of property relation and objectification: "The transformation of the commodity relation into a thing of 'ghostly objectivity' cannot therefore content itself with the reduction of all objects for the gratification of human needs to commodities. . . . And there is no

natural form in which human relations can be cast, no way in which man can bring his physical and psychic 'qualities' into play without their being subjected increasingly to this reifying process. We need only think of marriage, and . . . remind ourselves of the way in which Kant, for example, described the situation with the naïvely cynical frankness peculiar to great thinkers" (History and Class Consciousness 100). Theodor Adorno and Max Horkheimer level a similar critique against Kant in their discussion of his work alongside that of Sade; see Dialectic of Enlightenment, trans. John Cumming (New York: Continuum, 1995), 81–119. See also Jacques Lacan's essay, "Kant with Sade," October 51 (winter 1989): 55–104. Kant's justification of marriage in terms of property ownership, that is, the mutual ownership of "organs," is also mentioned in Gilles Deleuze and Félix Guattari, Anti-Oedipus: Capitalism and Schizophrenia, trans. Robert Hurley, Mark Seem, and Helen R. Lane (Minneapolis: U of Minnesota P, 1983), 71–72.

19 Pepita Haezrahi, "The Concept of Man as End-in-Himself," in Kant: A Collection of Critical Essays, ed. Robert Paul Wolff (New York: Anchor Books, 1967), 292; original emphasis. Haezrahi goes on to indicate further difficulties in Kant's reasoning, on its own terms: ". . . Kant's deduction is seen to move in a circle: He presupposes the freedom of the human will as a necessary condition for the possibility, i.e. existence and reality of moral obligation and responsibility; and then attributes dignity to men because they have free will, i.e. are morally responsible. Now a categorical judgment cannot be deduced from two hypothetical judgments. The objective reality of the dignity of man cannot be deduced from the hypothetical reality of freedom, much less can the universality of its application be so deduced" (297). Because of these logical difficulties, Haezrahi concludes that the "synthetic proposition 'All men-qua-men are possessed of dignity' is therefore incapable of any proof whatsoever, including the transcendental proof for the objective necessity of categories" (311). Haezrahi's objections are based on logical procedures; I would add to this the historically specific predications of rational free subjects built into Kant's system as defining limits as well. This essay was first published in Kant-Studien 53 (1962). See also Thomas E. Hill Jr., Dignity and Practical Reason in Kant's Moral Theory (Ithaca: Cornell UP, 1992), 38–57.

20 Haezrahi, "Concept of Man" 292–93.

21 Henry Abelove has written an enormously suggestive and insightful analysis of the reorganization of sexual practices and their value-codings in relation to the transformation of production and work rhythms in early English industrial capitalism. Abelove suggests that the rise in importance of what has come to be known as "sexual intercourse," relative to the importance of other practices that could be called sexual, correlates with new conceptualizations and practices associated with industrial production; see "Some Speculations on the History of 'Sexual Intercourse' During the 'Long Eighteenth Century' in England," in Nationalisms and Sexualities, ed. Andrew Parker, Mary Russo, Doris Sommer, and Patricia Yaeger (New York: Routledge, 1992), 335–42. It is from this essay that I have borrowed the intentionally denaturalizing terminology used to designate what is commonly referred to as "sexual intercourse." It is much too tempting to resist mentioning here that ambiguous demarcations of the sexual acquired quite public visibility

in the media coverage of President Bill Clinton's relationship with former White House intern Monica Lewinsky. To watch personalities in broadcast media debate whether or not Bill Clinton thinks that "oral sex" (presumably meaning a penis in the mouth of someone else, although this presumption is itself suspect) counts as "sexual relations" was a rather unexpected turn of affairs.

22 Fredric Jameson has pointed to the tendency of morality to posit as universal "what are in reality the historical and institutional specifics of a determinate type of group solidarity or class cohesion" (*The Political Unconscious: Narrative as a Socially Symbolic Act* [Ithaca: Cornell UP, 1981], 59). He also indicates the propensity of morality to maintain the eternal conditional of the subjunctive in its ideal-typical formulations: "For moral obligation presupposes a gap between being and duty, and cannot be satisfied with the accomplishment of a single duty and the latter's consequent transformation into being. In order to retain its own characteristic satisfactions, ethics must constantly propose the unrealizable and the unattainable to itself" (194). Adorno summarized this difficulty with characteristic succinctness in his discussion of Kant's moral theory: "The more the freedom of the subject—and the community of subjects—ascribes to itself, the greater the responsibility; and before this responsibility it must fail in a bourgeois life which in practice has never yet endowed a subject with the unabridged autonomy accorded to it in theory. Hence the subject must feel guilty" (*Negative Dialectics* 221; *Negative Dialektik* 220). Consequently, Kant's supreme moral law, the categorical imperative, must be rendered subjunctively: "Freedom is only grasped in determinate negation, corresponding to the concrete form of unfreedom. Positively it becomes an 'as if'" (231; 230).

23 Etienne Balibar has recently, and productively, revisited this problem in *Masses, Classes, Ideas: Studies on Politics and Philosophy Before and After Marx*, trans. James Swenson (New York: Routledge, 1994), 39–60. My analysis has also benefited from Wendy Brown's illuminating discussion of rights in *States of Injury: Power and Freedom in Late Modernity* (Princeton: Princeton UP, 1995).

24 This view has become so prevalent in the lesbian and gay media's accounts of what queers supposedly think that it has arguably acquired the status of a dominant common sense. Some of the more prominent advocates of this position are cited in the introduction with regard to the assimilationist impulses of lesbian and gay visibility politics. These advocates typically use HIV and AIDS as an alibi for a conservative sexual morality. Also of note is recent concern over the rise of "bareback" or unprotected anal sex among gay men. That this is an issue of concern there can be no doubt. But many have turned it into another reason why "long-term committed relationships" are the only responsible and lifesaving form in which gay male sex can be practiced. That such relationships in and of themselves can ward off HIV infection is an extremely dangerous view. It is both illogical and irresponsible to argue, for example, that "cheating" within committed relationships, or indeed within heterosexual marriages, indicates a crisis of individual morals, as is usually countered by sexual conservatives when infidelity is brought up as evidence against monogamy-as-prophylactic. Rather, the difficulties of monogamy should lead us to conclude that there may be something wrong with the way monogamy

itself is understood, at the very least as a universal moral imperative. Here the dangers of a moral individualism can have life-threatening consequences. The imperatives of Douglas Crimp's courageous defense of gay male promiscuity within the constraints of safer sex, it would seem, have not been historically exhausted; see "How to Have Promiscuity in an Epidemic," in *AIDS: Cultural Analysis, Cultural Activism* 237–71. Cindy Patton's *Fatal Advice* also provides an urgent and necessary analysis of sexual mores and practices in relation to the changing politics of AIDS.

As an aside, I would point to Adorno's attack on Karl Jaspers for arguing that "Eroticism becomes humanly meaningful only in the exclusiveness of unconditioned commitment." Adorno sees this as an "unreasonable demand for discipline": "Commitments [*Bindungen*] are classed under mental hygiene and, for that reason, undermine the transcendence which they prescribe. . . . The genuineness [*Echtheit*] of need and belief, which is questionable anyway, has to turn itself into the criterion for the desired [*Ersehnten*] and believed, and becomes counterfeit [*unecht*]" (*Jargon of Authenticity* 69–70; *Jargon der Eigentlichkeit* 459–60). Perhaps Adorno overstates his case; nevertheless his comments present a much needed tonic to the disciplining hyperbole of "commitment" as it circulates today.

25 Larry Kramer, "Sex and Sensibility," *Advocate*, 27 May 1997: 59.

26 Kathy D. Lessa, Letter to the Editor, *Advocate*, 24 June 1997: 8.

27 Bruce Bawer, "Sex Negative Me," *Advocate*, 23 August 1994; reprinted in *Beyond Queer* 172.

28 Ibid. 173.

29 Habermas, *Moral Consciousness and Communicative Action* 210.

30 Habermas, *Between Facts and Norms* 490.

31 G. W. F. Hegel, *Phenomenology of Spirit*, trans. A. V. Miller (Oxford: Oxford UP, 1977), 223.

32 Ibid. 224.

33 Ibid. 227.

34 G. W. F. Hegel, *Philosophy of Right*, trans. T. M. Knox (Oxford: Oxford UP, 1967), 58–59.

FOUR Inseminating the Orient, Disseminating Identity

1 Percy Bysshe Shelley, *Shelley's Prose or the Trumpet of Prophecy*, corr. ed., ed. David Lee Clark (Albuquerque: U of New Mexico P, 1966), 222; emphasis added. For a useful discussion of *Hellas* in its historical moment, see Mark Kipperman, "Macropolitics of Utopia: Shelley's *Hellas* in Context," in *Macropolitics of Nineteenth-Century Literature: Nationalism, Exoticism, Imperialism*, ed. Jonathan Arac and Harriet Ritvo (Durham: Duke UP, 1995), 86–101.

2 Percy Bysshe Shelley, *Shelley's Poetry and Prose*, ed. Donald H. Reiman and Sharon B. Powers (New York: Norton, 1977), 409.

3 Eve Kosofsky Sedgwick has usefully reminded us that the sexual cannot simply be cordoned off from other sites of social power: "[B]ecause the structuring of same-sex bonds can't, in any historical situation marked by inequality and contest between genders, fail to be a site of intensive regulation that intersects virtually every issue of power and gender,

lines can never be drawn to circumscribe within some proper domain of sexuality (whatever that might be) the consequences of a shift in sexual discourse" (*Epistemology of the Closet* 2–3; original emphasis).

More specific analyses of the relation between geopolitical and male same-sex sexual politics that have been helpful in formulating my concerns here include Robert Aldrich, *The Seduction of the Mediterranean: Writing, Art and Homosexual Fantasy* (London: Routledge, 1993); Parminder Kaur Bakshi, "Homosexuality and Orientalism: Edward Carpenter's Journey to the East," in *Edward Carpenter and Late Victorian Radicalism*, ed. Tony Brown (London: Frank Cass, 1990), 151–77; Rudi C. Bleys, *The Geography of Perversion: Male-to-Male Sexual Behavior Outside the West and the Ethnographic Imagination, 1750–1918* (New York: New York UP, 1995); Joseph A. Boone, "Vacation Cruises; or, The Homoerotics of Orientalism," *PMLA* 110.1 (January 1995): 89–107; Ronald Hyam, *Empire and Sexuality: The British Experience* (Manchester: Manchester UP, 1990); Christopher Lane, *The Ruling Passion: British Colonial Allegory and the Paradox of Homosexual Desire* (Durham: Duke UP, 1995); and Eve Kosofsky Sedgwick, *Between Men: English Literature and Male Homosocial Desire* (New York: Columbia UP, 1985), 161–79.

4   David M. Halperin offers an exemplary discussion of how imaginings of ancient Greece continue to have a normalizing function. The purportedly objective classical scholarship on Greek pederasty in the person of Harald Patzer, Halperin argues, deploys an interpretive strategy that "enables the ancient historian to exonerate the Greeks from the charge of actually experiencing homoerotic longings; it allows classicists to normalize Greek desire and to recuperate it for the cause of exclusive heterosexuality" (*One Hundred Years of Homosexuality and Other Essays on Greek Love* [New York: Routledge, 1990], 61). Interpreting ancient Greece continues to bear on the contemporary West, Halperin argues, because "the Greeks are all about us insofar as they represent one of the codes in which we transact our own cultural business: we use our 'truths' about the Greeks to explain ourselves to ourselves and to construct our own experiences, including our sexual experiences" (70). The historical record, he goes on to argue, "should not be pressed into the service of some sort of collective disavowal or used to interpose a false clinical distance between the interpreter and the objects of cultural interpretation. If there is indeed a way to free ourselves from the conceptual tyranny of current sexual categories, it lies not in an attempt to do away with those categories by means of a methodological sleight of hand but in an effort to understand them better as historically conditioned cultural representations — or, to be exact, as instances of an ideology which we not only fashion but also inhabit" (61).

5   Timothy Webb, *English Romantic Hellenism 1700–1824* (Manchester: Manchester UP; New York: Barnes and Noble, 1982), 161. See also Linda Dowling, *Hellenism and Homosexuality in Victorian Oxford* (Ithaca: Cornell UP, 1994), and Richard Jenkyns, *The Victorians and Ancient Greece* (Cambridge, MA: Harvard UP, 1980).

6   Terence Spencer, *Fair Greece Sad Relic: Literary Philhellenism from Shakespeare to Byron* (Athens: Denise Harvey, 1986), 171. For other general studies of European philhellenism, see Helen Angelomatis-Tsourgarakis, *The Eve of the Greek Revival: British Travellers' Perceptions of*

Early Nineteenth-Century Greece (New York: Routledge, 1990); Robert Eisner, Travelers to an Antique Land: The History and Literature of Travel to Greece (Ann Arbor: U of Michigan P, 1991); and Hugh Tregaskis, Beyond the Grand Tour: The Levant Lunatics (London: Ascent, 1979).

7   Quoted in Gregory Jusdanis, Belated Modernity and Aesthetic Culture: Inventing National Literature (Minneapolis: U of Minnesota P, 1991), 15.

8   Quoted in Tregaskis, Beyond the Grand Tour 7.

9   Quoted in Eisner, Travelers to an Antique Land 100.

10 It should be noted that erotic mappings of the "Orient" were by no means clear cut, given the association with southern and eastern Mediterranean areas, such as southern Italy, with non-normative sexual practices as well as more "strictly" oriental areas such as Persia.

11 Jeremy Bentham, "Offences Against Reputation," quoted in Louis Crompton, Byron and Greek Love: Homophobia in Nineteenth-Century England (Berkeley: U of California P, 1985), 111. "Crimes against nature" most often refer to sodomy. However, sodomy in Britain and the rest of western Europe in the eighteenth and nineteenth centuries did not simply denote a penis in a man's anus, as is often assumed. Following Foucault, Jonathan Goldberg correctly notes that sodomy "identifies neither persons nor acts with any coherence or specificity" ("Sodomy in the New World: Anthropologies Old and New," Social Text 29 [1991]: 46). Jeffrey Weeks infers that the "law against sodomy was a central aspect of the taboo on all non-procreative sex" (Coming Out: Homosexual Politics in Britain, from the Nineteenth Century to the Present [London: Quartet, 1977], 12). Yet even Weeks's general formulation does not entirely convey the semiotic slipperiness of sodomy, what Foucault rightly called "that utterly confused category." Such enabling ambiguities continue in the sodomy laws in twenty-three U.S. states, most potently exemplified in the Georgia law upheld by the U.S. Supreme Court in the 1986 Bowers v. Hardwick decision.

    I should note that Bentham's writings on male same-sex sexual activity, most of which remain unpublished, were reasoned attempts to argue for the decriminalization of such activities. He deployed non-Western examples in order to invalidate the argument that these activities were "unnatural"; see, for example, his comments on "Otahite" (Tahiti) in "Offences Against One's Self: Paederasty," Part 1, ed. Louis Crompton, Journal of Homosexuality 3.4 (summer 1978): 399.

12 Sedgwick, Epistemology of the Closet 136.

13 Ibid. 45; original emphasis.

14 Sigmund Freud, "The Relation of the Poet to Day-Dreaming" (1908), The Standard Edition of the Complete Psychological Works of Sigmund Freud, ed. and trans. James Strachey et al., 24 vols. (London: Hogarth, 1955–74), 9:147–48; emphasis added.

15 Meaghan Morris, "Identity Anecdotes," camera obscura 12 (summer 1984): 45; original emphasis.

16 The specificities of the term "phantasy" (as opposed to "fantasy") within psychoanalytic theory will not be broached here, although they are of interest; see the entry for "phantasy" in Jean Laplanche and Jean-Bertrand Pontalis, The Language of Psycho-Analysis, trans. Donald Nicholson-Smith (New York: Norton, 1973).

17 Freud, "A Disturbance of Memory on the Acropolis" (1937), Standard Edition 22:241.

18 Ibid. 22:246.

19 Ibid. 22:243.

20 Ibid. 22:247.

21 Ibid.; emphasis added.

22 Arthur N. Gilbert has documented the rise in sodomy convictions during the Napoleonic Wars, as well as the cultural function of such convictions during a xenophobic moral panic; see his "Buggery and the British Navy, 1700–1861," *Journal of Social History* 10.1 (fall 1976): 72–98, and "Sexual Deviance and Disaster During the Napoleonic Wars," *Albion* 9.1 (spring 1977): 98–113.

23 Quoted in Webb, *English Romantic Hellenism* 116–17. Webb excerpts passages from Henry Fuseli's 1765 translation of Winckelmann's 1755 *Gedancken über die Nachahmung der grie-chischen Wercke in der Mahlerey und Bildhauer-Kunst.*

24 Quoted in Webb, *English Romantic Hellenism* 117–18.

25 Quoted in Richard Dellamora, *Masculine Desire: The Sexual Politics of Victorian Aestheticism* (Chapel Hill: U of North Carolina P, 1990), 111.

26 Dellamora points out that "[i]n the nineteenth century, 'effeminacy' as a term of personal abuse often connotes male-male desire, a threat of deviance that seems to haunt gentlemen should they become too gentle, refined, or glamorous" (*Masculine Desire* 199). For a more detailed discussion of how male same-sex eroticism informed Winckelmann's aesthetics, see also Dennis Sweet, "The Personal, the Political, and the Aesthetic: Johann Joachim Winckelmann's German Enlightenment Life," *Journal of Homosexuality* 16.1–2 (1988): 147–62. Winckelmann's invocation of Sybaris is rather complex, as it value-codes southern Italy as liminally European, and connotes religious differences between Roman Catholic and Protestant. Anglo-Catholicism in mid-nineteenth-century Britain was often coded as a breeding ground for male homoeroticism by its detractors; see David Hilliard, "Unenglish and Unmanly: Anglo-Catholicism and Homosexuality," *Victorian Studies* 25 (1982): 181–210.

27 Quoted in Webb, *English Romantic Hellenism* 118.

28 As Crompton observes, Byron "liked to boast of his expertise in Turkish history" (*Byron and Greek Love* 111), and had written in a letter to his attorney John Hanson in 1808 that he wished "to study India and Asiatic policy and manners" (George Gordon, Lord Byron, *Byron's Letters and Journals*, vol. 1, ed. Leslie A. Marchand [Cambridge, MA: Harvard UP, 1973–82], 175). All further references to Byron's letters will be given in the text, indicated by the abbreviation LJ and followed by volume and page number.

29 Quoted in Crompton, *Byron and Greek Love* 134.

30 Quoted in ibid. 117.

31 Jerome Christensen has argued that the codes used to refer to male same-sex sexual encounters by Byron and his like-minded friends do not indicate "the formation of a gay sense of identity in response to real or imagined persecution" but rather "the deliberate formation of a *literary* sense of identity, a shared sense of what Matthews calls a profession" ("Setting Byron Straight: Class, Sexuality, and the Poet," in *Literature and the Body: Essays on Populations and Persons*, ed. Elaine Scarry [Baltimore: Johns Hopkins UP, 1988], 135; original emphasis). While Christensen is right to argue that "gay" would be anach-

ronistic, and that Byron's male same-sex sexual encounters were more often than not written through literary codes, he overemphasizes the extent to which such encounters were nothing more than literary, or rather, that "gay" and "literary" would be somehow mutually exclusive. This kind of literary functionalism seems to motivate Christensen's subtle and quite suspect questioning of the very real material persecution of men who engaged in same-sex sex—a persecution, he writes, that was "real or imagined." Christensen claims Byron may have "learned" his "homosexuality from books—old books" (130), without recognizing the anachronism of "homosexuality" he duplicates as he argues against an anachronistic reading of Byron as having a gay identity. Moreover, Christensen too quickly assumes that Byron's public *and* private writings accomplish a "fluent translation of the domain of sexuality into nationality" (130). In Byron's private correspondence he did not automatically identify ancient and modern Greece as a transhistorical "nation" distinct from its contemporary Ottoman rulers, though this is a distinct feature of his *public* writings.

32 Jonathan Dollimore, *Sexual Dissidence: Augustine to Wilde, Freud to Foucault* (Oxford: Clarendon, 1991), 342.

33 According to the *Oxford English Dictionary*, a "pathic" refers generally to the "passive" partner in male same-sex sexual activities, though it leaves unclear what "passive" might more precisely signify and in relation to what activities.

34 Jusdanis, *Belated Modernity* 16. All quotations from Byron's poetry and drama are from Jerome McGann's edition of Byron's *The Complete Poetical Works* (Oxford: Clarendon, 1980–86). Citations from *Childe Harold's Pilgrimage* are by canto and stanza; citations from *Sardanapalus* are by act, scene, and line.

35 Christensen, "Setting Byron Straight" 130.

36 Jusdanis, *Belated Modernity* 14.

37 Ibid. 16.

38 Sir Richard F. Burton, *The Sotadic Zone* (Boston: Longwood, 1977), 17–18; emphasis added.

39 George L. Mosse, *Nationalism and Sexuality: Middle-Class Morality and Sexual Norms in Modern Europe* (Madison: U of Wisconsin P, 1985), 13. See also Ed Cohen, *Talk on the Wilde Side: Toward a Genealogy of a Discourse on Male Sexualities* (New York: Routledge, 1993); and Michael Mason, *The Making of Victorian Sexual Attitudes* (Oxford: Oxford UP, 1994). Roy Porter and Lesley Hall's argument about the role of evangelicalism in shifting sexual mores from Georgian "pleasures of procreation" to "a new emphasis on public character and civic probity, a reidealization of love over sensuality, of the moral law over personal impulse or the vertigo of sensibility" is pertinent here (Roy Porter and Lesley Hall, *The Facts of Life: The Creation of Sexual Knowledge in Britain, 1650–1950* [New Haven: Yale UP, 1995], 126).

40 Mosse, *Nationalism and Sexuality* 30–31.

41 Weeks, *Coming Out* 52; original emphasis.

42 David Newsome, *Godliness and Good Learning: Four Studies on a Victorian Ideal* (London: Cassell, 1961), 216.

43 John Addington Symonds, "A Problem in Greek Ethics," in Symonds, *Sexual Inversion* (New York: Bell, 1984), 62. Further citations to this edition will be given in the text. See Halperin (*One Hundred Years of Homosexuality* 154 n. 12) for more detailed information on

the publication of Symond's essay, Ellis's inclusion of it in 1897, as well as the eventual suppression of Ellis's own book.

44 Sedgwick, *Between Men* 216, 217.

FIVE *Shelley's Heart*

1 I have borrowed here from Sedgwick's powerful analysis of minoritizing and universalizing paradigms of homosexuality; see *Epistemology of the Closet* 27–35.

2 Edward Carpenter and George Barnefield, *The Psychology of the Poet Shelley* (New York: E. P. Dutton, 1925).

3 Exemplary arguments about the historicity of cultural value can be found in John Guillory, *Cultural Capital: The Problem of Literary Canon Formation* (Chicago: U of Chicago P, 1993); Barbara Herrnstein Smith, *Contingencies of Value: Alternative Perspectives for Critical Theory* (Cambridge, MA: Harvard UP, 1988); and Jane Tompkins, *Sensational Designs: The Cultural Work of American Fiction 1790–1860* (New York: Oxford UP, 1985).

4 Neil Fraistat has recently examined the production of a normative cultural interest in Shelley in terms of the mutual imbrication of class divisions and cultural divisions — those between "high" and "low" — as they are made salient in early editions of his poems. Fraistat's analysis is particularly useful for its emphasis on the textual edition as part of a "monumentalizing" rhetoric, for its connection of the "textual space" to the "social space of its production, distribution, and reception" ("Illegitimate Shelley: Radical Piracy and the Textual Edition as Cultural Performance," *PMLA* 109.3 [May 1994]: 419).

5 I have borrowed here from Fredric Jameson's discussion of the dialectics structuring the thematics, forms, and cultural work of the nineteenth-century European novel in *The Political Unconscious*. He argues that "in its generic form, a specific narrative paradigm continues to emit its ideological signals long after its original content has become historically obsolete" (186). While my argument about Shelley is not about the generic forms or contents of the poet's texts per se, Jameson's dialectical understanding of the relationships between history, ideology, and textual form has nevertheless been important in the formulation of my concerns here.

6 Karsten Engelberg explains that Shelley's heart was part of "an extraordinary memorial display at Boscombe Manor, where the Shelley family resided." He adds: "The copy of the Pisa edition of Shelley's *Adonais*, in which the heart was said to have been found wrapped after Mary's death, is now in the Bodleian Library along with a letter in which the heart is described as a piece of leather" ("The Sentimental Appeal in Shelley Criticism, 1822–1860," in *The Romantic Heritage: A Collection of Critical Essays*, ed. Karsten Engelberg [Copenhagen: Publications of the University of Copenhagen Department of English, 1983], 158). Legend has it that Shelley's heart was buried along with Sir Percy Florence Shelley in the graveyard of the parish church in Bournemouth. Boscombe Manor now houses the Shelley Rooms, which are comprised of two museum and study rooms and whose collections concentrate on the period of Shelley's residence at Casa Magni in 1822. Along with books owned by and written about Shelley, the Shelley Rooms also have displays of poetic tributes to him and a quite substantial collection of his hair. My thanks to

Norman Hixon, Yvonne Hixon, and Andrea Magon for patiently escorting me around Bournemouth in search of these rather macabre artifacts.

7 Sylva Norman, *Flight of the Skylark: The Development of Shelley's Reputation* (Norman: U of Oklahoma P, 1954), 12; emphasis added. For studies and bibliographies of Shelley's critical reputation, see Miriam Allot, "Attitudes to Shelley: The Vagaries of a Critical Reputation," in *Essays on Shelley*, ed. Miriam Allott (Tottowa, NJ: Barnes and Noble, 1982), 1–38; James E. Barcus, ed., *Shelley: The Critical Heritage* (London: Routledge and Kegan Paul, 1975); Clement Dunbar, *A Bibliography of Shelley Studies: 1823–1950* (New York: Garland, 1976); Karsten Engelberg, *The Making of the Shelley Myth: An Annotated Bibliography of Criticism of Percy Bysshe Shelley, 1822–1860* (London: Mansell, 1988); Nancy Fogarty, *Shelley in the Twentieth Century: A Study of the Development of Shelley Criticism in England and America 1916–1971* (Salzburg: Institut für Englische Sprache und Literatur, 1976); Frederick A. Pottle, "The Case of Shelley," in *English Romantic Poets: Modern Essays in Criticism*, ed. M. H. Abrams (New York: Oxford UP, 1960), 289–306; Robert Metcalf Smith et al., *The Shelley Legend* (New York: Charles Scribner's Sons, 1945); and Newman Ivey White, *Shelley*, vol. 2 (New York: Alfred A. Knopf, 1940), 389–418.

George Edward Woodberry, a late-Victorian editor of Shelley, also notes retrospectively the development of what many would call the "Shelley cult": "The natural charm by which Shelley fascinated his familiar friends lives after him, and has gathered about him for his defense a group of men whose affection for him seems no whit lessened because they never knew him face to face. The one common characteristic prominent in all who have written of him with sympathy, however meager or valuable their individual contributions of praise, criticism, or information, is this sentiment of direct, intimate, intense personal loyalty which he has inspired in them to a degree rare, if not unparalleled in literary annals" (*Literary Memoirs of the Nineteenth Century* [New York: Harcourt, Brace and Company, 1921], 3). While they do not figure in my analysis here, Tennyson and the Cambridge Apostles were also influential in shaping a particular image of Shelley as a disembodied and androgynous aesthete; see Richard Cronin, "Shelley, Tennyson, and the Apostles, 1828–1832," *Keats-Shelley Review* 5 (1990): 14–40. For the differences between Shelley's radicalism and the more compromising stances of Tennyson and the Apostles, particularly as they relate to the impacted relations between normative homosociality and proscribed homoeroticism, see Dellamora, *Masculine Desire* 16–41.

8 Lady Jane Shelley, ed., *Shelley Memorials* (London, 1859), 219.

9 See Foucault, *The History of Sexuality, Volume 1*; Halperin, *One Hundred Years of Homosexuality* 15–40; and Chauncey, "From Sexual Inversion to Homosexuality."

10 Anon., rev. of *Life of Percy Bysshe Shelley*, by Thomas Jefferson Hogg, "Memoir of Percy Bysshe Shelley," by Thomas Love Peacock, *Recollections of the Last Days of Shelley and Byron*, by Edward J. Trelawny, *Shelley Memorials*, ed. Lady Jane Shelley, and *The Works of Percy Bysshe Shelley*, ed. Mary Shelley, *Quarterly Review* 110.220 (1861): 281.

11 Quoted in Robert Metcalf Smith, *The Shelley Legend* 255.

12 Charles and Mary Cowden Clarke, *Recollections of Writers* (New York, 1878), 151.

13 Quoted in Charles Wells Moulton, ed., *The Library of Literary Criticism of English and American Authors*, vol. 4 (Buffalo: Moulton, 1910), 695.

14 William Michael Rossetti, "Memoir," *The Complete Poetical Works of Percy Bysshe Shelley*, vol. 1, ed. William Michael Rossetti (London, 1878), 1. I have preferred to use the revised edition of 1878, which reproduced the memoir and the preface with only a few minor changes.

15 William Michael Rossetti, comp., *The Rossetti Papers* (New York: Scribner's, 1903), 55–56. My thanks to Jean Ferguson Carr for pointing out the probability of Eliza Lynn Linton as the identity of the letter writer. Rossetti also received a letter from Seymour Barone Kirkup in April 1870, in which Kirkup claims that he possessed Shelley's bed and had "slept for months on it in hopes of seeing Shelley's ghost" (*Rossetti Papers* 531).

16 Rossetti, "Memoir" 122.

17 Robert Browning, *An Essay on Percy Bysshe Shelley* (London, 1888), 19. Susan J. Wolfson has detailed a similar feminization of Keats in nineteenth-century critical commentary in "Feminizing Keats," in *Critical Essays on John Keats*, ed. Hermione de Almeida (Boston: G. K. Hall, 1990), 317–56. Browning's essay is also of particular interest for its representation of the avowedly atheist Shelley as, at heart, a Christian.

18 Ideals of androgynous manliness, however, were often opposed to "effeminacy" per se; middle-class manliness usually included only what were seen as feminine "virtues." See Norman Vance, *Sinews of the Spirit: The Ideal of Christian Manliness in Victorian Literature and Religious Thought* (Cambridge: Cambridge UP, 1985); Leonore Davidoff and Catherine Hall, *Family Fortunes*; and Mosse, *Nationalism and Sexuality*.

19 Claudia Nelson, "Sex and the Single Boy: Ideals of Manliness and Sexuality in Victorian Literature for Boys," *Victorian Studies* 32.4 (summer 1989): 530–31.

20 J. A. Mangan and James Walvin, eds., *Manliness and Morality: Middle-Class Masculinity in Britain and America 1800–1940* (New York: St. Martin's, 1987), 2.

21 Weeks, *Sex, Politics and Society: The Regulation of Sexuality since 1800* (London: Longman, 1981), 40.

22 Nelson, "Sex and the Single Boy" 549.

23 R. R. Madden, *Infirmities of Genius*, vol. 1 (Philadelphia, 1833), 16. Fraistat's "Illegitimate Shelley" is particularly useful for its discussion of Mary Shelley's role in securing an angelic and depoliticized image of Shelley for middle- and upper-class readers. See also Susan J. Wolfson, "Editorial Privilege: Mary Shelley and Percy Shelley's Audiences," in *The Other Mary Shelley*, ed. Audrey A. Fisch, Anne K. Mellor, and Esther H. Schor (New York: Oxford UP, 1993), 39–72.

24 Leigh Hunt, *The Autobiography of Leigh Hunt*, ed. J. E. Marpurgo (London: Cresset, 1948), 359. See also Hunt's comments on Shelley in *Lord Byron and Some of His Contemporaries* (Philadelphia, 1828), and his essay "Shelley" in *Leigh Hunt as Poet and Essayist*, ed. Charles Kent (London, 1891), 476–78.

25 Thomas Jefferson Hogg, *The Life of Percy Bysshe Shelley* (New York: E. P. Dutton, 1906), 46.

26 Ernest Dowden, *Life of Percy Bysshe Shelley* (New York: Barnes and Noble, 1966), 5–6.

27 W. R. Greg, *Literary and Social Judgments* (New York, 1876), 131.

28 Rossetti, "Memoir" 8.

29 Anon., rev. of *Life* 291.

30 Jeffrey Richards, " 'Passing the Love of Women': Manly Love and Victorian Society," in Mangan and Walvin, *Manliness and Morality* 113–14.

31 Thomas De Quincey, "Notes on Gilfillan's Literary Portraits," *The Collected Writings of Thomas De Quincey*, vol. 11, ed. David Masson (Edinburgh, 1890), 376–77.

32 Thomas Medwin, *Life of Percy Bysshe Shelley*, rev. ed. (London: Oxford UP, 1913), 18.

33 J. A. Symonds, *Shelley* (London, 1878), 26.

34 De Quincey, "Notes on Gilfillan's Literary Portraits" 377; Edward J. Trelawny, *Recollections of the Last Days of Shelley and Byron*, 2nd ed. (Boston, 1859), 89; Coventry Patmore, *Principle in Art* (London, 1889), 92; Peter George Patmore, *Personal Recollections of Lamb, Hazlitt, and Others*, ed. Richard Henry Stoddard (New York, 1875), 164; Medwin, *Life of Percy Bysshe Shelley* 15; Anon., rev. of *Life* 282.

35 De Quincey, "Notes on Gilfillan's Literary Portraits" 377; James Anthony Froude, "A Leaf from the Real Life of Lord Byron," *The Nineteenth Century* 14 (August 1883): 232.

36 Arthur Symons, *The Romantic Movement in English Poetry* (New York: E. P. Dutton, 1909), 271; emphasis added.

37 Ibid. 273; emphasis added.

38 Matthew Arnold, "Byron," *The Complete Works of Matthew Arnold*, vol. 9, ed. R. H. Super (Ann Arbor: U of Michigan P, 1973), 237. I should note that the image of Shelley as an ineffectual angel, which places him within a feminized private sphere, was quite far removed from the long tradition of a more public, radical Shelley that survived among working-class organizations in the nineteenth century. For documents on and commentary about this tradition, see Edward Aveling and Eleanor Marx, *Shelley's Socialism* (1888; London: Journeyman P, 1975); Siddiq M. Kalim, *The Social Orpheus: Shelley and the Owenites* (Lahore: Research Council, Government College, 1973); Henry S. Salt, *Shelley's Principles: Has Time Refuted or Confirmed Them? A Retrospect and Forecast* (1892; Brooklyn: Haskell House, 1977), *Percy Bysshe Shelley: A Monograph* (London, 1888), *A Shelley Primer* (London, 1887), and *Poet and Pioneer* (London, 1896); Bouthaina Shaaban, "Shelley in the Chartist Press," *Keats-Shelley Memorial Bulletin* 34 (1983): 41–60; and George Bernard Shaw, "Shaming the Devil About Shelley," *The Collected Works of Bernard Shaw*, vol. 29 (New York: Wm. Wise, 1930–32), 248–59.

    The use of gender to dichotomize the politics of interpreting Shelley's own politics has been persistent. Henry S. Salt, for one, attempted to recoup the radical Shelley as "virile." More recently, Paul Foot has championed the truer, more masculine and radical Shelley over the supposedly false, effeminate one. Foot figures the dominant, apolitical image of Shelley as a type of castration, recalling the times when Oxford undergraduates, back from crew games, would chisel off the testicles of the Shelley memorial statue at University College: " 'We've got Shelley's balls!' was the plummy cry of triumph which would echo through the quadrangles at three or four in the morning." "The castration of Shelley at British places of learning," Foot explains, "has not been confined to rowing oafs. Ladies and gentleman of letters have been at it far longer, and with far greater effect" (*Red Shelley* [London: Sidgwick and Jackson, 1980], 9–10). Foot notes that Friedrich Engels also used the castration metaphor to describe the depoliticization of Shelley in *The Condition of the Working Class in England*.

39 Matthew Arnold, "Shelley," *The Complete Works* 11:320.

40 Ibid. 326.

41 Quoted in Ronald A. Duerksen, *Shelleyan Ideas in Victorian Literature* (The Hague: Mouton, 1966), 124.

42 John Ruskin, "The Imagination Contemplative," *The Literary Criticism of John Ruskin*, ed. Harold Bloom (New York: Da Capo, 1965), 34.

43 Charles Kingsley, "Thoughts on Shelley and Byron," *Fraser's Magazine* 48 (November 1853): 570. It was not until fifteen to twenty years later that many other critics and reviewers would begin to mention the increased interest in Shelley among middle-class readers. Mathilde Blind, who would later become a founding member of the Shelley Society, notes in an 1870 lecture that Shelley's fame "is spreading year by year into ever-widening circles" (*Shelley. A lecture delivered to the Church of Progress, in St. George's Hall, Langham Place, London, W., on Sunday evening, January 9th, 1870* [London, 1870], 3). In the memoir preceding his 1874 edition of Shelley's poems, William B. Scott exclaims, "Now, at the distance of half a century, how great is the change! One edition after another is printed, and still they succeed each other year by year, without any sign of cessation" ("Memoir," *The Poetical Works of Percy Bysshe Shelley*, ed. William B. Scott [London, 1874], xv). And in an anonymous review in the October 1887 *Church Quarterly Review*, we are told that "[t]he popularity of Shelley has been increasing, and at the present time is at its height. There is certainly no limit to either the size or the number of editions of his works which are published. . . . He enjoys many devoted adherents, many enthusiastic admirers, who lavish their money, time, and energies on his service; and perhaps it is this excessive enthusiasm which interferes with the true appreciation of his merits. Certainly, neither his own nor his worshippers' reputation for sanity is increased by the existence of the Shelley Society" (Anon., "Shelley and the Shelley Society," *Church Quarterly Review* [October 1887]: 51–52). Proceedings of the Shelley Society, founded in London in 1886, have been reprinted; see Shelley Society, ed., *The Shelley Society's Papers* (London, 1888–91; New York: AMS P, 1975), and *Note–Book of the Shelley Society* (London, 1888; New York: AMS P, 1975).

44 Kingsley, "Thoughts on Shelley and Byron" 571.

45 David Hilliard, "Unenglish and Unmanly: Anglo-Catholicism and Homosexuality," *Victorian Studies* 25.2 (winter 1982): 190.

46 Vance, *Sinews of the Spirit* 112–13.

47 Anon., rev. of *Shelley Memorials*, ed. Lady Jane Shelley, *Quarterly Review* (October 1859): 361.

48 Thornton Hunt, "Shelley—By One Who Knew Him," in *Shelley and Keats as They Struck Their Contemporaries*, ed. Edmund Blunden (London: Beaumont, 1925), 21.

49 Ibid. 50–51.

50 T. N. Talfourd, *Speech for the Defendant in the Prosecution of The Queen v. Moxon, for the Publication of Shelley's Works* (London, 1841), 18–19; emphasis added.

51 Anon., "Shelley," *Westminster Review* 2 (1870): 78.

52 William Michael Rossetti, *The Diary of William Michael Rossetti*, ed. Odette Bornand (Oxford: Clarendon, 1977), 171.

53 The following section on fetishism was first presented as a paper at the Fourth Annual Lesbian, Bisexual, and Gay Studies Conference, Harvard University, November 1990. For useful contemporary openings of fetishism as an important epistemological and political problematic, see Emily Apter and William Pietz, eds., *Fetishism as Cultural Discourse*

(Ithaca: Cornell UP, 1993). My critique of Shelley's authoritative texts that follows owes much to, but also departs from, Terry Eagleton's "Ideology and Scholarship," in *Historical Studies and Literary Criticism*, ed. Jerome J. McGann (Madison: U of Wisconsin P, 1985), 114–25; and Jerome J. McGann's *A Critique of Modern Textual Criticism* (Chicago: U of Chicago P, 1983).

54 Anon., rev. of *Shelley Memorials* 374; emphasis added. This conflation of the poet's body and his corpus can be found in nearly every critical commentary on him during the nineteenth century. The belief in the enduring presence of the poet through his texts takes an intriguing detour in the work of twentieth-century mediums like Herman Behr, and especially Shirley Carson Jenney, who bypassed his extant texts altogether and claim to have actually "channeled" Shelley's spirit; see Herman Behr, *Letters from Eternity* (New York: Privately printed, 1930), and the following by Shirley Carson Jenney: *The Fortune of Eternity* (Ilfracombe: Arthur H. Stockwell, 1950); *The Fortunes of Heaven* (London: Arthur H. Stockwell, [1937]); *The Great War-Cloud* (London: Arthur H. Stockwell, [1938]); and *Moments with Shelley* (Culver City, CA: Highland Press, [c. 1950]). All of Jenney's texts, in fact, are catalogued in the British Library under "Suppositious Works" of Shelley himself.

55 Freud, *Standard Edition* 7:153.

56 Ibid. 21:156–57.

57 Richard von Krafft-Ebing, *Psychopathia Sexualis*, 12th ed., trans. Franklin S. Klaf (New York: Stein and Day, 1965), 146.

58 Havelock Ellis, *Studies in the Psychology of Sex*, vol. 5 (Philadelphia: F. A. Davis, 1930), 8.

59 Jacques Lacan, *The Four Fundamental Concepts of Psycho-Analysis*, ed. Jacques-Alain Miller, trans. Alan Sheridan (New York: Norton, 1981), 182.

60 Symons, *The Romantic Movement in English Poetry* 282.

61 After Mary Shelley's editions of Shelley's works in 1824 and 1839, two important editions appeared that indicate in their titles the hagiographic conflation of the poet's body and texts, further reinforcing Forman's notion of editing as disinterment: Lady Jane Shelley's *Shelley Memorials* (London, 1859), and Richard Garnett's *Relics of Shelley* (London, 1862). The importance Shelley editors placed on "correcting" his texts, whatever their guiding principle, cannot be overestimated. In his edition of *Alastor*, for example, Forman provides a lengthy footnote on a controversy between Rossetti and Swinburne over a particular line. Swinburne insists that if Rossetti's emendation were the correct one, "we should have here from one of the mightiest masters of language the most monstrous example on record of verbal deformity, of distorted and convulsed inversion or perversion of words" (Percy Bysshe Shelley, *Alastor, or the Spirit of Solitude: And Other Poems*, ed. Harry Buxton Forman [London, 1876], 31 n. 2).

62 Rossetti, "Memoir" 1.

63 William Michael Rossetti, "Preface," *The Complete Poetical Works of Percy Bysshe Shelley*, vol. 1, ed. William Michael Rossetti (London, 1878), xviii; emphasis added.

64 Donald H. Reiman, *Romantic Texts and Contexts* (Columbia: U of Missouri P, 1987), 87; Anon., "Shelley," *Westminster Review* 2 (1870): 78.

65 Rossetti, "Preface" xiii–xiv.

66 Harry Buxton Forman, "Preface," *The Poetical Works of Percy Bysshe Shelley*, vol. 1, ed. Harry Buxton Forman (London, 1876), xxxiii.

67 Ibid. xxx, xvi.

68 Ibid. xiv; original emphasis.

69 Ibid. xxxvi.

70 H. Buxton Forman, "Shelley, 'Peterloo,' and 'The Mask of Anarchy,'" *The Gentleman's Magazine* 3 (1887): 252.

EPILOGUE

1 Immanuel Kant, *The Conflict of the Faculties*, trans. Mary J. Gregor (Lincoln: U of Nebraska P, 1992), 163. Subsequent page references in the text refer to this edition.

BIBLIOGRAPHY

Abelove, Henry. "Some Speculations on the History of 'Sexual Intercourse' During the 'Long Eighteenth Century' in England." *Nationalisms and Sexualities.* Ed. Andrew Parker, Mary Russo, Doris Sommer, and Patricia Yaeger. New York: Routledge, 1992. 335–42.

Adorno, Theodor. *Critical Models: Interventions and Catchwords.* Trans. Henry W. Pickford. New York: Columbia UP, 1998.

———. *Gesammelte Schriften.* Ed. Rolf Tiedemann with Gretel Adorno, Susan Buck-Morss, and Klaus Schultz. 20 vols. Frankfurt am Main: Suhrkamp, 1970–86.

———. *The Jargon of Authenticity.* Trans. Knut Tarnowski and Frederick Will. Evanston: Northwestern UP, 1973.

———. *Minima Moralia: Reflections from Damaged Life.* Trans. E. F. N. Jephcott. London: Verso, 1974.

———. *Negative Dialectics.* Trans. E. B. Ashton. New York: Continuum, 1973.

Aldrich, Robert. *The Seduction of the Mediterranean: Writing, Art and Homosexual Fantasy.* London: Routledge, 1993.

Alexander, M. Jacqui. "Redrafting Morality: The Postcolonial State and the Sexual Offences Bill of Trinidad and Tobago." *Third World Women and the Politics of Feminism.* Ed. Chandra Talpade Mohanty, Ann Russo, and Lourdes Torres. Bloomington: Indiana UP, 1991. 133–52.

Allott, Miriam. "Attitudes to Shelley: The Vagaries of a Critical Reputation." *Essays on Shelley.* Ed. Miriam Allott. Tottowa, NJ: Barnes and Noble, 1982. 1–38.

Angelomatis-Tsourgarakis, Helen. *The Eve of the Greek Revival: British Travellers' Perceptions of Early Nineteenth-Century Greece.* New York: Routledge, 1990.

Apel, Karl-Otto. "Normatively Grounding 'Critical Theory' through Recourse to the Lifeworld? A Transcendental-Pragmatic Attempt to Think with Habermas against Habermas." *Philosophical Interventions in the Unfinished Project of Enlightenment.* Ed. Axel Honneth, Thomas McCarthy, Claus Offe, and Albrecht Wellmer. Cambridge, MA: MIT P, 1992. 125–70.

Apter, Emily, and William Pietz, eds. *Fetishism as Cultural Discourse.* Ithaca: Cornell UP, 1993.

Armstrong, Nancy. *Desire and Domestic Fiction: A Political History of the Novel.* New York: Oxford UP, 1987.

Arnold, Matthew. *The Complete Works of Matthew Arnold.* Ed. R. H. Super. 11 vols. Ann Arbor: U of Michigan P, 1973–77.

Aveling, Edward, and Eleanor Marx. *Shelley's Socialism.* 1888. London: Journeyman, 1975.

Bakshi, Parminder Kaur. "Homosexuality and Orientalism: Edward Carpenter's Journey to the East." *Edward Carpenter and Late Victorian Radicalism.* Ed. Tony Brown. London: Frank Cass, 1990. 151–77.

Balibar, Etienne. *Masses, Classes, Ideas: Studies on Politics and Philosophy Before and After Marx.* Trans. James Swenson. New York: Routledge, 1994.

Barcus, James E., ed. *Shelley: The Critical Heritage.* London: Routledge and Kegan Paul, 1975.

Bawer, Bruce. *A Place at the Table: The Gay Individual in American Society.* New York: Simon and Schuster, 1993.

———. *Beyond Queer: Challenging Gay Left Orthodoxy.* New York: Free P, 1996.

Behr, Herman. *Letters from Eternity.* New York: Privately printed, 1930.

Beiner, Ronald, and William James Booth, eds. *Kant and Political Philosophy: The Contemporary Legacy.* New Haven: Yale UP, 1993.

Benhabib, Seyla. *Situating the Self.* New York: Routledge, 1991.

Bentham, Jeremy. "Offences Against One's Self: Paederasty." Parts 1 and 2. Ed. Louis Crompton. *Journal of Homosexuality* 3.4 (summer 1978): 383–405; 4.1 (fall 1978): 91–107.

———. *The Theory of Fictions.* Ed. C. K. Ogden. Paterson, NJ: Littlefield, Adams and Co., 1959.

Berlant, Lauren. *The Queen of America Goes to Washington City: Essays on Sex and Citizenship.* Durham: Duke UP, 1997.

Berlant, Lauren, and Michael Warner. "Sex in Public." *Critical Inquiry* 24 (winter 1998): 547–66.

Bersani, Leo. "Is the Rectum a Grave?" *AIDS: Cultural Analysis, Cultural Activism.* Ed. Douglas Crimp. Cambridge, MA: MIT P, 1988. 197–222.

———. *Homos.* Cambridge, MA: Harvard UP, 1995.

Blasius, Mark. *Gay and Lesbian Politics: Sexuality and the Emergence of a New Ethic.* Philadelphia: Temple UP, 1994.

Bleys, Rudy C. *The Geography of Perversion: Male-to-Male Sexual Behavior Outside the West and the Ethnographic Imagination, 1750–1918.* New York: New York UP, 1995.

Blind, Mathilde. *Shelley. A lecture delivered to the Church of Progress, in St. George's Hall, Langham Place, London, W., on Sunday evening, January 9th, 1870.* London, 1870.

Bloch, Ernst. *Natural Law and Human Dignity.* Trans. Dennis J. Schmidt. Cambridge, MA: MIT P, 1986.

Blunden, Edmund, ed. *Shelley and Keats as They Struck Their Contemporaries.* London: Beaumont, 1925.

Boone, Joseph A. "Vacation Cruises; or, the Homoerotics of Imperialism." *PMLA* 110.1 (January 1995): 89–107.

Bové, Paul A. *In the Wake of Theory.* Hanover, NH: Wesleyan UP/UP of New England, 1992.

Brandt, Reinhard, and Werner Stark, eds. *Neue Autographen und Dokumente zu Kants Leben, Schriften und Vorlesungen (Kant-Forschungen I).* Hamburg: Felix Meiner, 1987.

Brown, Wendy. *States of Injury: Power and Freedom in Late Modernity.* Princeton: Princeton UP, 1995.

Browning, Robert. *An Essay on Percy Bysshe Shelley*. 1852. London: Reeves and Turner for the Shelley Society, 1888.

Burton, Sir Richard F. *The Sotadic Zone*. 1886. Boston: Longwood P, 1977.

Butler, Judith. *Bodies That Matter: On the Discursive Limits of "Sex."* New York: Routledge, 1993.

———. "Contingent Foundations: Feminism and the Question of "Postmodernism.' " *Feminists Theorize the Political*. Ed. Judith Butler and Joan W. Scott. New York: Routledge, 1992. 3–21.

Byron, George Gordon. *Lord Byron's Letters and Journals*. Ed. Leslie A. Marchand. 8 vols. Cambridge, MA: Harvard UP, 1973–82.

———. *The Complete Poetical Works*. Ed. Jerome J. McGann. 6 vols. Oxford: Clarendon, 1980–86.

Califia, Pat. *Public Sex: The Culture of Radical Sex*. Pittsburgh: Cleis P, 1994.

Carpenter, Edward, and George Barnefield. *The Psychology of the Poet Shelley*. New York: E. P. Dutton, 1925.

Chambers, Simone. "Discourse and Democratic Practices." *The Cambridge Companion to Habermas*. Ed. Stephen K. White. Cambridge: Cambridge UP, 1995. 233–59.

Champagne, John. *The Ethics of Marginality: A New Approach to Gay Studies*. Minneapolis: U of Minnesota P, 1995.

Chauncey, George, Jr. "From Sexual Inversion to Homosexuality: Medicine and the Changing Conceptualization of Female Deviance." *Salmagundi* 58–59 (fall 1982–winter 1983): 114–46.

Christ, Carol. "Victorian Masculinity and the Angel in the House." *A Widening Sphere: Changing Roles of Victorian Women*. Ed. Martha Vicinus. Bloomington: Indiana UP, 1977. 146–62.

Christensen, Jerome. "Setting Byron Straight: Class, Sexuality, and the Poet." *Literature and the Body: Essays on Populations and Persons*. Ed. Elaine Scarry. Baltimore: Johns Hopkins UP, 1988. 125–59.

Clarke, Charles Cowden, and Mary Cowden Clarke. *Recollections of Writers*. New York, 1878.

Clarke, Eric O. "All About Eve." *GLQ* 3 (1996): 109–23.

Clarke, Eric O., and Mathew Henson. "Hot Damme! Reflections on Gay Publicity." *Boys: Masculinities in Contemporary Culture*. Ed. Paul Smith. New York: Westview/Harper Collins, 1996. 131–50.

Cohen, Ed. *Talk on the Wilde Side: Toward a Genealogy of a Discourse on Male Sexualities*. New York: Routledge, 1993.

Cohen, Jean L., and Andrew Arato. *Civil Society and Political Theory*. Cambridge, MA: MIT P, 1992.

———. "Politics and the Reconstruction of the Concept of Civil Society." *Cultural-Political Interventions in the Unfinished Project of Enlightenment*. Ed. Axel Honneth, Thomas McCarthy, Claus Offe, and Albrecht Wellmer. Cambridge, MA: MIT P, 1992. 121–42.

Cott, Nancy F. "Passionlessness: An Interpretation of Victorian Sexual Ideology, 1790–1850." *Signs* 4.2 (winter 1978): 219–36.

Crimp, Douglas. "How to Have Promiscuity in an Epidemic." *AIDS: Cultural Analysis, Cultural Activism*. Ed. Douglas Crimp. Cambridge, MA: MIT P, 1988. 237–71.

———. "Portraits of People with AIDS." *Cultural Studies*. Ed. Lawrence Grossberg, Cary Nelson, and Paula Treichler. New York: Routledge, 1992. 117–30.

Crimp, Douglas, and Adam Rolston. *AIDS Demo Graphics.* Seattle: Bay P, 1990.

Crompton, Louis. *Byron and Greek Love: Homophobia in Nineteenth-Century England.* Berkeley: U of California P, 1985.

Cronin, Richard. "Shelley, Tennyson, and the Apostles, 1828–1832." *Keats-Shelley Review* 5 (1990): 14–40.

Culler, Jonathan. *Framing the Sign: Criticism and Its Institutions.* Norman: U of Oklahoma P, 1988.

Dangerous Bedfellows, eds. *Policing Public Sex: Queer Politics and the Future of* AIDS *Activism.* Boston: South End P, 1996.

Davidoff, Leonore, and Catherine Hall. *Family Fortunes: Men and Women of the English Middle Class, 1780–1850.* Chicago: U of Chicago P, 1987.

Deleuze, Gilles, and Félix Guattari. *Anti-Oedipus: Capitalism and Schizophrenia.* Trans. Robert Hurley, Mark Seem, and Helen R. Lane. Minneapolis: U of Minnesota P, 1983.

Dellamora, Richard. *Masculine Desire: The Sexual Politics of Victorian Aestheticism.* Chapel Hill: U of North Carolina P, 1990.

D'Emilio, John. "Capitalism and Gay Identity." *Powers of Desire: The Politics of Sexuality.* Ed. Ann Snitow, Christine Stansell, and Sharon Thompson. New York: Monthly Review P, 1983. 100–13.

De Quincey, Thomas. *The Collected Writings of Thomas De Quincey.* Ed. David Masson. 14 vols. Edinburgh, 1890.

Derrida, Jacques. *Limited Inc.* Evanston: Northwestern UP, 1988.

Dollimore, Jonathan. *Sexual Dissidence: Augustine to Wilde, Freud to Foucault.* Oxford: Clarendon, 1991.

Dowden, Ernest. *Life of Percy Bysshe Shelley.* 1886. New York: Barnes and Noble, 1966.

Dowling, Linda. *Hellenism and Homosexuality in Victorian Oxford.* Ithaca: Cornell UP, 1994.

Duerksen, Roland A. *Shelleyan Ideas in Victorian Literature.* The Hague: Mouton, 1966.

Duggan, Lisa, and Nan D. Hunter. *Sex Wars: Sexual Dissent and Political Culture.* New York: Routledge, 1995.

Dunbar, Clement. *A Bibliography of Shelley Studies: 1823–1950.* Folkestone, Kent: Wm. Dawson and Sons; New York: Garland, 1976.

Eagleton, Terry. "Ideology and Scholarship." *Historical Studies and Literary Criticism.* Ed. Jerome J. McGann. Madison: U of Wisconsin P, 1985. 114–25.

Edelman, Lee. *Homographesis: Essays in Gay Literary and Cultural Theory.* New York: Routledge, 1994.

Eisner, Robert. *Travelers to an Antique Land: The History and Literature of Travel to Greece.* Ann Arbor: U of Michigan P, 1991.

Ellis, Havelock. *Studies in the Psychology of Sex.* 6 vols. Philadelphia: F. A. Davis, 1930.

Engelberg, Karsten. "The Sentimental Appeal in Criticism of Shelley, 1822–1860." *The Romantic Heritage: A Collection of Critical Essays.* Ed. Karsten Engelberg. Copenhagen: Publications of the University of Copenhagen Department of English, 1983. 153–72.

———. *The Making of the Shelley Myth: An Annotated Bibliography of Criticism of Percy Bysshe Shelley 1822–1860.* London: Mensell, 1988.

Evans, David T. *Sexual Citizenship: The Material Construction of Sexualities.* London: Routledge, 1993.

Fogarty, Nancy. *Shelley in the Twentieth Century: A Study of the Development of Shelley Criticism in England and America 1916–1971*. Salzburg: Institut für Englische Sprache und Literatur, 1976.

Foot, Paul. *Red Shelley*. London: Sidgwick and Jackson, 1980.

Forman, Harry Buxton. "Preface." *The Poetical Works of Percy Bysshe Shelley*. Ed. Harry Buxton Forman. Vol. 1. London, 1876. 4 vols. xi–xl.

———. "Shelley, 'Peterloo,' and 'The Mask of Anarchy.' " *The Gentleman's Magazine* 3 (1887): 250–52.

Foucault, Michel. *The Archaeology of Knowledge*. Trans. A. M. Sheridan Smith. New York: Pantheon, 1972.

———. *Ethics: Subjectivity and Truth*. Ed. Paul Rabinow. Trans. Robert Hurley et al. New York: New P, 1997.

———. *Foucault Live (Interviews, 1966–84)*. Trans. John Johnston. Ed. Sylvère Lotringer. New York: Semiotext(e), 1989.

———. *The History of Sexuality, Volume 1: An Introduction*. Trans. Robert Hurley. New York: Vintage, 1980.

———. *The History of Sexuality, Volume 2: The Use of Pleasure*. Trans. Robert Hurley. New York: Vintage, 1986.

———. *The History of Sexuality, Volume 3: The Care of the Self*. Trans. Robert Hurley. New York: Vintage, 1988.

———. *The Politics of Truth*. Ed. Sylvère Lotringer. New York: Semiotext(e), 1997.

———. *Power/Knowledge: Selected Interviews and Other Writings 1972–1977*. Ed. Colin Gordon. Trans. Colin Gordon, Leo Marshall, John Mepham, and Kate Soper. New York: Pantheon, 1980.

Fraistat, Neil. "Illegitimate Shelley: Radical Piracy and the Textual Edition as Cultural Performance." *PMLA* 109.3 (May 1994): 409–23.

Fraser, Nancy. "From Recognition to Redistribution: Dilemmas of Justice in a 'Post-Socialist' Age." *New Left Review* 212 (1996): 68–93.

———. *Unruly Practices: Power, Discourse, and Gender in Contemporary Social Theory*. Minneapolis: U of Minnesota P, 1989.

Fraser, Nancy, and Linda Gordon. "Contract versus Charity: Why Is There No Social Citizenship in the United States?" *Socialist Review* 22.3 (1992): 45–67.

Freud, Sigmund. *The Standard Edition of the Complete Psychological Works of Sigmund Freud*. Ed. and trans. James Strachey et al. 24 vols. London: Hogarth, 1955–74.

Froude, James Anthony. "A Leaf from the Real Life of Lord Byron." *The Nineteenth Century* 14 (August 1883): 228–42.

Frutkin, Alan, and Gerry Kroll. "Gays on the Tube." *Advocate* 20 August 1996: 20.

Gallop, Jane. *Reading Lacan*. Ithaca: Cornell UP, 1985.

Garnett, Richard, ed. *Relics of Shelley*. London: Moxon, 1862.

Giddens, Anthony. *The Transformation of Intimacy: Sexuality, Love and Eroticism in Modern Societies*. Stanford: Stanford UP, 1992.

Gide, André. *The Immoralist*. Trans. Richard Howard. New York: Vintage, 1996.

Gilbert, Arthur N. "Buggery and the British Navy, 1700–1861." *Journal of Social History* 10.1 (fall 1976): 72–98.

————. "Sexual Deviance and Disaster During the Napoleonic Wars." *Albion* 9.1 (Spring 1977): 98–113.

Gluckman, Amy, and Betsy Reed, eds. *Homo Economics: Capitalism, Community, and Lesbian and Gay Life.* New York: Routledge, 1997.

Goldberg, Jonathan. "Sodomy in the New World: Anthropologies Old and New." *Social Text* 29 (1991): 46–56.

Greg, W. R. *Literary and Social Judgments.* 1873. New York: H. Holt, 1876.

Guillory, John. *Cultural Capital: The Problem of Literary Canon Formation.* Chicago: U of Chicago P, 1993.

Habermas, Jürgen. *Autonomy and Solidarity: Interviews with Jürgen Habermas.* Ed. Peter Dews. London: Verso, 1986.

————. *Between Facts and Norms: Contributions to a Discourse Theory of Law and Democracy.* Trans. William Rehg. Cambridge, MA: MIT P, 1995.

————. *Communication and the Evolution of Society.* Trans. Thomas McCarthy. Boston: Beacon P, 1979.

————. "Further Reflections on the Public Sphere." *Habermas and the Public Sphere.* Ed. Craig Calhoun. Cambridge, MA: MIT P, 1992. 421–61.

————. *The Inclusion of the Other: Studies in Political Theory.* Ed. Ciaran Cronin and Pablo De Greiff. Trans. Ciaran Cronin et al. Cambridge, MA: MIT P, 1998.

————. *Justification and Application: Remarks on Discourse Ethics.* Trans. Ciaran Cronin. Cambridge, MA: MIT P, 1993.

————. *Legitimation Crisis.* Trans. Thomas McCarthy. Boston: Beacon P, 1975.

————. "Modernity—An Incomplete Project." *The Anti-Aesthetic: Essays on Postmodern Culture.* Ed. Hal Foster. Port Townsend, WA: Bay P, 1983.

————. *Moral Consciousness and Communicative Action.* Trans. Thomas McCarthy. Cambridge, MA: MIT P, 1990.

————. *The New Conservatism: Cultural Criticism and the Historians' Debate.* Trans., ed. Shierry Weber Nicholsen. Cambridge, MA: MIT P, 1989.

————. *On the Pragmatics of Communication.* Ed. Maeve Cook. Cambridge, MA: MIT P, 1998.

————. *The Past as Future.* Ed., trans. Max Pensky. Lincoln: U of Nebraska P, 1994.

————. *The Philosophical Discourse of Modernity: Twelve Lectures.* Trans. Frederick Lawrence. Cambridge, MA: MIT P, 1987.

————. *Postmetaphysical Thinking: Philosophical Essays.* Trans. William Mark Hohengarten. Cambridge, MA: MIT P, 1992.

————. *The Structural Transformation of the Public Sphere: An Inquiry into a Category of Bourgeois Society.* Trans. Thomas Burger. Cambridge, MA: MIT P, 1989.

————. *Theory and Practice.* Trans. John Viertel. Boston: Beacon P, 1973.

————. *The Theory of Communicative Action. Volume 1: Reason and the Rationalization of Society.* Trans. Thomas McCarthy. Boston: Beacon P, 1984.

————. *The Theory of Communicative Action. Volume 2: Lifeworld and System: A Critique of Functionalist Reason.* Trans. Thomas McCarthy. Boston: Beacon P, 1987.

————. *Toward a Rational Society: Student Protest, Science, and Politics.* Trans. Jeremy J. Shapiro. Boston: Beacon P, 1970.

Haezrahi, Pepita. "The Concept of Man as End-in-Himself." *Kant: A Collection of Critical Essays.* Ed. Robert Paul Wolff. New York: Anchor Books, 1967. 291–313.

Hagland, Paul Eenam Park. "International Theory and LGBT Politics: Testing the Limits of a Human Rights-Based Strategy." *GLQ* 3.4 (1997): 357–84.

Halley, Janet E. "The Politics of the Closet: Towards Equal Protection for Gay, Lesbian and Bisexual Identity." *Reclaiming Sodom.* Ed. Jonathan Goldberg. New York: Routledge, 1994. 145–204.

———. "The Status/Conduct Distinction in the 1993 Revisions to Military Anti-Gay Policy: A Legal Archaeology." *GLQ* 3.2–3 (1996): 159–252.

Halperin, David M. "More or Less Gay-Specific." *London Review of Books* 18.10 (23 May 1996): 24–27.

———. *One Hundred Years of Homosexuality and Other Essays on Greek Love.* New York: Routledge, 1990.

———. *Saint Foucault: Towards a Gay Hagiography.* New York: Oxford UP, 1995.

Handy, Bruce. "He Called Me Ellen Degenerate?" *Time* 14 April 1997: 86.

Harper, Philip Brian. "Gay Male Identities, Personal Privacy, and Relations of Public Exchange: Notes on Directions for Queer Critique." *Social Text* 52/53 (fall/winter 1997): 4–29.

———. "Play in the Dark: Privacy, Public Sex, and the Erotics of the Cinema Venue." *camera obscura* 30 (May 1992): 93–111.

———. "Private Affairs: Race, Sex, Property, and Persons." *GLQ* 1.2 (1994): 111–34.

Harris, Daniel. *The Rise and Fall of Gay Culture.* New York: Hyperion, 1997.

Harrison, Fraser. *The Dark Angel: Aspects of Victorian Sexuality.* New York: Universe, 1977.

Hazlitt, William. *The Complete Works of William Hazlitt.* Ed. P. P. Howe. 21 vols. London: J. M. Dent and Sons, 1930–34.

Hegel, G. W. F. *Phenomenology of Spirit.* Trans. A. V. Miller. Oxford: Oxford UP, 1977.

———. *Philosophy of Right.* Trans. T. M. Knox. Oxford: Oxford UP, 1967.

Hennesy, Rosemary. "Queer Visibility and Commodity Culture." *Cultural Critique* 29 (winter 1994/95): 31–76.

Hill, Thomas E., Jr. *Dignity and Practical Reason in Kant's Moral Theory.* Ithaca: Cornell UP, 1992.

Hilliard, David. "Unenglish and Unmanly: Anglo-Catholicism and Homosexuality." *Victorian Studies* 25 (1982): 181–210.

Hirschman, Albert O. *The Passions and the Interests: Political Arguments for Capitalism before Its Triumph.* Princeton: Princeton UP, 1977.

Hogg, Thomas Jefferson. *The Life of Percy Bysshe Shelley.* 1858. New York: E. P. Dutton, 1906.

Hohendahl, Peter Uwe. *The Institution of Criticism.* Ithaca: Cornell UP, 1982.

Honneth, Axel. *The Critique of Power: Reflective Stages in a Critical Social Theory.* Trans. Kenneth Baynes. Cambridge, MA: MIT P, 1991.

———. *The Fragmented World of the Social: Essays in Social and Political Philosophy.* Ed. Charles W. Wright. Albany: SUNY P, 1995.

Honneth, Axel, and Hans Joas, eds. *Communicative Action: Essays on Jürgen Habermas's The Theory of Communicative Action.* Cambridge, MA: MIT P, 1990.

Hull, Isabel V. *Sexuality, State, and Civil Society in Germany, 1700–1815.* Ithaca: Cornell UP, 1996.

Hunt, Leigh. *The Autobiography of Leigh Hunt*. 1859. Ed. J. E. Marpurgo. London: Cresset, 1948.

———. *Leigh Hunt as Poet and Essayist*. Ed. Charles Kent. London, 1891.

———. *Lord Byron and Some of His Contemporaries*. Philadelphia, 1828.

Hunt, Thornton. "Shelley—By One Who Knew Him." *Shelley and Keats as They Struck Their Contemporaries*. Ed. Edmund Blunden. London: Beaumont, 1925. 11–53.

Hyam, Ronald. *Empire and Sexuality: The British Experience*. Manchester: Manchester UP, 1990.

Jäger, Wolfgang. *Öffentlichkeit und Parlamentarismus: Eine Kritik an Jürgen Habermas*. Stuttgart: W. Kohlhammer, 1973.

Jameson, Fredric. *Late Marxism: Adorno, or, The Persistence of the Dialectic*. London: Verso, 1990.

———. *The Political Unconscious: Narrative as a Socially Symbolic Act*. Ithaca: Cornell UP, 1981.

Jay, Martin. "The Debate over Performative Contradiction: Habermas versus the Poststructuralists." *Philosophical Interventions in the Unfinished Project of Enlightenment*. Ed. Axel Honneth, Thomas McCarthy, Claus Offe, and Albrecht Wellmer. Cambridge, MA: MIT P, 1992. 261–79.

Jenkyns, Richard. *The Victorians and Ancient Greece*. Cambridge, MA: Harvard UP, 1980.

Jenney, Shirley Carson. *The Fortune of Eternity*. Ilfracombe: Arthur H. Stockwell, 1950.

———. *The Fortunes of Heaven*. London: Arthur H. Stockwell, [1937].

———. *The Great War-Cloud*. London: Arthur H. Stockwell, [1938].

———. *Moments with Shelley*. Culver City, CA: Highland Press, [c. 1950].

Judy, Ronald A. T. *(Dis)Forming the American Canon: African-Arabic Slave Narratives and the Vernacular*. Minneapolis: U of Minnesota P, 1993.

———. "On the Question of Nigga Authenticity." *boundary 2* 21.3 (1994): 211–30.

Juhasz, Alexandra. AIDS TV: *Identity, Community, and Alternative Video*. Durham: Duke UP, 1996.

Jusdanis, Gregory. *Belated Modernity and Aesthetic Culture: Inventing National Literature*. Minneapolis: U of Minnesota P, 1991.

Kalim, Siddiq M. *The Social Orpheus: Shelley and the Owenites*. Lahore: Research Council, Government College, 1973.

Kant, Immanuel. *The Conflict of the Faculties*. Trans. Mary J. Gregor. Lincoln: U of Nebraska P, 1992.

———. *Eine Vorlesung Kants über Ethik*. Ed. Paul Menzer. Berlin: Pan Verlag Rolf Heise, 1924.

———. *Kant's gesammelte Schriften*. Ed. Königliche Preussische Akademie der Wissenschaften/ Akademie der Wissenschaften der DDR. 29 vols. to date. Berlin: George Reimer, later Walter de Gruyter and Co., 1900–.

———. *Lectures on Ethics*. Trans. Louis Infield. 1930. New York: Harper and Row, 1963.

———. *Lectures on Ethics*. Ed. Peter Heath and J. B. Schneewind. Trans. J. B. Schneewind. The Cambridge Edition of the Works of Immanuel Kant. Paul Guyer and Allen W. Wood, gen. eds. Cambridge: Cambridge UP, 1997.

———. *Practical Philosophy*. Trans., ed. Mary J. Gregor. The Cambridge Edition of the Works of Immanuel Kant. Paul Guyer and Allen W. Wood, gen. eds. Cambridge: Cambridge UP, 1996.

Kaplan, Morris B. *Sexual Justice: Democratic Citizenship and the Politics of Desire*. New York: Routledge, 1997.

Kelly, Michael, ed. *Critique and Power: Recasting the Foucault/Habermas Debate*. Cambridge, MA: MIT P, 1994.

[Kingsley, Charles.] "Thoughts on Shelley and Byron." *Fraser's Magazine* 48 (November 1853): 568–76.

Kipperman, Mark. "Macropolitics of Utopia: Shelley's *Hellas* in Context." *Macropolitics of Nineteenth-Century Literature: Nationalism, Exoticism, Imperialism*. Ed. Jonathan Arac and Harriet Ritvo. Durham: Duke UP, 1995. 86–101.

Kirk, Marshall, and Hunter Madsen. *After the Ball: How America Will Conquer Its Fear and Hatred of Gays in the '90s*. New York: Doubleday, 1989.

Krafft-Ebing, Richard von. *Psychopathia Sexualis*. 1877. Trans. Franklin S. Klaf. 12th ed. New York: Stein and Day, 1965.

Kramer, Larry. "Gay Culture, Redefined." *New York Times* 12 December 1997: A35.

———. "Sex and Sensibility." *Advocate* 27 May 1997: 59–70.

Lacan, Jacques. *The Four Fundamental Concepts of Psycho-Analysis*. Ed. Jacques-Alain Miller. Trans. Alan Sheridan. New York: Norton, 1981.

———. "Kant with Sade." *October* 51 (winter 1989): 55–104.

Lane, Christopher. *The Ruling Passion: British Colonial Allegory and the Paradox of Homosexual Desire*. Durham: Duke UP, 1995.

Laplanche, Jean, and Jean-Bertrand Pontalis. *The Language of Psycho-Analysis*. Trans. Donald Nicholson-Smith. New York: Norton, 1973.

Lessa, Kathy D. Letter to the Editor. *Advocate* 24 June 1997: 8.

Rev. of *Life of Percy Bysshe Shelley*, by Thomas Jefferson Hogg; "Memoir of Percy Bysshe Shelley," by Thomas Love Peacock; *Recollections of the Last Days of Shelley and Byron*, by Edward J. Trelawny; *Shelley Memorials*, ed. Lady Jane Shelley; and *The Works of Percy Bysshe Shelley*, ed. Mary Shelley. *Quarterly Review* 110.220 (1861): 289–328.

Lukács, Georg. *History and Class Consciousness: Studies in Marxist Dialectics*. Trans. Rodney Livingstone. Cambridge, MA: MIT P, 1986.

Lukenbill, Grant. *Untold Millions: Positioning Your Business for the Gay and Lesbian Consumer Revolution*. New York: HarperCollins, 1995.

Lyotard, Jean-François. *The Differend: Phrases in Dispute*. Trans. Georges Van Den Abbeele. Minneapolis: U of Minnesota P, 1988.

Madden, R. R. *Infirmities of Genius*. 2 vols. Philadelphia, 1833.

Mangan, J. A., and James Walvin, eds. *Manliness and Morality: Middle-Class Masculinity in Britain and America 1800–1940*. New York: St. Martin's, 1987.

Marcuse, Herbert. *Reason and Revolution: Hegel and the Rise of Social Theory*. Boston: Beacon P, 1960.

Martin, Biddy. "Extraordinary Homosexuals and the Fear of Being Ordinary." *differences* 6.2–3 (1994): 101–25.

———. "Sexualities Without Genders and Other Queer Utopias." *diacritics* 24.2–3 (1994): 104–21.

Marx, Karl. *Capital: A Critique of Political Economy*. Vol. 1. Trans. Ben Fowkes. London: Penguin, 1990.

————. *Grundrisse: Foundations of the Critique of Political Economy.* Trans. Martin Nicolaus. London: Penguin, 1993.

————. *Karl Marx: Selected Writings.* Ed. David McLellan. Oxford: Oxford UP, 1977.

Mason, Edward T. *Personal Traits of British Authors.* New York: Charles Scribner's Sons, 1885.

Mason, Michael. *The Making of Victorian Sexual Attitudes.* Oxford: Oxford UP, 1994.

McCarthy, Thomas. *Ideals and Illusions: On Reconstruction and Deconstruction in Contemporary Critical Theory.* Cambridge, MA: MIT P, 1991.

McGann, Jerome J. *A Critique of Modern Textual Criticism.* Chicago: U of Chicago P, 1983.

Medwin, Thomas. *Conversations of Lord Byron.* London, 1824.

————. *Life of Percy Bysshe Shelley.* 1847. Rev. ed. London: Oxford UP, 1913.

Merck, Mandy. "Death Camp: Feminism vs. Queer Theory." *New Sexual Agendas.* Ed. Lynne Segal. New York: New York UP, 1997. 232–37.

Merle, W. H. "Shelley at Eton." 1848. *Shelley and Keats as They Struck Their Contemporaries.* Ed. Edmund Blunden. London: Beaumont, 1925. 1–5.

"Missing the Boat." *Advocate* 13 May 1997: 13–14.

Morris, Meaghan. "Identity Anecdotes." *camera obscura* 12 (summer 1984): 41–65.

Mosse, George L. *Nationalism and Sexuality: Middle-Class Morality and Sexual Norms in Modern Europe.* Madison: U of Wisconsin P, 1985.

Moulton, Charles Wells, ed. *The Library of Literary Criticism of English and American Authors.* Vol. 4. Buffalo: Moulton, 1910. 8 vols.

Negt, Oskar. "What Is a Revival of Marxism and Why Do We Need One Today?: Centennial Lecture Commemorating the Death of Marx." *Marxism and the Interpretation of Culture.* Ed. Cary Nelson and Lawrence Grossberg. Urbana: U of Illinois P, 1988. 211–234.

Negt, Oskar, and Alexander Kluge. *Public Sphere and Experience: Towards an Analysis of the Bourgeois and Proletarian Public Sphere.* Trans. Peter Labanyi, Jamie Owen Daniel, and Assenka Oksiloff. Minneapolis: U of Minnesota P, 1993.

Nelson, Claudia. "Sex and the Single Boy: Ideals of Manliness and Sexuality in Victorian Literature for Boys." *Victorian Studies* 32.4 (summer 1989): 525–50.

Newsome, David. *Godliness and Good Learning: Four Studies in a Victorian Ideal.* London: John Murray, 1961.

Norman, Sylva. *Flight of the Skylark: The Development of Shelley's Reputation.* Norman: U of Oklahoma P, 1954.

Nussbaum, Martha C. "Objectification." *The Philosophy of Sex: Critical Readings.* 3rd ed. Ed. Alan Soble. Lanham, MD: Rowman and Littlefield, 1997. 283–321.

O'Neill, Onora. *Constructions of Reason: Explorations of Kant's Practical Philosophy.* Cambridge: Cambridge UP, 1989.

Ouida [Marie Louise de la Ramée]. "A New View of Shelley." *North American Review* 150 (February 1890): 246–62.

Patmore, Coventry. *Principle in Art, etc.* London, 1889.

Patmore, Peter George. *Personal Recollections of Lamb, Hazlitt, and Others.* Ed. Richard Henry Stoddard. New York, 1875.

Patton, Cindy. *Fatal Advice: How Safe-Sex Education Went Wrong.* Durham: Duke UP, 1996.

———. "Tremble, Hetero Swine!" *Fear of a Queer Planet: Queer Politics and Social Theory.* Ed. Michael Warner. Minneapolis: U of Minnesota P, 1993. 143–77.

Perkin, Harold. *Origins of Modern English Society.* London: Routledge and Kegan Paul, 1969.

Porter, Roy, and Lesley Hall. *The Facts of Life: The Creation of Sexual Knowledge in Britain, 1650–1950.* New Haven: Yale UP, 1995.

Pottle, Frederick A. "The Case of Shelley." *English Romantic Poets: Modern Essays in Criticism.* Ed. M. H. Abrams. New York: Oxford UP, 1960. 289–306.

Quine, W. V. *Methods of Logic.* 4th ed. Cambridge, MA: Harvard UP, 1982.

Rasmussen, David, ed. *Universalism vs. Communitarianism: Contemporary Debates in Ethics.* Cambridge, MA: MIT P, 1990.

Rehg, William. *Insight and Solidarity: The Discourse Ethics of Jürgen Habermas.* Berkeley: U of California P, 1997.

Reiman, Donald H. *Romantic Texts and Contexts.* Columbia: U of Missouri P, 1987.

Richards, Jeffrey. " 'Passing the Love of Women': Manly Love and Victorian Society." *Manliness and Morality: Middle-Class Masculinity in Britain and America 1800–1940.* Ed. J. A. Mangan and James Walvin. New York: St. Martin's, 1987. 92–122.

Rossetti, William Michael. *The Diary of William Michael Rossetti.* Ed. Odette Bornand. Oxford: Clarendon, 1977.

———. "Memoir." *The Complete Poetical Works of Percy Bysshe Shelley.* Ed. William Michael Rossetti. Vol. 1. London: Moxon, 1878. 3 vols. 1–154.

———. "Preface." *The Complete Poetical Works of Percy Bysshe Shelley.* Ed. William Michael Rossetti. Vol. 1. London: Moxon, 1878. 3 vols. xi–xviii.

———. *The Rossetti Papers.* Comp. William Michael Rossetti. New York: Scribner's, 1903.

Rotello, Gabriel. *Sexual Ecology: AIDS and the Destiny of Gay Men.* New York: Dutton, 1997.

Rubin, Gayle. "Thinking Sex: Notes Towards a Radical Theory of the Politics of Sexuality." *Pleasure and Danger: Exploring Female Sexuality.* Ed. Carole S. Vance. Boston: Routledge and Kegan Paul, 1984. 267–319.

Ruskin, John. "The Imagination Contemplative." 1846. *The Literary Criticism of John Ruskin.* Ed. Harold Bloom. New York: Da Capo, 1965. 25–35.

Salt, Henry S. *Percy Bysshe Shelley: A Monograph.* London, 1888.

———. *Poet and Pioneer.* London, 1896.

———. *Shelley's Principles: Has Time Refuted or Confirmed Them? A Retrospect and Forecast.* 1892. New York: Haskell House, 1977.

Sandel, Michael J. *Liberalism and the Limits of Justice.* 1982. 2nd ed. Cambridge: Cambridge UP, 1998.

———. "The Procedural Republic and the Unencumbered Self." *Political Theory* 12 (1984): 81–96; reprinted in *Contemporary Political Philosophy.* Ed. Robert E. Goodin and Philip Pettit. Oxford: Blackwell, 1997. 247–55.

Schiller, Friedrich. *On the Aesthetic Education of Man.* Ed., trans. Elizabeth M. Wilkinson and L. A. Willoughby. Oxford: Clarendon P, 1967.

Schneewind, J. B. "Autonomy, Obligation, and Virtue: An Overview of Kant's Moral Philosophy." *The Cambridge Companion to Kant.* Ed. Paul Guyer. Cambridge: Cambridge UP, 1991. 309–41.

Scott, William B. "Memoir." *The Poetical Works of Percy Bysshe Shelley.* Ed. William B. Scott. London: George Routledge and Sons, 1874. xi–xxxiv.

Sedgwick, Eve Kosofsky. *Between Men: English Literature and Male Homosocial Desire.* New York: Columbia UP, 1985.

———. *Epistemology of the Closet.* Berkeley: U of California P, 1990.

———. "Queer Performativity: Henry James's *The Art of the Novel.*" *GLQ* 1.1 (1993): 1–15.

Shaaban, Bouthaina. "Shelley in the Chartist Press." *Keats-Shelley Memorial Bulletin* 34 (1983): 41–60.

Shaw, George Bernard. *The Collected Works of Bernard Shaw.* 32 vols. New York: Wm. H. Wise, 1930–32.

Shell, Susan Meld. *The Embodiment of Reason: Kant on Spirit, Generation, and Community.* Chicago: U of Chicago P, 1996.

"Shelley." Rev. of *The Poetical Works of Percy Bysshe Shelley,* ed. William Michael Rossetti. *Westminster Review* 2 (1870): 75–97.

"Shelley and the Shelley Society." Rev. of *Life of Percy Bysshe Shelley,* by Ernest Dowden, and *Publications of the Shelley Society. Church Quarterly Review* (October 1887): 51–77.

Shelley, Lady Jane, ed. *Shelley Memorials.* London, 1859.

Rev. of *Shelley Memorials,* ed. Lady Jane Shelley. *Quarterly Review* (October 1859): 360–91.

Shelley, Percy Bysshe. *Alastor, or the Spirit of Solitude: And Other Poems.* Ed. Harry Buxton Forman. London, 1876.

———. *Shelley's Poetry and Prose.* Ed. Donald H. Reiman and Sharon B. Powers. New York: Norton, 1977.

———. *Shelley's Prose or the Trumpet of Prophecy.* Corr. ed. Ed. David Lee Clark. Albuquerque: U of New Mexico P, 1966.

Shelley Society, ed. *The Shelley Society's Papers.* London, 1888–91; New York: AMS P, 1975.

———. *Note-Book of the Shelley Society.* London, 1888; New York: AMS P, 1975.

Simmel, Georg. *The Philosophy of Money.* Trans. Tom Bottomore and David Frisby. Ed. David Frisby. 2nd ed. London: Routledge, 1990.

Simpson, Mark, ed. *Anti-Gay.* London: Cassell, 1996.

Singer, Linda. *Erotic Welfare: Sexual Theory and Politics in the Age of Epidemic.* Ed. Judith Butler and Maureen MacGrogan. New York: Routledge, 1993.

Smith, Anna Marie. "The Good Homosexual and the Dangerous Queer: Resisting the 'New Homophobia.'" *New Sexual Agendas.* Ed. Lynne Segal. New York: New York University P, 1997. 214–31.

Smith, Barbara Herrnstein. *Contingencies of Value: Alternative Perspectives for Critical Theory.* Cambridge, MA: Harvard UP, 1988.

Smith, Robert Metcalf, et al. *The Shelley Legend.* New York: Charles Scribner's Sons, 1945.

Spencer, Terence. *Fair Greece Sad Relic: Literary Philhellenism from Shakespeare to Byron.* 1954. Athens: Denise Harvey, 1986.

Spivak, Gayatri Chakravorty. *In Other Worlds: Essays in Cultural Politics.* New York: Routledge, 1988.

———. *Outside in the Teaching Machine.* New York: Routledge, 1993.

Streitmatter, Rodger. *Unspeakable: The Rise of the Gay and Lesbian Press in America.* Boston: Faber and Faber, 1995.

Stychin, Carl F. *Law's Desire: Sexuality and the Limits of Justice.* London: Routledge, 1995.

Sullivan, Andrew. "The Marriage Moment." *Advocate* 20 January 1998: 59–67.

———. *Virtually Normal: An Argument about Homosexuality.* New York: Alfred A. Knopf, 1995.

Sweet, Denis M. "The Personal, the Political, and the Aesthetic: Johann Joachim Winckelmann's German Enlightenment Life." *Journal of Homosexuality* 16.1–2 (1988): 147–62.

Symonds, John Addington. *Sexual Inversion.* New York: Bell, 1984.

———. *Shelley.* London: Macmillan, 1878.

Symons, Arthur. *The Romantic Movement in English Poetry.* New York: E. P. Dutton, 1909.

Talfourd, T. N. *Speech for the Defendant in the Prosecution of The Queen v. Moxon, for the Publication of Shelley's Works.* London, 1841.

Thompson, E. P. "The Moral Economy of the English Crowd in the Eighteenth Century." *Past and Present* 50 (1971): 76–136.

Thompson, F. M. L. *The Rise of Respectable Society: A Social History of Victorian Britain, 1830–1900.* London: HarperCollins, 1988.

Thompson, Mark, ed. *The Long Road to Freedom: The Advocate History of the Gay and Lesbian Movement.* New York: St. Martin's, 1994.

Tilly, Charles. "Parliamentarization of Popular Contention in Great Britain, 1758–1854." *Theory and Society* 26 (1997): 245–73.

Tompkins, Jane. *Sensational Designs: The Cultural Work of American Fiction 1790–1860.* New York: Oxford UP, 1985.

Tregaskis, Hugh. *Beyond the Grand Tour: The Levant Lunatics.* London: Ascent, 1979.

Trelawny, Edward J. *Recollections of the Last Days of Shelley and Byron.* 2nd ed. Boston: Ticknor and Fields, 1859.

Vaid, Urvashi. *Virtual Equality: The Mainstreaming of Gay and Lesbian Liberation.* New York: Doubleday, 1995.

Vance, Norman. *Sinews of the Spirit: The Ideal of Christian Manliness in Victorian Literature and Religious Thought.* Cambridge: Cambridge UP, 1985.

Warner, Michael. "Introduction." *Fear of a Queer Planet: Queer Politics and Social Theory.* Ed. Michael Warner. Minneapolis: U of Minnesota P, 1993. vii–xxxi.

———. *The Letters of the Republic: Publication and the Public Sphere in Eighteenth-Century America.* Cambridge, MA: Harvard UP, 1990.

———. "The Mass Public and the Mass Subject." *Habermas and the Public Sphere.* Ed. Craig Calhoun. Cambridge, MA: MIT P, 1992. 377–401.

———. "Normal and Normaller: Beyond Gay Marriage." *GLQ* 5.2 (1999): 119–71.

Webb, Timothy. *English Romantic Hellenism 1700–1824.* Manchester: Manchester UP; New York: Barnes and Noble, 1982.

Weber, Max. *Economy and Society: An Outline of Interpretive Sociology.* Vol. 1. Trans. Ephraim Fischoff et al. Ed. Guenther Ross and Claus Wittich. Berkeley: U of California P, 1968. 2 vols.

———. *From Max Weber: Essays in Sociology.* Trans., ed. H. H. Gerth and C. Wright Mills. New York: Oxford UP, 1958.

————. *Methodologische Schriften*. Frankfurt am Main: S. Fischer, 1968.

————. *The Methodology of the Social Sciences*. Trans., ed. Edward A. Shils and Henry A. Finch. New York: Free P, 1964.

Weeks, Jeffrey. *Coming Out: Homosexual Politics in Britain, from the Nineteenth Century to the Present*. London: Quartet, 1977.

————. *Sex, Politics and Society: The Regulation of Sexuality since 1800*. London: Longman, 1981.

Whipple, Edwin P. *Essays and Reviews*. 2 vols. New York, 1848.

White, Newman Ivey. *Shelley*. 2 vols. New York: Alfred A. Knopf, 1940.

Wilde, Oscar. "The Critic as Artist." *The Artist as Critic: Critical Writings of Oscar Wilde*. Ed. Richard Ellmann. New York: Vintage, 1968. 341–408.

Wolfson, Susan J. "Editorial Privilege: Mary Shelley and Percy Shelley's Audiences." *The Other Mary Shelley*. Ed. Audrey A. Fisch, Anne K. Mellor, and Esther H. Schor. New York: Oxford UP, 1993. 39–72.

————. "Feminizing Keats." *Critical Essays on John Keats*. Ed. Hermione de Almeida. Boston: G. K. Hall, 1990. 317–56.

Woodberry, George Edward. *Literary Memoirs of the Nineteenth Century*. New York: Harcourt, Brace and Company, 1921.

Woodring, Carl Ray. *Victorian Samplers: William and Mary Howitt*. Lawrence: U of Kansas P, 1952.

Young, Iris Marion. *Intersecting Voices: Dilemmas of Gender, Political Philosophy, and Policy*. Princeton: Princeton UP, 1997.

————. *Justice and the Politics of Difference*. Princeton: Princeton UP, 1990.

————. "Polity and Group Difference: A Critique of the Ideal of Universal Citizenship." *Ethics* 99 (1989): 250–74; rpt. in *Contemporary Political Philosophy*. Ed. Robert E. Goodin and Philip Pettit. Oxford: Blackwell, 1997. 256–72.

————. "Unruly Categories: A Critique of Nancy Fraser's Dual Systems Theory." *New Left Review* 222 (1997): 147–60.

INDEX

Abelove, Henry, 200 n.21
ACT UP, 47–49, 55, 71–72
Adorno, Theodor, 61, 64, 75–76, 78, 81, 169,
    172, 179 n.26, 183 n.9, 186 n.32, 190–91
    n.11, 201 n.22, 202 n.24
Affect, 58–59, 61–62, 130–32, 151
Affirmation, 11, 12, 30, 32, 46, 52–53, 59,
    88, 90–94, 97, 147, 177 n.21. *See also*
    Stereotypes; Politics, U.S. lesbian and
    gay
AIDS, 45, 48, 53, 71–73, 101, 121
Anglo-Catholicism, 160
Antihomophobia, 18–19, 21, 24, 40, 44, 59,
    61, 90
Apel, Karl-Otto, 192 n.23
Armstrong, Nancy, 23
Arnold, Matthew, 149, 158–59
Authenticity, 12, 21, 30, 49, 60–67, 147
Autonomy, 21, 68–98, 103–4, 117, 123–24,
    154

Bawer, Bruce, 41–42, 122
Bentham, Jeremy, 63, 138, 139, 204 n.11
Berlant, Lauren, 5–6, 39–40, 174 n.8, 178
    n.24
Bersani, Leo, 182–83 n.9
Blind, Mathilde, 163
Bloch, Ernst, 101
Brown, Ford Maddox, 162
Browning, Robert, 153
Burton, Sir Richard, 142–43
Butler, Judith, 95, 96, 186 n.32, 195–96 n.59

Byron, George Gordon, Lord, 23, 129–31,
    135–46, 158–61, 205 n.28

Canonicity (literary), 24, 150–68
Capitalism, 8–9, 11, 13, 15, 50–52, 56–60,
    63–66, 74, 78; legitimation profits of,
    31, 53–54; as social formation, 13, 15,
    60, 63–64, 174 n.9. *See also* Commodity;
    Habermas, Jürgen; Marx, Karl; Value
Carlyle, Thomas, 159
Chandler, Richard, 129
Christensen, Jerome, 140, 205–6 n.31
Citizenship, 12–14, 22, 24, 37–46, 51, 61–63,
    69, 101–5, 110, 115–18, 123–25, 126, 175
    n.11, 181 n.6, 196–97 n.5. *See also* Kant,
    Immanuel
Civil society, 2, 3, 63, 103–4, 115, 120
Clarke, Charles, and Mary Cowden Clarke,
    152
Class, 2–3, 10, 21–23, 39, 51, 56, 64, 74–
    79, 147, 153, 162, 176 n.19, 210 n.38; and
    bourgeois publicity, 3–4, 8–9, 21–22, 39,
    51–52, 56, 61, 74–80, 103, 106, 171; work-
    ing class, 76–78. *See also* Middle class;
    Public sphere
Closet, 19, 59, 126, 141
Commodity, 12, 56–59, 61–64, 66, 163. *See
    also* Affect; Marx, Karl
Communicative action: *See* Habermas,
    Jürgen
Complicity, 24–25, 48, 65–67, 88–93, 96,
    97, 132

Middle class, (*continued*)
106, 171; hegemony of, 2–3, 14, 37, 75–78.
See also Class; Gender; Public sphere
Modernity, 13, 15, 57, 64, 86. *See also* Capi-
talism; Enlightenment; Habermas,
Jürgen
Morality, 6, 11, 37–46, 51, 58, 81–83, 102,
103, 111, 151, 171, 182 n.9. *See also* Haber-
mas, Jürgen; Kant, Immanuel; Value
Morris, Meaghan, 133
Mosse, George, 143

Negt, Oskar, and Alexander Kluge, 8–9, 20–
21, 51–52, 55–56, 173 n.2, 186–87 n.35,
189 n.6. *See also* Counterpublic spheres;
Public sphere
Nelson, Claudia, 153–54
Nineteenth-century Britain, 15, 20, 24, 25,
76–77, 129, 151–68, 191 n.15; cultural
public sphere of, 23, 126–68
Normalcy, 1, 9–10, 14–15, 20–21, 25, 26,
30–35, 43, 49, 52, 66–67, 150, 164; as
assimilation, 13, 18, 77, 87, 93, 96, 97. *See
also* Heteronormativity; Public sphere
Norman, Sylva, 150–51

Orient, the, 126, 128–30, 135–45
Orientalism, 23, 137–47
Ottoman Empire, 23, 128–30, 137–41, 143.
See also Greece

Parliament (British), 76–77, 169–70
Patmore, Coventry, 157
Patton, Cindy, 177 n.21
Pederasty, 127, 139, 142–44
Philhellenism, 128–31, 136–41, 143. *See
also* Greece; Orientalism; Winckelmann,
Johann Joachim
Politics, U.S. lesbian and gay, 15, 18, 25, 29–
30, 34, 36, 43, 49, 92–93, 96–97, 121–22,
171, 177 n.21; visibility politics, 12, 19–21,
29–67, 88, 91, 93, 95–96, 146–47. *See also*
Affirmation; Legitimation; Media; Public
sphere; Stereotypes
Pouqueville, François, 138, 139
Power, 70, 81–84, 86, 88–96, 103, 169. *See
also* Foucault, Michel

Property: ownership of, 3, 4, 8–9, 22, 38,
42–44, 51, 61, 77, 103, 108, 111–25; and
propriety, 4; rights, 43–44. *See also* Kant,
Immanuel
Public interest, 2, 5, 7, 10, 22, 23, 39–40, 46,
52, 69, 74, 81, 126, 182 n.8. *See also* Public
sphere
Public sphere, 1–3, 7–8, 12–15, 25, 30, 35,
38, 56, 59, 62, 67, 69–70, 72, 87, 125, 147,
172; as bourgeois, 3–4, 8–9, 21–22, 39,
51–52, 56, 61, 74–80, 103, 106, 171; as
commercial, 30–31, 32, 47–69, 75–76,
78, 146–47, 175–76 n.19; as cultural, 24,
58, 126–68; and democracy, 2–18, 36–
40, 62, 67, 74–79, 86, 97, 142, 169–72;
exclusion from, 4–5, 7, 11, 13–14, 16–20,
44, 61, 65–66, 70, 74, 78, 81; and gender,
4–5, 135, 137, 140, 144–45, 153–62, 197
n.6, 205 n.26, 210 n.38; as general, 20,
53; as ideal, 2–3, 7–11, 14–17, 21, 26, 39,
51, 61, 67–80, 93, 169–72, 76, 173 n.2,
178 n.24; inclusion within, 1–21, 24, 26,
30, 31, 33, 37–38, 41, 52–55, 58, 60, 65–
67, 70–71, 81–98, 105, 147–48, 171, 177
n.21, 183 n.9; and literature, 23; political,
60; and race, 4, 126–47; self-correction
of, 4–9, 14–18, 78–81; subjunctive mood
of, 7, 9, 12–18, 21, 38, 41, 55, 60, 64–65,
67, 74–75, 85–87, 170, 174 n.9, 175 n.11,
178 n.24, 178–79 n.26. *See also* Counterpublic spheres; Habermas, Jürgen; Kant,
Immanuel; Negt, Oskar, and Alexander
Kluge
Publicity. *See* Public sphere
Publicness. *See* Public sphere

Quine, W. V., 174 n.9

Race, 4, 10, 23, 128–29, 131, 135–46, 196
n.4. *See also* Orientalism; Public sphere
Reiman, Donald, 166
Richards, Jeffrey, 156
Rights, 16, 18, 22, 40, 54, 70, 82, 86–87, 93,
98, 104–5, 111–25, 170, 180 n.3, 196–97
n.5; civil, 18, 29, 48, 101; as discourse, 16,
22, 40; equal, 10, 44, 122; human, 54, 70;
marriage, 44–46, 121–23; property, 43;

"special," 43. *See also* Citizenship; Enfranchisement; Equality; Habermas, Jürgen; Kant, Immanuel; Marriage
Rossetti, William Michael, 152–53, 155, 162–63, 166–68
Rotello, Gabriel, 45–46
Ruskin, John, 158, 159

Schiller, Friedrich, 68
Sedgwick, Eve Kosofsky, 65, 131, 145, 179 n.31, 179 n.32, 195 n.56, 202–3 n.3
Self-determination, 2, 6, 39, 51, 57–58, 68–71, 79, 85, 95–96, 170–72. *See also* Autonomy; Enlightenment
Sexuality, 10, 13, 18–19, 21, 23, 26, 32, 44, 70, 84, 87–89, 95–97, 104–5, 132, 151–52; indeterminate erotic expression, 26, 41–46, 102, 104, 119–22, 124–25, 201–2 n.24; promiscuity, 45, 101, 121–22. *See also* Identity; Heteronormativity; Heterosexuality; Homoeroticism; Homosexuality
Shelley, Lady Jane, 150, 151, 163
Shelley, Mary, 150
Shelley, Percy Bysshe, 24, 127–28, 148–68; demonization of, 158–62; "A Discourse," 127–28, 148; Epipsychidion, 158; feminization of, 153–62; Hellas, 127–28; Laon and Cythna, 167; textual editions of, 24, 149–50, 163–68; veneration of, 150–58, 162, 165–68
Simmel, Georg, 176–77 n.20, 185 n.27, 187 n.42
Smith, Anna Marie, 177 n.21
Sodomy, 135, 139, 204 n.11. *See also* Pederasty
Sonnini, Nicolas, 138, 139
Spencer, Terence, 129
Spivak, Gayatri Chakravorty, 66, 67, 177 n.20, 187 n.43, 188 n.45
State, the, 2, 3, 36, 37, 51, 78, 79, 104, 171–72. *See also* Kant, Immanuel; Parliament (British)
Stereotypes, 20, 34–36, 52–53, 55, 60–61, 64, 66. *See also* Affirmation; Politics, U.S. lesbian and gay
Stoddard, Richard Henry, 152
Stonewall, 18, 47–48, 54, 184 n.22
Sullivan, Andrew, 44–46

Symonds, John Addington, 23–24, 130–31, 135, 136, 142–46, 156, 162
Symons, Arthur, 157–58, 165

Talfourd, T. N., 162
Television, 20, 29, 32–34, 47–49. *See also* Degeneres, Ellen; Media; Politics, U.S. lesbian and gay
Tilly, Charles, 76–77
Tolerance, 95, 101, 169–72
Trelawny, Edward, 150, 157, 163

Universalism, 25, 37–38, 67, 81–85, 94, 105, 116–21, 124–25, 171–72

Value, 6–7, 12–15, 19, 21, 25, 30, 61, 62, 64, 67, 78, 80, 83, 95, 97, 125, 129, 135, 136, 143, 145, 176–77 n.20; cultural, 135, 148–68; economic, 19, 30, 47–60, 92; erotic, 150, 162–68; extraction of, 19, 30–31, 53, 57, 75; as form, 10, 62–64, 150, 167; and history, 48, 149–50; political/civic, 11, 31, 33, 48, 50–60, 90–91, 103; and rationality, 73–80; as relation, 12, 19, 63. *See also* Capitalism; Marx, Karl; Value determination
Value determination, 4, 7, 10–16, 19–20, 24, 37–38, 60, 66, 77, 83, 96, 103, 170, 187 n.43; and authenticity, 31, 60–67; coordination of political and economic, 50–60, 62, 65; economic/commercial, 10–11, 31, 47–60, 62, 65–66, 176 n.19, 187 n.43; moral, 6, 10, 19, 30–31, 37–47, 51, 55, 57, 62, 69–70, 73. *See also* Value
Vance, Norman, 160
Visibility. *See* Politics, U.S. lesbian and gay

Warner, Michael, 5–6, 66, 175 n.11
Weber, Max, 78, 183 n.9, 185 n.27, 191 n.17
Weeks, Jeffrey, 144, 154
Wilde, Oscar, 135, 145, 148
Williams, Raymond, 6
Winckelmann, Johann Joachim, 136–37, 142, 143

Young, Iris Marion, 181 n.5

ł

Eric O. Clarke is Associate Professor of English at the
University of Pittsburgh.

Library of Congress Cataloging-in-Publication Data
Clarke, Eric O.
Virtuous vice : homoeroticism and the public sphere /
Eric O. Clarke.
p.   cm. — (Series Q)
Includes bibliographical references and index.
ISBN 0-8223-2477-6 (cloth : alk. paper).
ISBN 0-8223-2513-6 (pbk. : alk. paper)
1. Homosexuality.   2. Homosexuality—Public opinion.
3. Homosexuality and literature.   4. Gay liberation
movement.   5. Social values.   I. Title.   II. Series.
HQ76.25.C525   2000   306.76′6—dc21   99-44768 CIP